THE JOHN HARVARD LIBRARY

The John Harvard Library, founded in 1959, publishes essential
American writings, including novels, poetry, memoirs, criticism, and works of social and political history, representing all
periods, from the beginning of settlement in America to the
twenty-first century. The purpose of The John Harvard Library
is to make these works available to scholars and general readers
in affordable, authoritative editions.

J O H N
H A R V A R D
L I B R A R Y

ALEXANDER BERKMAN

HENRY BAUER

CARL NOLD

PRISON BLOSSOMS

ANARCHIST VOICES FROM THE
AMERICAN PAST

EDITED BY MIRIAM BRODY AND BONNIE BUETTNER

JOHN
HARVARD
LIBRARY

THE BELKNAP PRESS OF HARVARD UNIVERSITY PRESS
Cambridge, Massachusetts, and London, England   2011

Library of Congress Cataloging-in-Publication Data

Berkman, Alexander, 1870–1936.

Prison blossoms : anarchist voices from the American past / Alexander Berkman,
Henry Bauer, Carl Nold ; edited by Miriam Brody and Bonnie Buettner.

p.   cm.—(The John Harvard Library)

Includes bibliographical references.

ISBN 978-0-674-05056-3 (cloth)

1. Anarchists—United States—History.   2. Prisoners—Pennsylvania—
Biography.   3. State Penitentiary for the Western District of Pennsylvania.
I. Bauer, Henry, 1861–1934.   II. Nold, Carl, 1869–1934.
III. Brody, Miriam, 1940–   IV. Buettner, Bonnie Cleo, 1943–   V. Title.

HX843.5.B47 2011

335'.8309748—dc22   2010045391

Contents

Note on the Text

THE ORIGINAL MANUSCRIPTS that comprise *Prison Blossoms* are housed in the archive of the International Institute of Social History in Amsterdam, where they are described as "25 copies of a small illegal magazine published by [Alexander] Berkman and two other anarchists." Included in a collection of Emma Goldman's papers that came to the International Institute after her death in 1940, the manuscripts were handwritten in German and in English in booklets three by five inches in size, small enough to elude guards who searched the prison cells where, for the most part, they were composed and hidden. The contents of two of the twenty-five documents are identical, except that one was written in German and the other in English after the writers had acquired more facility in that language. The twenty-four separate chapters of essays, narratives, and poems published in this volume are published for the first time in their entirety, representing the complete collection of *Prison Blossoms* that found refuge in the archive. The remaining documents that originally formed a corpus of some sixty booklets, according to Alexander Berkman's comments in *Prison Memoirs of an Anarchist,* were lost as Berkman, Bauer, and Nold moved from place to place in the United States and, in Berkman's case, moved as a refugee abroad. Frequent searches of and the destruction of papers in the offices of anarchist publications where Berkman worked as a journalist also made their survival unlikely.

The anarchist writers of these manuscripts intended that the documents would form the basis of a larger work on anarchism and prison life in America that they hoped to publish after their release from prison. As they left no record of the organization they had intended for the book, we have placed the documents in a sequence that the contents suggested to us, honoring, we hope, the internal organization of material evident in the reading. For the most part, the English-written text is rendered just as it was produced, the copy having been written in a clear hand remarkably free of editorial deletions and additions. On those few occasions when the writers edited their own work, usually to choose more felicitous wording, their choices have been honored without our indicating that a revision took place. We have corrected minor errors in spelling, punctuation, and wording in the English text and, in a few instances, added a missing preposition or article in brackets, where the addition promotes clearer understanding. We have chosen not to alter occasional errors in the diction of these nonnative-English writers in order to retain a sense of their original voices.

Because the writers composed their texts with some sense of urgency and with a scarcity of paper, they often relied on abbreviations to refer to comrades and friends familiar to them, though not necessarily to us, as well as to refer to place names, titles, and other often-repeated terms. What was a space- and time-saving measure for them can be a source of irritation and confusion for the reader, and we have expanded such shorthand where it seemed advisable and possible. While we have supplied what information we could, we have had to leave some people mentioned in the text with no further identification than what the three authors provided. Some of the essays contain footnotes written by the authors or commentary on the text written by one of the other writers acting as editor. In these cases we have distinguished the comments of the original writers from our own by placing their comments in italic footnotes at the bottom of the page.

We have taken the literal translation of *Zuchthausblüthen* as a title for this work. It is the title that Berkman, Bauer, and Nold had given to their earliest exchanges with each other in their native language. When they began to write in English, they sometimes called their "magazinelet" the *Prison Bird* or *Jail Bird*, using the prison slang for messages sent sub rosa. In his first public appearance, newly released from the penitentiary and workhouse, Berkman gave "To Hell and Back" as the title of the book he and his comrades had written in prison. No mention of these alternative titles surfaces in his *Prison Memoirs of an Anarchist*, published six years later, as Berkman uses the English translation "Prison Blossoms" exclusively in reference to the prison writings.

Excerpts from the diary of Berkman's last days in the penitentiary, which he never intended to be a part of this collection, are included in an appendix, as a grace note to the years in which he bore witness to his prison experience in America. Two of the essays in *Prison Blossoms* were published separately during the lifetime of their writers. Henry Bauer published a slightly altered version of "A Fateful Leaflet" in *Free Society* on April 17, 1898. In August 1906, Alexander Berkman published portions of "Punishment: Its Nature and Effects" in the anarchist journal *Mother Earth.*

A Note on the German Texts

More than half of the *Prison Blossoms* texts were written in German; those by Henry Bauer and Carl Nold were written in *Kurrent,* a nineteenth-century form of German cursive script, those by Alexander Berkman in a Latin script. Transcription of the texts was sometimes difficult, not because their writing was not clear—all three authors wrote in remarkably clear hands—but because of the conditions under which they were written and the wear and tear of the intervening years. Poor-quality paper, water damage, words almost obliterated by rubbing, ink bleeding through from the other side of the paper, crumbling edges, the hand-stitching of the small pages that sometimes encroached on the writing—all of these conditions added to the challenge of deciphering what the authors had written.

The translation of the German attempts to do justice not only to the primary meaning of the authors' words and expressions but also to the underlying subjective context they wished to convey. They were, after all, not just describing what happened but were also putting a particular "spin" on the events. We have attempted to give the reader some sense of each author's voice by choosing expressions in English that might reflect the poetry of Carl Nold's prose, for example, the drama of Henry Bauer's stories, the elegance of Alexander Berkman's narratives, and the fervor and conviction of all three. Occasionally, long, complex sentences—more common and more acceptable in German than in English—have been split into more compact units to facilitate comprehension, though most have been left and may in this way give the reader some sense of the author's associative approach to an idea. We have tried not to beautify or censor what they wrote nor to change it beyond what is inevitable when one tries to render the thoughts of another. In that sense, every translation is an interpretation, but we have tried to remain true to the reality of the world, the society, and the age they inhabited, as well as to these three men and how they saw themselves in that world.

Bonnie Buettner translated and edited the German texts. Miriam Brody wrote the introduction to *Prison Blossoms* and edited the English texts.

Introduction

THIS COLLECTION OF DOCUMENTS called *Prison Blossoms* is part of a series of manuscripts written and edited by Henry Bauer, Alexander Berkman, and Carl Nold, all anarchists who were active in the late nineteenth-century American labor movement. The best known of these men, Alexander Berkman (1870–1936), was a prominent and eloquent spokesperson and writer in the international anarchist community, a man who was thrust suddenly onto the public stage in 1892 when he committed, in his words, "the first terrorist act" on American soil, the attempted assassination of steel tycoon Henry Clay Frick.[1]

Never before published, these documents open a window, an American window, to the tumult and turmoil that characterized rapidly industrializing fin-de-siècle Europe and America. From the Paris Commune in 1871 to the bitter labor strife of the American 1880s and 1890s, factories, railroads, and mines, as well as city squares, became

deadly contested arenas of class warfare. In *Prison Blossoms* the con-
tradictions of America's Gilded Age, European social theory, and
ruthless monopoly capitalism come together in the secret writings of
three jailed immigrant anarchists.

Most of the pieces in *Prison Blossoms* were written furtively from
1893 to 1897, during the overlapping years of the anarchists' imprisonment in Western Pennsylvania Penitentiary. Passing messages from
cell to cell via circuitous routes, these comrades risked grave retaliation if their clandestine writing was uncovered and they were perceived to be hatching an anarchist plot. In spite of this risk, the manuscript they completed, composed primarily under the roof of the
prison, contained sixty diminutive "booklets," as they called them,
each one only three by five inches in size, each concealed under the
floor of the prison broom shop after composition, and then mailed to
an outside friend by a guard bribed for his service. According to the
anarchists' plans, once beyond the prison walls the manuscript was to
be held in safekeeping, awaiting the release of Bauer and Nold, who
were to promote its publication as a single volume to be called *Prison
Blossoms.*

It is difficult to trace the trail of the *Prison Blossoms* writings once
they left Western Pennsylvania Penitentiary, or to account for all of
the booklets that comprised the original collection. We know that
some of them came into Berkman's possession for use in the preparation of his *Prison Memoirs,* the much praised book about his
confinement published in 1912, six years after his release from the
penitentiary and workhouse, and still in print. Berkman's lifelong anarchist comrade Emma Goldman had rescued some of the booklets
from the frequent police raids of her homes and sent them to Berkman when he began writing his *Memoirs.* Carl Nold, Henry Bauer,
and others of Berkman's friends had also retained copies that they
sent to Berkman. In 1940, twenty-five of the booklets were included

in Emma Goldman's papers when they came to reside in the International Institute of Social History's archive in Amsterdam. More than a hundred years after their composition, many of the *Prison Blossoms* writings are only now reaching the broader public audience for whom they were initially written—an audience beyond the prison walls—in the hope of acquainting readers with anarchism and with the dire conditions inside American penitentiaries.

The authors of *Prison Blossoms,* the Russian-Jewish anarchist Alexander Berkman and German anarchists Carl Nold and Henry Bauer, were imprisoned in Western Pennsylvania Penitentiary for the attempted assassination in July 1892 of industrial magnate Henry Frick, the man they held responsible for the outbreak of labor violence that had attracted worldwide attention at Andrew Carnegie's steelworks in Homestead, Pennsylvania, one of the world's largest steel mills. Sometime early in their confinement, the three men learned they could communicate with one another by speaking through empty water pipes that reached from the privies in their cells to the cells directly above or below. Once a message from one of the men was received, it could be carried by word of mouth from cell to cell along the corridor until it reached its destination. From this primitive telephone system a process began of speaking—and soon writing—to one another that ended in the more sophisticated exchange of essays, narratives, and literary parables that the three anarchists hoped to publish.

In the years they spent together inside the cell blocks, Berkman, Bauer, and Nold exchanged thousands of words, almost all carried as smuggled messages passed from hand to hand to a "rangeman," a privileged prisoner allowed outside his cell whose work was sweeping a corridor or pouring coffee. A message from one of the anarchists might be carried to a workroom, where another of the prisoners, if need be, could move it to a more distant cell block and ultimately into the hands of one of the other two. In such a way, along with hundreds of other messages about matters trivial and urgent, the plans for writing *Prison Blossoms* were refined. During these long years, Bauer, Berkman, and Nold were never actually in one another's presence. Only once was Alexander Berkman almost near enough to look Carl Nold in the face or to lay his hand upon his sleeve.

Nothing about Western Pennsylvania Penitentiary suggested it might be the setting for a literary and intellectual venture. The penitentiary was a singularly bleak place for prisoners enduring a lengthy confinement. Its long brick cell blocks, enclosed within a perimeter wall, were set on a large tract of land that lay on the banks of the Ohio River, five miles from the center of Pittsburgh. Breezes from the nearby river only sometimes tempered the noxious climate of the penitentiary. More frequently, when the river flooded its banks, the prison cells became damp and malodorous, the floors infested with rats and insects. Only a few years before the anarchists' arrival, the prison administration, notorious for corruption and cruel treatment of prisoners, had been investigated for malfeasance by a state committee.

Nold and Bauer, charged with complicity in the attack on Frick, faced five-year sentences in the penitentiary. Alexander Berkman, who had in fact acted alone, faced twenty-two years and was close to suicidal despair. But with the water-pipe telephone system, which facilitated written messages that were carried by a friendly prisoner called Horsethief, Berkman's spirits lifted. As they debated with each other the political events that had brought them to the prison, the three men recreated the arguments about revolution and strategy that had animated them earlier, in the saloons and cafés of their tenement neighborhoods. Nold, Bauer, and Berkman had come to America with the politics of reform and revolution bred in the social upheaval of their European birthplaces. Once in America, they had found like-minded men and women who believed an endless enmity was inevitable between the toilers who worked the mills of industry and the capitalists who owned them.

1. "Homestead!"

The events that led Berkman, Bauer, and Nold to prison began in the spring of 1892 during the management lockout at Andrew Carnegie's steel mills in Homestead, Pennsylvania, the mills an overlapping set of steelworks on a swath of land alongside the Monongahela River just outside of Pittsburgh. What happened in the Homestead works that year, events that would produce these "prison blossoms," epitomized the volatile social tensions that characterized late nineteenth-century America. In this period, when America was transforming itself from an agrarian economy into an industrial and commercial colossus, rapid industrialization and the presence of cheap labor among the crowds of jobless immigrants fueled disputes between workers and owners, disputes that frequently turned bloody. As fluctuations in market prices, dependent on an uneven demand for raw materials, drove a boom-and-bust economy, workers had no protection against sudden wage reductions or job losses. By the time of the events at Homestead, five state governors had recently called out their states' National Guard: against miners in eastern Tennessee and Idaho, against railroad workers in upstate New York, and against general strikers in Louisiana. But unlike earlier scenes of unrest that may have been unfocused or haphazard, the strike at Homestead was well organized by the powerful Amalgamated Association of Iron and Steel Workers, a union that had already emerged victorious in two previous strikes.

On July 1, 1892, the prevailing collective-bargaining agreement between Amalgamated and management at Homestead was due to ex-

pire, negotiations for a new contract having begun in February. En-
couraged that steel production at Homestead was at an all-time high,
Amalgamated asked for wage increases at the outset of its talks with
management. Frick, a notoriously anti-union negotiator who was
working with the approval of Andrew Carnegie, countered with pro-
posals for wage reductions, including provisions for cuts that would
affect vast numbers of Homestead's 3,800 workers. In April Carnegie
left for his annual trip to his hunting lodge in Scotland, leaving his
steelworks under the management of Frick, who had successfully put
down efforts to unionize workers at Carnegie's Duquesne plant a year
earlier, where he both broke the strike and fired the union employees
identified by company spies.[2] On May 30, Frick delivered an ultima-
tum to Amalgamated, insisting that if the union did not accept the
new contract he would negotiate individually with workers, effectively declaring Homestead a nonunion shop.

The violence that erupted at Homestead would expose the anoma-
lies of Andrew Carnegie's relationship with organized labor and deliver a blow to his reputation as a benevolent industrialist. A world-
famous philanthropist and donor of symphony halls and libraries,
Carnegie had already arranged to give away his fortune at his death,
adhering to principles he had proclaimed publicly in his *Gospel of
Wealth* (1889), which held that an inheritance should be passed on to
benefit the general community rather than to one's personal heirs.
Moreover, he had given public support to negotiating with labor leaders in the past and opposed calling in mercenaries or militias to sup-
press workers' grievances. At the same time, however, Carnegie the
industrialist hoped to control production and profits by adjusting
salaries downward while increasing the workday at the furnaces to a
dangerous and grueling twelve hours, and by employing the twin
processes of horizontal and vertical integration, in which he bought
out competitors and also owned all aspects of the production process, from the coal and iron fields to the barges that transported raw

materials to the mills where the steel was forged. Workers blacklisted at Homestead would not find employment elsewhere.

In later years Carnegie attempted to distance himself from Frick's handling of the Homestead strike, describing himself as a retired vacationer at the time, who had been trout fishing in Scotland. But in fact Carnegie had been in continual contact with Frick during the spring months that moved the face-off to a crisis, concerned that his younger colleague, despite his success at resisting the union at Duquesne, was not yet a fully tested combatant in such labor struggles. Frick's mettle proved equal to the fray that developed. With no concession from Amalgamated, by the end of June Frick had closed down the plant, surrounded it with barbed wire strung on top of wooden walls, declared the workers discharged, and locked them out.

With more than two thousand Homestead workers attending its meeting in response to the lockout, Amalgamated mobilized its forces and formed executive and advisory committees to patrol the river stations and the entrances to the town of Homestead. Endeavoring to maintain a peaceful protest and ensure that the first blow would have to be struck by management, Amalgamated took such steps as to warn saloon owners to control drunkenness that might lead to violence. At the same time, the union worked to control the messages sent out to the world, setting up a special committee to meet regularly with members of the press, whose response was largely sympathetic.

Workers at four other Carnegie plants struck in sympathy, as did the mechanics and transportation workers at Homestead represented by the radical labor union, the Knights of Labor. Meanwhile, the locked-out steelworkers and their families were determined to prevent Frick from shipping in replacements on the Monongahela River. A virtual military camp was organized, run by the strike committee; shifts of workers took up sentinel positions along the river and strangers were closely questioned before given entry.

On July 6, 1892, violent conflict broke out. Frick had called in 300 armed Pinkerton guards, an army of professional strike breakers with no ties to the local community that might impede their actions. Under cover of night, the Pinkertons were to travel down the Monongahela to the steelworks, where they would provide security for the replacement workers Frick was recruiting from distant cities and abroad. Alerted to their arrival by telegraph from sympathizers in Pittsburgh, strikers and their families crowded the banks of the river, exchanging shots with the Pinkertons when they attempted to disembark in early-morning darkness. Stranded on barges, the Pinkerton men were bombarded by bullets, explosives, and even firecrackers left over from the Fourth of July. They were set upon by a flaming riverborne raft and a burning railroad flatcar set adrift in their direction, so that some desperate men leaped into the river, terrified of the fire.

Meanwhile, newsmen, having taken up headquarters in town, began telegraphing the story out to the world, which alerted hundreds of steelworkers in nearby Pittsburgh who were preparing to join forces at Homestead. By late afternoon the Pinkertons had surrendered, and by the next day they had been spirited out of town by a strike committee eager to prevent mayhem, the guards only narrowly escaping further retaliation at the hands of the locked-out workers. When the smoke cleared, six steelworkers and two Pinkerton guards lay dead. But more astounding to the workers and their families, Frick's army had suffered a humiliating retreat, forced to run a bloody gauntlet of furious Homestead workers to reach the safety of the sheriff's office. For the moment, it would appear to a sympathetic newspaper-reading public that men, women, even children, defending their livelihoods and homes, had thwarted Henry Clay Frick's attempt to crush the union of iron- and steelworkers.

While the events at Homestead unfolded, Alexander Berkman, twenty-one years old and only four years in America, was working in a lunch parlor hundreds of miles to the northeast in Worcester, Massachusetts, frying pancakes, serving tea and ices. He had come to Worcester from New York with Emma Goldman, then his lover, and his cousin Modest Aronstam, hoping to earn enough money to pay for his ship fare back to Russia, where he believed he could do more useful work disseminating anarchist propaganda among peasants and newly industrialized workers. Emma Goldman chanced to see the headlines of a newspaper proclaiming that Frick had declared he'd rather see strikers dead than yield to their demands. Incensed to read that impoverished pregnant women—the wives of striking steelworkers—were evicted by sheriffs and left on the street, she rushed to the rooms she shared with Berkman, waving the newspaper and crying in outrage and excitement—"Homestead!"

For Berkman, the moment sounded a call to arms. All of his young life he had been in preparation for such a crisis. Born in Russia in 1870 into an educated and middle-class family, Berkman was inspired as a young boy by the ferment of political activity and the lure of forbidden books. He was familiar with Turgenev's 1862 novel *Fathers and Sons,* which documented the widening chasm between an older generation of Russian reformers whose model was Western liberalism and a younger generation of nihilists and Slavophiles who sought instead indigenously Russian models. Like so many other young Russians of his generation, he had read Nikolai Chernyshevsky's *What Is to Be Done* (1863), a novel in which a middle-class Russian couple sacrifices personal well-being for the sake of revolution, a model of nobility and asceticism for the early underground socialist movement to follow.

Berkman had listened to family whispers about the illegal proselytizing of his maternal uncle, Mark Natanson (1850–1919), a well-known Narodnik, or man of "the people's will," who preached to the peasantry in the hope of arousing them politically. As a gymnasium student, Berkman had boldly asserted his radicalism by writing an essay proclaiming himself an atheist, an act of boyish rebellion for which he lost a year of academic standing. When Sophia Perovskaya and her lover Andrei Zhelyabov were executed for the assassination of Czar Alexander II in 1881, Berkman was inspired by an exalted vision of revolutionary zeal and sacrifice that he carried with him to America.

Shortly before Berkman immigrated to the United States in 1888, he read about the four anarchists executed in the fallout of the 1886 Haymarket riot in Chicago prompted by workers' rallies for the eight-hour day. Albert Parsons, August Spies, George Engel, and Adolph Fischer were executed for their part in the violence that claimed the lives of seven policemen and an unknown number of protesters when a bomb was detonated toward the end of a rally against the McCormick Harvesting Machine Company in Chicago. A fifth convicted anarchist, Louis Lingg, took his own life on the eve of his execution. The lofty self-abnegation and idealism of the Haymarket martyrs when facing the gallows drew Berkman to their cause and to the shores of America, where he and hundreds of thousands of immigrants like him had come in search of a more hopeful world of labor relations.

By the time Berkman was working in the Worcester lunch parlor, he had learned that poverty, hunger, and what he perceived as an intractable hostility between labor and capital thrived in his adopted country. Upon hearing the cry "Homestead!" his instant resolve was to abandon his plan to join the struggle in Russia and instead to help arouse the great, slumbering American working class. He hoped to instill in the uprising anarchist ideals that would provide a model for a future reorganized society, believing "the vision of Anarchism alone could imbue discontent with conscious revolutionary purpose; it alone could lend wings to the aspirations of labor."[3]

As he first absorbed the labor strife at Homestead, Berkman intended only to distribute propaganda to the steelworkers in the form of leaflets. But as the violence grew, with the heavily armed Pinkerton guards killing numbers of steelworkers, including a small boy, his plans for agitation and propaganda were altered. Both Berkman and Goldman felt a sea change had occurred. The deaths of helpless family members and embattled workers, they maintained, would at last move the American working class, already widely sympathetic to the locked-out steelmen, to break their chains.

Berkman held Frick responsible for the bloodshed at Homestead and believed he must be made to bear the consequences. Retaliation was not only moral, it was expedient. As he explains in his *Prison Blossoms* essay "Autobiographical Sketches" (Chapter 3), "The eyes of all were on Homestead. Most sympathized with the workers. I wanted to use the opportunity offered me to demonstrate the solidarity of the anarchists with the working class—for the first time in this country—by means of an indisputable *deed* and thus win the sympathy of the people for anarchists and their endeavors." Assuming that in all likelihood he himself would die in the act, Berkman resolved to kill Frick. To sacrifice his own life in the cause of the people was an obligation he accepted joyously, in the revolutionary tradition of the nineteenth-century Russian rebels whose martyrdoms had fed the dreams of his youth.

His first plan was to explode a bomb that would kill Frick but leave Berkman alive long enough to explain that, far from being a criminal with a personal grudge, he had acted selflessly on behalf of the American worker. As for the morality of violence committed by bomb or bullet against tyrants, whether they wore crowns or top hats, Berkman had since boyhood known the revolutionary argument for assassination. Known as an *attentat,* a form of "propaganda by deed," the theory popular among European anarchists held that through an act of violence the attacker would wreak class vengeance on the oppressor. More subtly, through an act of political violence the crumbling base on which the powerful stood would be exposed in all its vulnerability. The *attentat* proved that the powerless could become powerful, the working man, with dynamite or a gun, could confront kings, state militia, Pinkerton guards, or the police on level ground.

From April 4, 1866, when the first assassin's bullet almost killed Russian Czar Alexander II, until after World War I, when most anarchists had abandoned the theory of propaganda by deed, the idea of the *attentat* held sway as a daring and dramatic act of revolutionary violence. Although approval for the *attentat* as a revolutionary strategy waned even in Europe during the lifetime of the authors of *Prison Blossoms*, sympathy remained for the man driven to commit such an act. In 1916, writing about violence and anarchism, Berkman was impatient with those who were slow to understand that any violence visited upon agents of the state was the whirlwind they had themselves stirred. "The bomb is the echo of your cannon, trained upon our starving brothers; it is the cry of the murdered striker; 'tis the voice of hungry women and children. . . . *The bomb is the ghost of your past crimes.*"[4]

To wreak vengeance upon Frick, Berkman had at his disposal the textbook for terrorist bomb-making, *The Science of Revolutionary Warfare*, written in 1885 by the German social democrat–turned-anarchist Johann Most (1846–1906). Most was an important leader in New York immigrant anarchist circles after his arrival in 1882 and an early mentor to both Goldman and Berkman. As an advocate of revolutionary violence, Most made a study of nitroglycerin for his how-to manual on making a bomb, and included as well some notes on toxicology, arson, and burglary. With Most's instructions at hand, Berkman removed himself to rural Staten Island in mid-July to prepare his bomb. To his chagrin his trial efforts failed. Forced to revise his plans, and with diminished savings, Berkman set forth alone by train for Pittsburgh, leaving Emma Goldman, who had longed to accompany him, behind in New York to raise more money for their enter-prise. Berkman told her he would buy a cheap revolver at a pawn shop and find lodgings with Carl Nold, a German comrade recommended to him.

Nold had not met Berkman before, nor had Henry Bauer, another German anarchist comrade with whom Berkman met in the few days before his attack on Frick. In fact, with Homestead workers' fears of company spies running high, Bauer was suspicious of Berkman when he arrived in Pittsburgh looking for a place to sleep. Johann Most, who had fallen out with Berkman for taking sides against him in a theoretical feud, had in fact warned Bauer to be wary of Berkman, whom he regarded as a renegade. The first night Alexander Berkman spent in Bauer's company, the German anarchist stayed awake and alert, bent on searching Berkman's luggage for anything suspicious, his own revolver at the ready if Berkman made a false move.

Henry Bauer (1861–1934), described by Berkman as tall, good-natured, and ruddy-complected, had come to the United States from Germany in 1880. A carpenter by trade, Bauer became an activist in America in the movement for the eight-hour day after the Haymarket riot galvanized him into political life, as it did so many other young immigrant anarchists. Bearing leaflets that described him as an "Agent for Labor Literature," Bauer and companions distributed their rally-ing cries among the steelworkers at Homestead, risking assault and death at the hands of a lynch mob that suspected them of being Pinkerton men. Later, on trial for incitement to riot, as well as for col-luding with Berkman in the attack on Frick, Bauer would refuse to name the men who distributed leaflets with him, earning further jail time for contempt of court.

Carl Nold (1869–1934) was slight of stature, sympathetic and intel-ligent in expression, bearing a black mustache and hair combed back from his forehead in a high pompadour, an "anarchistic" hairdo in the eyes of the unfriendly press. Born in Germany, the son of an army doctor who died in the Franco-German War, Nold was raised by his grandparents as a practicing Catholic. As a young man he joined his mother in America, where he endured harsh treatment while apprenticed to a relative as a locksmith. Having become acquainted with socialist and anarchist ideas as he worked in different cities, Nold eventually landed in Pittsburgh, where he served the anarchist movement well as a speaker and writer. By the time of Homestead, his political activities had drawn the attention of the local police, and his home, with a printing press on the third floor, had become a meeting place for local radical anarchists. Berkman grew fond of both of the men who, through writing, became his prison companions, but he was more immediately drawn to Carl Nold, whose philosophic turn of mind he found more congenial.

When he arrived at Homestead, Berkman was awestruck by his first sight of the battlefield that had opened up around the walled-in steelworks, now dubbed Fort Frick. Between the Monongahela River and Fort Frick, Berkman saw "men carrying Winchesters . . . hurrying by, their faces grimy, eyes bold yet anxious." Remembering the scene later, he wrote:

> From the mill-yard gape the black mouths of cannon, dismantled breastworks bar the passages, and the ground is strewn with burning cinders, empty shells, oil barrels, broken furnace stacks, and piles of steel and iron. The place looks the aftermath of a sanguinary conflict,—the symbol of our industrial life, of the ruthless struggle in which the *stronger*, the sturdy man of labor, is always the victim, because he acts *weakly*. But the charred hulks of the Pinkerton barges at the landing-place, and the blood-bespattered gangplank, bear mute witness that for once the battle went to the *really strong, to the victim who dared*. (*Memoirs*, 26–27)

The night before his attack on Frick, Berkman moved into a Pittsburgh hotel, hoping he would spare Nold and Bauer, who remained
unaware of his intentions, any notice by the police. He signed the hotel ledger with the name of Rakhmetov, the revolutionary hero in the
Chernyshevsky novel he had read as a boy. On July 23, he forced
his way into Frick's private office and raised his revolver at the "black-
bearded, well-knit figure at a table in the back of the room." At the
sight of Berkman and his revolver, Frick clutched the arm of his chair
and attempted to rise and "with a look of horror" averted his face.
There was, as Berkman described it, a "flash" as he fired his revolver.
Frick fell to his knees and Berkman stepped toward him to fire again,
when John Leishman, the vice president of Carnegie Steel, who happened to be in Frick's office, leapt upon him. "He looks slender and
small. I would not hurt him," Berkman recalled thinking, "I have
no business with him." Someone shouted "Murder! Help!" Berkman
aimed again at Frick and pulled the trigger, but the revolver did not
fire a second time. Hearing the shouts, carpenters from a nearby work
site rushed into the office, striking Berkman with hammers, one of
the carpenters knocking him down. Berkman managed to drag himself to where Frick sought safety behind a desk and with a dagger he
had concealed in his pocket struck at Frick's legs until finally the carpenters overwhelmed him and police surrounded him. At this moment, Berkman remembered having an odd and passing flicker of
doubt about what he had done.

> An officer pulls my head back by the hair, and my eyes meet Frick's.
> He stands in front of me, supported by several men. His face is
> ashen gray; the black beard is streaked with red, and blood is ooz-
> ing from his neck. For an instant a strange feeling, as of shame,
> comes over me; but the next moment I am filled with anger at the

sentiment, so unworthy of a revolutionist. With defiant hatred I look him full in the face. (*Memoirs*, 38)

The hatred he felt for Frick would be lifelong and shared by fellow anarchists and friends of labor. Less certain in his own mind and in the minds of his comrades was the conviction that assassination was a strategy for revolution. But through long and cruel years of imprisonment and exile, Berkman did not waver from the almost spiritual ideal of anarchist community that had inspired him to act.

2. The "Beautiful Ideal" of European Anarchism

Years later, in 1926, when he was writing a primer of anarchism in simple terms to reach working people, Berkman tried to obliterate the stereotype of the mad bomb-throwing anarchist that his own act had helped spread. "Anarchism is not bombs, disorder, or chaos. It is not robbery and murder. It is not a war of each against all. It is not a return to barbarism or to the wild state of man." Instead, he wrote, "I consider Anarchism the most rational and practical conception of a social life in freedom and harmony. I am convinced that its realization is a certainty in the course of human development." What stood in the way of this natural development toward social harmony and individual liberty, wrote Berkman, was the edifice of the state and its handmaidens—the church, the bank, and the military—by which every aspect of human life was constrained. "Only the abolition of coercive authority and material inequality can solve our political, economic, and national problems."[5]

In his invocation of rational harmony and natural development, Berkman echoes the anarchist communism of his mentor, the famous Russian theorist Peter Kropotkin (1842–1921), who envisioned an Edenic workers' paradise of voluntary associations of craftspeople in networks of shops, forming a society based on mutual aid. Kropotkin's vision of independent craftsmen engaged in work for mutual benefit borrowed models from a nostalgically remembered golden age: the free cities of the European Middle Ages, the communities of Essenes and early Christians, the tribal communities of Russian peasants, whose traditions suggested the sharing of goods.

Kropotkin did not share the apocalyptic revolutionary vision of the equally famous Russian anarchist Mikhail Bakunin (1814–1876), who believed anarchism would emerge only out of the ashes of a cataclysmic political destruction of the existing order. With the disciplined mind of a trained scientist and the gentler disposition of a philosopher, Kropotkin proposed that the anarchist networks of production should avail themselves of the knowledge the industrial age was producing, and not reject industrialism in the single-minded pursuit of a bygone age with its craft economy. Although Kropotkin's temperament prevented his condoning terror, his journal *Le Révolté* did accept that in autocratic countries with few opportunities for democratic protest, the *attentat,* one of the political strategies that fell under the notion of propaganda by deed, was legitimate.[6]

A profoundly moral sentiment of simplicity and communal sharing underlay Kropotkin's anarchist vision, such that anarchists like Berkman, Nold, and Bauer easily spoke of it as their "beautiful ideal." In this anarchist ideal, each craftsperson would contribute to the production of necessary goods and each in turn would consume only the goods he or she needed. Freed from the time-consuming production of luxurious items that no one needed, they would be able to produce goods to assure necessities for all, while left with the leisure to join societies of learning or of the arts.

Kropotkin based his anarchist vision of communal life on the method of scientific observation that he had used in his study of animal life. Unlike most social theorists influenced by Darwin, as Kropotkin applied Darwinian insights to human beings, he concluded that the survival of a species did not lie in competition and struggle but in cooperation, the giving of mutual aid. While Kropotkin named individual liberty as the highest value of anarchism, he saw no tension between the desires of one person and the needs of the community in which a human life was lived out. In his primer on anarchism, Berkman wrote that his hopes for the victory of anarchism lay in his reading of our species' history, as Kropotkin had explained it. "Mutual help and cooperation gradually multiplied man's strength and ability," wrote Berkman, "till he has succeeded in conquering nature, in applying her forces to his use, in chaining the lightning, bridging oceans, and mastering even the air." This natural impulse toward community or mutualism to "accomplish more than by strife and enmity" was basic to human nature, enabling Berkman to speak of the inevitability of progress and amelioration.[7] Yet only if disencumbered from the restraints and artificial fetters of the state would people behave in accordance with these natural cooperative instincts. Anarchists like Alexander Berkman would spend many years despairing that human beings had not risen to understand their better nature.

In their common opposition to social and economic inequality, Marxists and anarchists might seem to have been natural allies. But important distinctions separated them. Marx saw the proletariat seizing the state politically and then using its coercive force to communalize the means of production, which would produce a classless society and the "withering away" of the state. Bakunin's anarchist followers, worrying how temporary this dictatorship of the proletariat would be, wanted the economic and political revolutions to occur simultaneously. Their differences culminated in the dramatic split between Marx and Bakunin at the Internationale meeting in The Hague in 1872, a split that would be permanent. Ultimately, anarchists would become the first victims of the new Bolshevik state under Lenin's stewardship. Although the anarchists had rallied round the Bolshevik Revolution at the outset, hopeful a stateless society would emerge, they were hostile to all forms of state government. By their lights no government, no matter whose interests were in theory represented, could exist alongside true individual liberty.

Neither Marxist nor anarchist, most of the steelworkers at Homestead knew little of these incendiary doctrines that were, to their mind, both alien and foreign. But the Homestead workers needed little convincing of the righteousness of their struggle against bosses like Frick, a man who would lock them out of their jobs and take the food from their tables: rebellion against tyranny was a long-standing native American practice.

3. The Immigrant and Native Traditions of American Anarchism

The European communal anarchism of theorists like Kropotkin and Bakunin was less welcome on American soil, due in part to the nativism that flourished in late-nineteenth- and twentieth-century America. Although vibrant communities of recent immigrants speaking in German, Polish, Russian, or Yiddish preached anarchism in the cities and seaports of coastal America in this period, few English-speaking native American workers rallied to these banners. A simple fear of the foreign-born worker, too easily exploited as a blackleg, or strike-breaker, fueled some of the xenophobia that kept European anarchism at bay as a foreign and suspect ideology. In addition, the American press labeled anarchism a noxious foreign import, relevant, if at all, only in autocratic governments like Russia and Germany. When political violence was committed—in the attempt on the life of Kaiser Wilhelm in 1878, in the bombing of the Winter Palace in St. Peters-

burg in 1880, and in the successful assassination of Czar Alexander II
a year later—the upheaval envisioned seemed remote. But the Haymarket riot changed all that.

At the time of the riot, militant anarchism had reached a high-
water mark in its outreach to American workers in such urban centers
as Chicago. Witness to a history of violent labor upheavals and brutal police suppression, Chicago had swollen with immigrant workers
and their families, their impoverished and desperate living conditions
painfully visible as the gap between rich and poor widened in the
economic depression of 1884 to 1886. In such nurturant soil, radical
politics flourished, with many socialists and anarchists believing that
class warfare and revolution were imminent. More than five anarchist
newspapers, published in German, Russian, Bohemian, and English,
circulated in Chicago and Detroit at the time of Haymarket, with a
readership of more than 30,000. The International Working People's
Association, active in the rapidly expanding national movement for
the eight-hour day, was led by anarchists August Spies and Albert Parsons, the latter, no foreign immigrant, possessing an American lin-
eage that reached back to the Revolutionary War.

The bloody events at Haymarket began May 3, 1886, when police
fired at workers and their sympathizers who were striking at the Mc-
Cormick Harvesting Machine Company, wounding some of those
who had assembled to picket or support the strikers. Before the outbreak of violence, incendiary rhetoric had been running high in anarchist newspapers and in the mainstream press. Now, responding to
the police shootings, August Spies called for armed resistance from
the workers, while the mainstream press called for the arrest of Spies
and Parsons, urging they be made an example of if any trouble broke
out. When a bomb was thrown by an unknown assailant at a peaceful
demonstration in Chicago's Haymarket Square on May 4, mayhem
erupted. Seven policemen were killed and sixty policemen were in-

jured—either by the bomb itself or, some suggest, by police bullets fired in the confusion that followed—while an unknown number of protesters in the crowd were also killed or injured.

Now having in hand the reason it needed to silence the most visible agitators, the state struck back. In spite of no evidence linking them to the bombing, Spies and Parsons and six other leading anarchists were arrested, tried, and sentenced to death. When four of the anarchists, including Spies and Parsons, were executed a year later, the international outcry was loud enough to reach the ears of young Alexander Berkman, who was planning to come to America. But at the same time that Haymarket conferred martyrdom on men who would become the saints of the movement, the riots undermined the influence of European anarchism among American workers, forging fateful links between anarchy, violence, and terror that would be reinforced by the mainstream press. At the Haymarket trials, the state's attorney proclaimed that anarchy, compounded of foreign ideas, was itself on trial. The *New York Times* questioned the wisdom of permitting foreigners to immigrate, calling anarchists "shirkers" and "deadbeats," and adding "it is highly improbable that there is a single native anarchist in the United States."[8]

But there was indeed a vibrant native anarchist movement in late-nineteenth-century America, one that eschewed violence as the agent of social and political change, an anarchism quite free of European anarchism's nostalgia for a communal golden age of the past or its hopes for shared ownership in the future. While most American reformers in the last decades of the nineteenth century, such as the Populists and the early Progressives, turned to the state as the ally of poorer farmers, craftsmen, and workers, calling, for example, for nationalization of the railroads and the telegraph and for government regulation of trusts and monopolies, a vocal group of native anarchist advocates for the poor gave voice to the individualist, antigovernment, antistatist ideals of the people's champions from the early Republic. Those founding radical liberals were the voices heard in America's most influential anarchist journal, Benjamin Tucker's *Liberty,* published from 1881 to 1907. One was the proto-anarchist voice of Tom Paine, praising civil society as self-regulating and a blessing, while saying "government even in its best state is but a necessary evil."[9] Another was Thomas Jefferson's contention that the best government governs least, the "motto" with which Thoreau began his famous 1849 essay, *Resistance to Civil Government.* And another was the laissez-faire antistatism at the heart of radical attacks on wealth and privilege found in Jacksonian rhetoric.

> It is under the word *government* that the subtle danger lurks. Understood as a central consolidated power, managing and directing the various general interests of the society, all government is evil, and the parent of evil. A strong and active democratic government in the common sense of the term is an evil, differing only in degree and mode of operation, and not in nature, from a strong despotism . . . the best government is that which governs least. . . . Government should have as little as possible to do with the general business and interests of the people.[10]

The American anarchist movement never abandoned this native early aversion to the state, even as other reformers would turn to its potential as rescuer of the poor. American anarchists continued to see government as, inevitably, the tool of the powerful and well-to-do, whether they be monarchs, noblemen, and clerics, or bankers and monopolists. Its two leading nineteenth-century theorists, Josiah Warren (1798–1874) before the Civil War, his dalliance with utopian socialist communalism behind him, and Benjamin Tucker (1854–1939) after the Civil War, both spoke in this radical, individualistic, antigovernment language of spontaneous action, self-regulating civil society, free competition, and association, what they called the "voluntary principle." But there was, to be sure, an important foreign influence on both of them, the French writer Pierre-Joseph Proudhon (1809–1865), who coined the word *anarchism* and whose writings had been popularized in America by Horace Greeley's *New York Tribune* in 1849 and 1850.

Totally eschewing violence and utterly uninterested in militant destruction of the state, Proudhon's anarchist strategy, ridiculed by Marx, envisioned dissolving the state by first transforming the economy. Warren and Tucker shared Proudhon's conviction that the anarchist reorganization of society would occur through economic action, not political revolution. Worker and producer associations would replace government as people, mutually bargaining and contracting with one another, created networks of voluntary groups based on agreements among freely consenting individuals.

These individualist American anarchists were, by and large, committed to the moral legitimacy of private property when it was a product of personal labor and hard work, but they feared its corruption by monopolistic capital concentration, facilitated and guaranteed by the coercive institutions of the centralized state. One of Proudhon's proposed economic innovations, the "People's Bank," was particularly appealing to American anarchists as a powerful tool with which to subvert the financial foundation of that governmental-capital-monopoly nexus. People's banks, providing credit at cost, interest-free, based on mutual exchanges of labor, products, and services and signified by negotiable credit and labor "checks," would, Proudhon and his American followers believed, help produce the free contractual associations of workers, peasant-farmers, and craftsmen that ultimately and peacefully would create a new, restructured, cooperative, self-regulating social order, with no need for government and its inevitable restrictions on individual freedom.

During the years of increased centralization of state authority and the emergence of powerful industrial monopolies, Berkman's contemporary Benjamin Tucker raised a critical American voice in support of the sovereign individual's right of free access to the market and to capital. In very Lockean terms, he argued that private property was an extension of personhood and a guarantor of an individual's liberty. The acquisition of "monopolistic" capital, on the other hand, depended on thwarting competition through copyright, tariffs, patents, rents, and interest, all of which prevented equal entrance into the competitive marketplace. If capital were released from government-protected monopolies, as Tucker urged, and placed within the reach of individuals by people's banks, the market system could produce harmony and justice.

Optimistic, egalitarian, and individualistic, American anarchism joined its European cousin in calling for the scaffolding of the state to fall away from the individual, leaving him or her able to discover a better self, unconstrained by unnatural and coercive authority. But while the European variety of communal anarchists tended to march under the banner of cooperation, believed to be native to the human species, or under the banner of violence directed at political leaders, the American variety espoused by Benjamin Tucker preached social and economic transformation and singled out monopoly capitalists as the villains. Rather than on princes and kings, American individualist anarchism fixed its anger on Rockefellers and Vanderbilts.

To a certain extent, then, Alexander Berkman, immigrant anarchist, failed assassin of the industrialist Henry Clay Frick, absorbed some of the teachings of native American anarchism. While his anarchism was filled with communal socialist variations, there was some common ground with aspects of American individualist anarchism. They shared at least a common villain, bankers and monopoly capitalists, even if the idea of getting rid of them by violence would be a permanent and defining difference. No surprise, then, that the imprisoned Berkman wrote: "The real despotism of republican institutions . . . rests on the popular delusion of self-government and independence. . . . In modern capitalism, exploitation rather than oppression is the real enemy of the people. Oppression is but its handmaid. Hence the battle is to be waged in the economic, rather than the political field" (*Memoirs*, 424).

4. "The First Terrorist Act in America"

Choosing an industrialist as his target, Berkman claimed he had committed "the first terrorist act in America" (*Memoirs*, 60). With regret, Benjamin Tucker announced in the pages of *Liberty* that he had "no pity for Frick, no praise for Berkman." The act had not only failed in its purpose but had been, Tucker believed, a fool's mission at the outset.[11] Over the course of many years, Alexander Berkman had time to contemplate the cost of his attack on Frick and to weigh its revolutionary use. Still, by the end of his life he could not yet bring himself to say that individual acts of violence were completely without merit as a revolutionary strategy. But Berkman did realize that in expecting to precipitate a mass uprising, he had gravely misunderstood the mind of the American worker.

In prison, he was quickly disabused of his expectations. Only a short time after being jailed, Berkman was confronted by a prisoner who asked why he had tried to kill Frick: "What did I want to 'nose in' for? Help the strikers? I must be crazy to talk that way. Why, it was none of my 'cheese.' Didn't I come from New York? Yes? Well, then, how could the strike concern me? I must have some personal grudge against Frick. Ever had dealings with him? No? Sure? Then it's plain 'bughouse,' no use talking" (*Memoirs*, 51).

A short time later Berkman approached another prisoner, a steelworker from Homestead whom Berkman regarded as a natural ally. This man, too, was incredulous that Berkman's motive for shooting Frick was political. "Some business misunderstanding, eh?" he asks. When Berkman tells him, "It was for you, for your people," the steel-man interrupts him angrily, telling him the men at Homestead would only be harmed by Berkman's actions. "They don't believe in killing, they respect the law. . . . [T]hey had a right to defend their homes and families against unlawful invaders" but "the mill-workers have nothing to do with Anarchists" (*Memoirs*, 55).

Spurning Berkman and the assistance of anarchists to help win the strike, the steelworker echoed the opinions expressed in most American newspapers, which had labeled anarchism violent and alien in the wake of the Haymarket riot. The image of steelworkers defending workplace and home against Pinkerton gunmen may have resonated in the public mind with the pioneer standing armed before his prairie home, but the European anarchist argument against property itself would be met with disbelief by American workingmen, so the *New York Times* argued, men who wished to become property owners themselves. As editors of the *Times* wrote shortly after the Haymarket riot: "The great majority [of wage earners] already own property or hope and labor to own it. . . . Every man and woman of them who have laid aside a few dollars against old age or for the schooling of their children . . . need no argument as to whether their property is robbery, or as to what they have to gain from the lunatics and scoundrels who are spreading the doctrine of general anarchy."[12]

Nor would Berkman find supportive comradeship for his *attentat* among the American anarchists. The publisher of *Liberty* wholly disavowed Berkman's act and worked to separate American anarchism from the doctrine of propaganda by deed that named dynamite as the great equalizing force between monarchs or titans and ordinary working people. Although Tucker had kind words for Berkman and believed they could meet as friends, he saw no path to social improve-ment through the barrel of a gun. "The strengths of the Fricks," Tucker wrote, "rest on violence; now it is to violence that the Berkmans ap-peal. The peril of the Fricks lies in the spreading of the light; violence is the power of darkness. If the revolution comes by violence and in advance of light, the old struggle will have to be begun anew. The hope of humanity lies in the avoidance of that revolution by force which the Berkmans are trying to precipitate."[13]

Worse than the failure to find comradely approval, a cloud of sus-picion now hovered over Berkman, suggesting he had perhaps fatally injured the steelworkers' cause in their face-off with Carnegie's man-agement. Some said that the shooting sealed Frick's decision not to settle the strike, although the decision to call in the state militia after the Pinkertons surrendered had effectively ended the workers' resis-tance some days before Berkman arrived in Pittsburgh. Meanwhile, in Homestead it was a widespread belief among the strikers that Berk-man was a company man, hired to fake an attempt on Frick that would enflame public opinion against the steelworkers. Some years later John McLuckie, the worker-elected mayor of Homestead at the time of the strike, was startled to learn while visiting Emma Goldman that Berkman was still in prison, so broadly based was the belief that he had been secretly released years earlier, as a hired hand for Car-negie.[14]

But the unkindest cut came from anarchist Johann Most, the lead-ing spirit of the immigrant anarchist community in New York, a riv-eting, spell-binding orator and a powerful wielder of the pen. Already bloodied by anarchist agitation, a survivor of many prison terms, Most had welcomed the young Berkman into the movement, put him to work as a typesetter at his German-language journal *Freiheit,* and inspired him with his revolutionary speeches and writings, including his bomb-making manual *Science of Revolutionary Warfare,* with its incendiary advice that a pound of dynamite beat a bushel of ballots. But Berkman's and Most's paths had begun to diverge before Berkman boarded the train for Pittsburgh. Although they had worked amicably in New York for a few years, the older Most and his young comrade found themselves on opposite sides in an internecine anarchist quarrel fed by different visions of future anarchist collectives and by a challenge to Most's leadership in the German-American community. The bitterness of the argument became known as the "Brothers War," and it had repercussions that came back to haunt Berkman when he sought Most's support after his attack on Frick.

With Berkman's attack on Frick making front-page news, Johann Most openly broke with his former comrade, although he took note of Berkman's heroism and bravery in jail. At greater length, in the pages of *Freiheit* under the title "Reflections on Propaganda by Deed," the author of the bomb-making handbook called Berkman an "eccentric," repudiating his act and his hope of attracting more Americans to anarchism. Most wrote: "In a country where we are so poorly represented, and so little understood as in America, we simply cannot afford the luxury of assassination."[15] Privately, he joked that Berkman had used a toy pistol, infuriating Emma Goldman, who accosted him at one of his public lectures and lashed him across the face with a horsewhip. The division in the anarchist community over Berkman's act was profound and lasting, deepening and broadening the schism that had opened in the Brothers War and effectively enervating anarchist political agitation in America. Emma Goldman, who emerged as anarchism's most visible advocate in the early years of the twentieth century, was now anathema among those who remained faithful to Johann Most.

Perhaps some of the more generous responses to Berkman's deed came from Henry Bauer and Carl Nold, who would each suffer five years' imprisonment on Berkman's account. Accused of compromising anarchist principles themselves because they accepted representation by an attorney, Nold and Bauer repudiated Most's criticism of Berkman. Carl Nold, in his *Prison Blossoms* essay "The Red Bugbear" (Chapter 9), poignantly observes that it is "quite impossible as well as undesirable that in the great anarchistic movement all feet should beat time to the same tune."

For his part, the young would-be assassin Alexander Berkman received the news of Most's repudiation with incredulity and despair. Thought a madman by fellow prisoners, thought a fool or worse by fellow anarchists, Berkman felt himself to be wholly deserted. "Now I stand alone," he wrote (*Memoirs*, 83).

5. The Evolution of *Prison Blossoms*

In his *Prison Memoirs*, Berkman remembered the heroic fantasies he and Emma Goldman had shared as young activists, imagining themselves imprisoned for revolutionary crimes, chained to dungeon walls, attacked by vermin, enduring bodily torment. Rather than facing a long imprisonment, Berkman had assumed he would die at the hands of police when he attacked Frick; if left alive, he had decided he would postpone suicide to defend his act at his trial, at which, consistent with anarchist principles, he would permit no defense attorney. But events, when they overtook Berkman, worked against his purpose. Although the judge said he would allow him to read from a testimonial he had prepared in German, his translator was ill prepared for Berkman's syntax, and the truncated, halting English version of Berkman's defense bore little resemblance to the expansive text Berkman had written, even before the judge peremptorily ended the reading. Charged with six separate counts, including not only the attempted murder of Frick but also an intention to harm his associate John Leishman, which Berkman denied, he was given a sentence of twenty-one years in the penitentiary and one year in the workhouse, more than three times the legal sentence for assault; it was later commuted to fourteen years.

Consigned to a long prison term, Berkman had little to reflect upon with satisfaction. The judge had cut short the trial speech that he had hoped would galvanize anarchist propaganda worldwide. As additional insult, Frick's presence on the witness stand, apparently recovered from his wounds, seemed to mock Berkman's skill as an assassin, though the propaganda value of his attack did not depend on Frick's death. Some comfort came from imagining his suicide, but a spoon he was honing as a sharp tool was taken away by guards. In letters from friends, Berkman sensed "disapproving surprise" that he was still alive. Meanwhile, fellow prisoners around him were driven into insane stupors by their brutal treatment, poor diet, and inadequate medical care. He had imagined prison as a place where "social distinctions are abolished, artificial barriers destroyed; . . . one could be his real self, shedding all hypocrisy and artifice at the prison gates." Instead he found "an aggravated counterpart of the outside world . . . the flatterer, the backbiter, the spy" (*Memoirs*, 151).

Although his older fellow prisoners were notably uninterested in his anarchism, they treated Berkman kindly, calling him "the kid," regretting the many years he had to serve. Tutored by them, Berkman learned of a sub-rosa mail route, bypassing the prison censor by paying friendly guards to post letters to comrades on the outside. When not in solitary confinement, he learned he could ignore the injunction against conversation in the workrooms by moving his lips as little as possible when he talked, to avoid detection. His informal education in the subterfuge prisoners used to communicate with each other soon deepened.

Several months after arriving at Western Pennsylvania Penitentiary, Berkman was taken to appear as a witness at the trials of Carl

Nold and Henry Bauer, in spite of Berkman's testimony that he had acted alone. Nold made light of his five-year sentence, calling it a "long-needed vacation from many years of ceaseless factory toil," teasing Bauer that capitalism would suffer the loss of his talented carpentry work (*Memoirs*, 180). Berkman was amazed, then profoundly heartened, when Horsethief, a friendly prisoner with some freedom to travel the cell-block halls, told him Nold and Bauer were housed in the same cell block several tiers above, reachable via communication through the pipes or messages Horsethief himself could carry in his job as a rangeman, or sweeper of corridors.

We know little about this friendly messenger Robert Richards, aka Horsethief, without whom it is unlikely that *Prison Blossoms* would exist in its present expansive form. Convicted in fact for stealing horses, Richards had already served two separate terms at Western Pennsylvania Penitentiary and was a year into his third term when Berkman arrived in 1892. A friend to Berkman, Bauer, and Nold, Richards was an old hand with the prison routine and found no problem in purloining paper from the workrooms when the anarchists' writing threatened to exceed their supply. With Horsethief as mailman, the stranglehold of isolation and despair lifted from Berkman. The three anarchists forged a friendship as a fragile web of communication enabled them to share anarchist theory and trial anecdotes within the prison walls.

Describing the development of these early exchanges, Berkman wrote, "The personal tenor of our correspondence is gradually broadening into the larger scope of socio-political theories, methods of agitation, and applied tactics. The discussions, prolonged and often heated, absorb our interest." Such volubility posed the immediate problem of requiring, as Berkman warned, "greater circumspection" (*Memoirs*, 180, 182). The cells of the notorious anarchists were frequently searched and any indication of collusion among them, particularly their correspondence, which was carried on in German, would have been rapidly interpreted as plotting insurrection. The reaction would have been harshly punitive: indefinite confinement in the "hole," a damp cell below ground level, with a daily diet of water and two ounces of bread. In fact, none of the early messages among the three men has survived. "I destroyed them only very reluctantly," Bauer writes in his essay "Our Prison Life" (Chapter 11), since "our cells were searched for every trifling reason." In addition to harassment by guards, the infant correspondence was threatened by a limited reserve of writing paper. As Berkman notes in *Prison Memoirs of an Anarchist*, "Every available scrap of paper is exhausted; margins of stray newspapers and magazines have been penciled on, the contents repeatedly erased, and the frayed tatters microscopically covered with ink. Even an occasional fly-leaf from library books has been sacrilegiously forced to leave its covers, and every evidence of its previous association dexterously removed. The problem threatens to terminate our correspondence, and fills us with dismay" (*Memoirs*, 182).

When Horsethief promised to provide sheets of smooth yellow wrapping paper from the broom shop where he was employed, Berkman, Bauer, and Nold, elated by their sudden riches, ambitiously converted their informal correspondence into a "magazinelet," which they named *Zuchthausblüthen*, the German term from which the later English "Prison Blossoms" would be derived. They planned "more pretentious issues," to be the same small size, three by five inches, but with an increased number of pages, "each issue to have a different editor, to ensure equality of opportunity; the readers to serve as contributing editors." Berkman described the process by which the tiny magazine gathered material as Horsethief carried the diminutive manuscript from cell to cell.

The appearance of the *Blüthen* is to be regulated by the time required to complete the circle of readers, whose identity is to be masked with certain initials, to protect them against discovery. Henceforth, Bauer, physically a giant, is to be known as "G" [*der Grosse*]; because of my [Berkman's] medium stature, I shall be designated with the letter "M" [*der Mittlere*]; and Nold, as the smallest, by "K" [*der Kleine*]. . . . "M," "K," or "G," are to act, in turn, as editors in chief, whose province it is to start the *Blüthen* on its way, each reader contributing to the issue till it is returned to the original editor, to enable him to read and comment upon his fellow-contributors. The publication, its content growing in transit, is finally to reach the second contributor, upon whom will devolve the editorial management of the following issue. (*Memoirs*, 182, 183)

Amid the dreariness, the boredom, and the humiliation of prison life, the *Zuchthausblüthen* project offered the pleasures of intellectual and aesthetic work. Berkman praised "the little magazine" as "rich in contents and varied in style," distinctive in its varied handwritings, which he suggested "stimulates speculation on the personality of our increasing reader-contributors" (*Memoirs*, 183). Henry Bauer's essay "Penitentiary Administration and the Treatment of Prisoners," testily edited by Berkman when the manuscript reached him in his cell, best preserves the sense of a conversation among editors created by this process of composition.

To Berkman, Bauer, and Nold, the *Zuchthausblüthen* captured the political talk that had animated the sidewalk taverns where anarchists and socialists debated the virtues of imagined communities. For Berkman, in particular, the writing meant the renewal of a sense of political purpose that inspired hope that he might survive imprisonment, versed as he was in the manner in which notable nineteenth-century political prisoners like Chernyshevsky and Kropotkin had triumphed while confined. Chernyshevsky's classic utopian novel *What Is to Be Done* had been spirited out of a St. Petersburg prison. While imprisoned in France during a roundup of anarchists, Berkman's mentor Kropotkin had conducted classes for prisoners in physics, astronomy, geometry, and foreign languages. If Berkman had not indeed found a method to kill himself, as had the Haymarket martyr Louis Lingg, who cheated the hangman on the eve of execution, then the prospect of useful political work through writing was redemptive, and more so if a larger audience for *Zuchthausblüthen* could be found.

In fact, a larger audience was at hand. Imprisoned at the same time as Berkman were prominent leaders of the radical trade union Knights of Labor, Hugh F. Dempsey and Robert J. Beatty, who had been sentenced to seven-year terms at Western Pennsylvania Penitentiary for arranging to poison strikebreakers at the Homestead plant. The men denied the charges, but Berkman hailed them as terrorizers of "scabbery," whether guilty or innocent, and hoped that by including them in the readership of the anarchists' magazine, they could provide "propaganda among workers representing the more radical element of American labor." Painstakingly, a route of communication was established from cell block to cell block, workroom to workroom, again with the help of Horsethief. Several other men joined the correspondence, and Berkman found himself "transcending the limits" of his paper supply as he defended and explained the "historic role of the *Attentäter*," the anarchist who commits a revolutionary deed, "and the social significance of conscious individual protest." More proficient in English after a few years' imprisonment and hoping to do valuable political work, Berkman, Bauer, and Nold suspended the German-composed *Zuchthausblüthen* and began publishing their magazine in the language of their prison readers (*Memoirs*, 184–185).

To be sure, communication among the anarchists, difficult to maintain at best, often broke down arbitrarily. During Berkman's first year of captivity, prison officials were suspicious that clandestine communication was taking place to foment prison unrest or to organize testimony before commissions appointed to investigate prison abuses. Alarmed, they removed Berkman without warning to a different location within the prison, beyond the access of the helpful Horsethief or another friendly rangeman. At such times, when moved to separate cell blocks, the three men were rarely able to communicate, and then only Horsethief's faithful and daring services enabled them to exchange an occasional note. Determined to maintain his revolutionary dignity, despising the sycophant and flatterer, Berkman was often outspoken with prison officials, bringing down on himself the full measure of prison retaliation. Equally defiant, Henry Bauer, who had scorned a judge's order to name the comrades who distributed leaflets with him at Homestead, suffered a demotion in grade during his first year. Such resistance to capricious authority, they believed, was the responsibility of the political prisoner. Shortly after "publishing" the first English edition of their magazine, Berkman was consigned to many days in the hole, suspected of having incited protest among prison workers in the hosiery shop. Close on the heels of imprisonment in the hole, he was given a month in the cell Henry Bauer describes as the "basket," from which Berkman emerged skeletal and enervated. In and out of punishment cells, almost always in solitary confinement, Berkman spent most of his long years in Western Pennsylvania Penitentiary without visitors, and with only limited access to mail.

Yet unexpectedly in his second year of confinement, Berkman was let out of his cell for a limited time and given a range job pouring coffee and sweeping corridors, enabling him to have more contact with Horsethief, who effected the passage of written messages to Nold and Bauer. Berkman's sudden freedom from confinement, the walks along the range and the hushed, secretive conversations with other prisoners, usually about the "rotten grub," the brutal "screws," the "stomach-robber of a Warden," lent him a familiarity with the institution and its inhabitants, from the warden's office to the dungeon, that found its way into the discussions of penal life in *Prison Blossoms*.

These more relaxed conditions permitted a revival of the magazine. The Knights of Labor leaders were released, but propaganda possibilities still loomed attractively in the presence of other workers radicalized by Homestead. Now their readership was broadened to include strikers from Carnegie's Duquesne plant, men who had closed down the steelworks in sympathy with the Homesteaders and had been charged with assault and rioting against strikebreakers. "Subscribers," as Berkman called them, were not only steelworkers, prized in the work of radicalizing the labor force, but also the prison librarian, a former university student, a lawyer, and a writer/novelist, burglars, professional gamblers, and confidence men, all of whom were also enlisted as contributors, with Nold, Bauer, and Berkman acting as alternate editors. Illustrated with pen and ink drawings, the diminutive publication, still small enough to be readily concealed against cell searches, offered a variety of genres, from serious essays to humorous sketches. Nold wrote poetry in German and Berkman expanded reminiscences of an early romance into a short novel set in the New York neighborhoods of revolutionaries and reformers.

During the third year of their imprisonment, the anarchist comrades were able to reflect on what they had achieved under the most dire of circumstances. Berkman, who in the penitentiary was reading his way through a vast collection of literature including the Bible, Shakespeare, the Romantic poets, and many important European and American novels, had become proficient in English, indeed able to mimic the rich, expressive slang in the range of American dialects of the prison-house speakers. Suggesting they preserve their writing for a larger readership, Bauer speculated that their prison writings might be published for an audience beyond the prison, if some way might be found to smuggle the manuscripts out into daylight. Again the resourceful Horsethief was reassuring. Berkman paraphrased Horsethief's response: "Youse fellows jest go ahead an' write, an' don't bother about nothin'. Think I can walk off all right with a team of horses, but ain't got brains enough to get away with a bit of scribbling, eh? Jest leave that to th' Horsethief, an' write till you bust th' paper works, see?" With Horsethief's confident backing, the men "form the ambitious project of publishing a book" under their pseudonyms "MKG" (*Memoirs*, 284).

In the year or more left of Bauer and Nold's confinement, the production of the anarchists was impressive. Berkman said that as many as sixty booklets had been composed and smuggled out to a comrade nearby in Pennsylvania. Again, it was Horsethief who had enabled them to secure these manuscripts against discovery by prison officials. Berkman wrote, "The repeated searches have failed to unearth them. With characteristic daring, the faithful Bob [Horsethief] has secreted them in a hole in the floor of his shop, almost under the very seat of the guard. One by one they have been smuggled outside by a friendly officer." In 1897, as Carl Nold and Henry Bauer made preparations to leave Western Pennsylvania Penitentiary, they were entrusted with arrangements for the publication of their book. Throughout the preceding long four years, only messages had passed between Nold, Bauer, and Berkman. They never worked in the same workrooms, nor shared space along the same corridor. "The loneliness seems heavier," Berkman wrote after Nold and Bauer's release, "the void more painful" (*Memoirs*, 335–336).

In 1900 the names of the three anarchists, Nold, Bauer, and Berkman, were once again linked in the public mind when a daring escape plan of Berkman's was discovered, a plan conceived while Berkman's hope was waning that he'd survive imprisonment. During these years Berkman had entertained some slim hopes for an official pardon, despite the offense to his anarchist principles if he made the appeal himself. At the behest of friends, he consented to have his name put forward by others, repugnant though it was to acknowledge even indirectly the authority of a pardons board or to imply that a revolutionary deed required forgiving. When asked at an interview if he would refrain from anarchist activity if pardoned, he replied he would not. After the appeals were denied, he resigned himself to having to serve out his long sentence unless he found a means of escape. Berkman had become skeletally thin, prone to sleeplessness and bodily pains from exposure to the damp prison climate. He had been made familiar with punishment cells, beatings, and bread-and-water diets. In an environment in which tuberculosis and mental breakdowns were epidemic, his health was at grave risk. Physical survival seemed uncertain.

To escape from prison, Berkman arranged to have a tunnel dug from a house rented nearby, the tunnel connecting at its end to a concealed spot in the prison yard. Anarchist friends raised the money, notes were passed sub rosa and in cipher, Emma Goldman was won over, but ultimately the plans went awry and the excavation was uncovered.[16] The newspapers and prison officials assumed an anarchist plot to rescue Berkman had been fortunately thwarted. Suspicious of such anarchist conspiracies for years, the warden of Western Pennsylvania Penitentiary, Edward S. Wright, was prepared to convict both Nold and Bauer as confederates in the planning along with Berkman, had evidence not securely placed the two released comrades elsewhere. Carl Nold, in fact, had assisted in planning the tunnel's excavation, but was safely in St. Louis and at work while the tunnel was being dug. Henry Bauer remained active in official committees to secure Berkman's release, but his commitment to anarchism seemed less fervent to Berkman after his release, so much so that Berkman referred to Bauer as an "ex-comrade" at the time of the tunnel's discovery. Although no evidence linked him to the escape plan, Berkman was placed for a year in strict solitary confinement, a harrowing year of isolation from which he emerged profoundly shaken physically and mentally. He had passed, he explained in a letter to Emma Goldman, through a "great crisis" (*Memoirs*, 413).

Alexander Berkman was released from Western Pennsylvania Penitentiary in 1905, having received an unexpected commutation of his sentence after passage of a Pennsylvania statute intended to benefit two highly placed tobacco manufacturers who had been convicted of fraud. He was sent directly to a workhouse to serve the last year of his sentence, from which he was released in 1906. His last years in prison had offered him a brief respite from his unmitigated solitude. A new warden had permitted him a visit from Emma Goldman, although he was so stunned by her presence he was unable to speak during their brief encounter. Their friendship forged in a disastrous plan to commit a revolutionary *attentat,* Goldman had remained Berkman's most faithful correspondent during the long years of his imprisonment, his misfortunes and suffering shadowing her life. They would remain loyal compatriots during their future years of political activism in the United States and through shared years of exile in Europe. Their belief in their "beautiful ideal" had known only one serious moment of rupture, and that in 1901, while Berkman was still in prison, when self-proclaimed anarchist Leon Czolgosz assassinated President William McKinley.

Writing to Goldman after Czolgosz's execution, the imprisoned Berkman expressed sympathy for the young assassin but wholly denied the "social value" of his act. Berkman repeated that the battle must be waged in America against persons who are known to be economic exploiters, not statesmen. In America, where "the popular delusion of self-government" prevails, no widespread support will follow for an *attentat* against a political figure. His own act, Berkman explained to Goldman, was far more significant since "it was directed against a tangible, real oppressor, visualized as such by the people" (*Memoirs*, 424). Years later, corresponding from different refuges in

Europe, the two anarchists would still argue over the worthiness of Czolgosz's act of assassination, Goldman acknowledging no difference between the killing of a Frick and the killing of a McKinley, both in her mind being "utterly useless."[17]

6. Release, Activism, and Exile

The authors of *Prison Blossoms* lived into the middle of the fourth decade of the twentieth century, witnesses to the First World War, the Russian Revolution, and the emergence of European fascism. Carl Nold had been a loyal correspondent while Berkman remained in prison in Pennsylvania. He was in St. Louis at the time of McKinley's assassination and helped to hustle Emma Goldman out of the city when newspapers were falsely implicating her in McKinley's death. He was on hand again in the train station in Detroit, where he had settled, to greet the pale and enervated Berkman when he traveled there immediately after his release from the workhouse. While in Detroit, Nold wrote for several anarchist periodicals and taught at the Detroit Modern School, one of twenty such schools in the country founded on the liberatory pedagogy of the Spanish anarchist and educator Francisco Ferrer (1859–1909). Described as a man with a wonderful sense of humor, Nold seems to have won the affection of everyone he met. Toward the end of his life, he amassed material on radicalism in America for the Labadie Collection at the University of Michigan. A member of a dwindling community of anarchists in Detroit, Nold died in 1934.

Henry Bauer died in the same year. Like Nold, after his release from prison Bauer had worked to commute Berkman's sentence, serving as the secretary for the Berkman Defense Committee in Pittsburgh. There he became a distributor of English- and German-language anarchist publications, including *The Firebrand, Free Soci-*

ety, and *Freiheit.* Later he moved to Cleveland, where his interests diverged, cultivating a private garden of rare plants that merited some brief notice in a Cleveland newspaper, a far cry from the incendiary headlines he had garnered as the alleged accomplice of the notorious Berkman.[18] Some mystery clouds Berkman's opinion of Bauer by 1910, when he referred to "developments following his [Bauer's] release having characterized him as a man of loose principle and weak character."[19] Berkman did not explain his comment, but Carl Nold, in correspondence with Berkman when the latter was living as a refugee in France, accused Bauer of having kept money raised in support of Berkman's prison appeals for his own personal use.[20] In spite of the suspicion cast on Bauer, he and Berkman seem to have been on friendly terms when they briefly corresponded toward the end of their lives. Bauer sent news of mutual anarchist friends and described plans to meet the German anarchist Rudolf Rocker, whose writings on anarchism and the labor movement placed him in the forefront of anarchists writing on theoretical matters in the twentieth century. Beyond these associations, however, Bauer seems to have withdrawn from anarchist work.

The life of Alexander Berkman after his release from prison was less quiet. He lived in New York and worked as an editor and writer for Emma Goldman's journal *Mother Earth,* raising that periodical to the status of the primary international publication of the anarchist community. But the circle in which Goldman flourished was uncongenial to Berkman, who found the radical and progressive community surrounding his old friend more literary than revolutionary, more middle-class than working class. In his first years of freedom, he was able to keep at bay some of the malaise that haunted him by exorcizing the nightmare of his long confinement in writing the *Prison Memoirs of an Anarchist,* published by Mother Earth Press in 1912. But while Berkman deliberated like an intellectual, he was by temperament a political activist, impatient with becoming a mere chronicler of events rather than a shaper of them. Posting a report of his travels back to *Mother Earth* when he was en route to California, he was ill at ease with the work of the journalist, remembering the streets that were "haunted by emaciated and bedraggled unemployed." Of them he wrote, "If words could thaw out their frozen misery and send the burning love of their suffering flowing through the heart of a callous world—I would write and write."[21]

After the publication of his *Prison Memoirs* in 1912, Berkman spent only seven more years in America, and he would be jailed again for two of them. But in the time before his deportation to Russia, he remained committed to political struggle in the streets, organizing demonstrations against unemployment, against the militancy of the antilabor movement, and finally against conscription into the army in World War I, for which he was imprisoned again and ultimately deported. In 1914 he organized demonstrations at the home of mine-owner John D. Rockefeller in Tarrytown, New York, after militiamen attacked striking coal miners in Ludlow, Colorado, killing twenty-two strikers, including two women who were suffocated in their tents by fire. When a bomb that may have been intended for Rockefeller's home exploded prematurely in an apartment in Manhattan, some anarchist comrades claimed Berkman had masterminded the plan, although Berkman himself, in a letter to Emma Goldman, wrote that the bomb makers had acted alone.[22]

A year later Berkman moved to San Francisco and founded his own journal, *The Blast,* a more incendiary and less philosophical newspaper than Goldman's *Mother Earth.* In California, he worked in defense of radical labor activists, the victims of judicial reprisals in the tradition of the Haymarket convictions. He was active in the defense of anarchists Matthew Schmidt and David Caplan, arrested for bombing the Los Angeles Times Building in 1910. He led the popular defense of Warren Billings and Tom Mooney, labor radicals arrested without evidence and charged with murder after a bomb exploded during a Preparedness Day parade in San Francisco, killing ten and injuring many. Mooney's death sentence was ultimately commuted after an international outcry organized by Berkman forced President Woodrow Wilson to intervene with the governor of California. When Congress passed the Selective Service Act in 1917, requiring all men between the ages of twenty-one and thirty-three to register for conscription, Berkman's campaign against militarism intensified. With *The Blast* under siege by police, Berkman moved back to New York and organized the No Conscription League with Emma Goldman.

In June 1917, Berkman and Goldman were arrested and charged, under the newly enacted Espionage Act, with conspiracy to induce persons not to register for the draft. He served two years in the Atlanta Federal Penitentiary, seven months of them in solitary confinement for protesting the beating of other prisoners, and emerged from prison broken in health, its horrors, said Goldman, "burned into his soul."[23] A few months after his release, Berkman and Goldman were hustled on board the SS *Buford* sailing out of New York Harbor en route to the new Soviet Union, deported from their adopted country. At a farewell dinner in Chicago shortly before his removal to Ellis Island, Berkman, learning from reporters that Henry Frick had just died, said wryly that Frick was "deported by God."[24]

Berkman spent almost two years observing the Bolshevik Revolution at work in a land he had once thought to be the most backward among nations, now in his mind triumphantly in the vanguard. As an anarchist he was committed to the ideal of social change without the intermediary of a state apparatus, however temporary and transitional such an apparatus was intended to be. But as a revolutionary he pledged himself wholly to the new day he believed the Bolsheviks had begun in a country that had for so long been enslaved. Gradually, though, he became disillusioned and dispirited, watching a cumbersome and corrupt party bureaucracy impede the rebuilding of a new order while a freezing and hungry populace was left without resources. Meanwhile, tolerating no dissent, the Communist Party began imprisoning and executing anarchists. The Cheka, the Soviet secret police, was omnipresent. When the Kronstadt sailors, heroes of the Revolution, backed anti-Bolshevik strikers in St. Petersburg, Berkman worked to effect a compromise with Leon Trotsky, who was preparing to call the Kronstadt sailors enemies of the state. Berkman's efforts failed, Trotsky's army attacked, and to Berkman's horror the Kronstadt heroes were slain in the streets. In 1921, with Emma Goldman, who had shared his Russian travels, Berkman fled Russia.

He would live out the remainder of his life as an exile in France, supported by friends in America and earning what money he could as a translator and writer. In 1922 he published the pamphlets *Kronstadt* and *The Russian Tragedy*. In 1925 he published the diaries of his Russian experience in a book titled *The Bolshevik Myth*. To simplify anarchist theory for ordinary readers, he published *What Is Communist Anarchism?* in 1929. In 1936, terminally ill and in great pain, Alexander Berkman took his own life in Nice, where he is buried. Although the "beautiful ideal" to which he had dedicated his life seemed perilously illusory in his later years, he had not abandoned his belief that international cooperation and individual liberty—anarchism, in his mind —would someday prevail.

Nor, in spite of acknowledging the failure of the anarchist mission in America, did he wholly disavow the act of terror for which he had given fourteen years of his life, although, with some vagueness, he once added in a letter to Emma Goldman, "I am in general now not in favor of terroristic tactics, except under very exceptional conditions."[25] Berkman had lived long enough to witness the influence of

anarchism diminishing, its numbers of followers dwindling as political radicals looked increasingly to economic and political centralization as the solution to social ills, the supremacy of the individual sub-
ordinated to collective values. Taking stock of his life of activism only
months before he died, he wrote to Emma Goldman that their years
in service to their beautiful ideal had not brought its realization closer.
"We have failed to create a mass movement," he conceded, adding,
"How that is to be done, that's another question, and a very difficult
one."[26]

In the long years of his activism, Berkman had not fully compre-
hended or appreciated the nature of the resistance anarchism met in
America. The incredulity and disdain with which American workers
had greeted Berkman as the failed assassin of Henry Clay Frick was
emblematic of the more widespread nativist rejection of anarchism
as alien and violent. The notion of the unkempt, dangerous anarchist
that had begun as a popular prejudice at the time of the Haymarket
riot was fanned into greater animus during the economic downturn
of the 1890s and was hardened into abomination by anarchist agitation against America's entry into World War I. Against a national enthusiasm for military intervention and patriotic loyalty, images of
anarchists blurred with socialists and radicals of all persuasions—
immigrants, for the most part, so it was believed, who had carried
their unsavory politics with them from eastern and southern Europe.
An emerging pseudoscience of eugenics, in the service of the new
American nativism, was quick to label such foreigners as members of
an inferior race, hostile to the Anglo-Saxon traditions of the nation's
founding.

To be sure, the growing hostility toward immigrants, whose numbers swelled in the 1890s and the first decades of the twentieth century, clashed uncomfortably with traditions based on America as a
refuge from European tyranny and a melting pot of assimilation into

bedrock American values, such as the promise of advancement as a
return for hard work. Still, as an inflexible plutocracy of millionaires
remained uncompromising in labor disputes, and as the American
dream of climbing a ladder to material success fell under assault, anarchism's vague dream of a future in which networks of craftsmen
would be free from the iron grip of state laws seemed increasingly illusory, perhaps irrelevant. When the Industrial Workers of the World
(IWW) convened in 1905 to found "one big union," their numbers
included anarchists as well as socialists and trade unionists. However,
the movement toward centralization was inconsistent with anarchist
beliefs in localism, and while anarchists worked within the IWW,
their integration was strained.[27]

From his vantage points in New York City, as an editor of *Mother
Earth,* and San Francisco, as editor of *The Blast,* Alexander Berkman
sought to reverse anarchism's apparent declining influence, asking
anarchists to achieve solidarity with working-class grievances "to
rouse the social consciousness throughout the land" against the
"growing menace" of national repression.[28] Such repression was most
fatefully inflicted by the Palmer Raids after World War I, when hundreds of foreign-born anarchists, many of them only theoretical anarchists, were deported from American shores, effectively marginal-
izing the political work of activists like Berkman.[29] Ultimately,
however, it was communism, not anarchism, that attracted younger
radicals to its barricades, in the wake of the successful Bolshevik Revolution that seemed to promise to redress social and economic grievances through the Soviet state.

Their ranks thinning, their comrades aging, anarchists became
more invested in education than in agitation. From exile in France,
Berkman argued for a new literature to achieve the intellectual revolution without which no agitation could be effective. Indeed, toward

this end his *What Is Communist Anarchism?*—with its simple language and contemporary political references—models the kind of liberatory education he believed the next generation of anarchists must provide. In Detroit, Berkman's old comrade Carl Nold spoke at the Ferrer School, keeping the black banner of anarchism alive as his community dwindled around him. And if Henry Bauer's garden in Pittsburgh drew only passing interest in the 1930s, another generation of anarchists, not yet conceived, would in the 1960s and '70s herald the virtues of local food as well as communes, locally organized day care centers, theater groups, and clinics, all in resistance to the militancy and obduracy of states that no longer seemed to provide a model anywhere for the redress of grievances.

But these brief flickers of anarchist resurgence in the United States would not have altered the sad finality with which Alexander Berkman wrote of the failure of the mission to create a mass movement. And yet, when comrades despaired of social progress Berkman chided them for their pessimism. As fascism threatened and the promise of the Bolshevik Revolution faded in the Soviet Union, Berkman insisted there were reasons to be hopeful. In a 1935 letter to a friend, he wrote that while, tragically, men might struggle for false ideals, "it all proves that men DO long and fight for ideals. And in THAT is the great hope of humanity. Some day people will find the REAL ideal— and they will fight for it and realize it. . . . Fascism and nationalism are nothing new. Under different names they existed in old Rome and Greece and in feudal times. They PASSED and so will the modern fascism pass—and that is why I do not doubt my anarchism."[30]

It was with such hopefulness, and with such a refusal to be cowed and constrained, that Berkman, Bauer, and Nold wrote, hid, and circulated their *Prison Blossoms* in Western Pennsylvania Penitentiary. Those documents that survived cell searches, police raids, and the losses that befall the belongings of stateless refugees are published here in their entirety for the first time.

Notes

1. Alexander Berkman, *Prison Memoirs of an Anarchist* (New York: New York Review Books, 1970), 60.

2. For a thorough analysis of Andrew Carnegie's complex relationship with Henry Clay Frick, see David Nasaw, *Andrew Carnegie* (New York: Penguin Press, 2006).

3. Berkman, *Memoirs*, 8. All subsequent references to Berkman's *Prison Memoirs of an Anarchist* will be made as in-text citations.

4. Alexander Berkman, "Violence and Anarchism," *The Blast: Complete Collection of the Incendiary San Francisco Bi-Monthly Anarchist Newspaper* (Edinburgh and Oakland: AK Press, 2005), vol. 1, no. 17, 142.

5. Alexander Berkman, *What Is Anarchism?* (Edinburgh and Oakland: AK Press, 2003), xii–xiii.

6. For a discussion of Kropotkin's work in *Le Révolté*, the influential journal he founded in 1878, and the evolution of the idea of "propaganda by deed," see George Woodcock, *Anarchism: A History of Libertarian Ideas and Movements* (Cleveland: Meridian Books, 1962), 198–199, 210–211, 329.

7. Berkman, *What Is Anarchism?*, 172.

8. "Anarchy's Red Hand," *New York Times*, May 5, 1886, 1.

9. Thomas Paine, *Common Sense*, ed. Isaac Kramnick (Harmondsworth: Penguin Classics, 1986), 65.

10. "Introduction," *The United States Magazine and Democratic Review*, ed. John L. O'Sullivan, vol. 1, no. 1 (October 1837): 6.

11. Benjamin Tucker, "Save Labor from Its Friends," in *The Individualist Anarchists: An Anthology of "Liberty" (1881–1908)*, ed. Frank H. Brooks (New Brunswick, N.J.: Transaction Publishers, 1994), 308.

12. *New York Times*, May 7, 1888, 4. For a well-documented description of the American reception of nineteenth-century anarchism in the mainstream press, see Billie Jeanne Hackley Stevenson, "Ideology of American Anarchism 1880–1910," Ph.D. diss., University of Iowa, 1972, 257–309.

13. Tucker, "Save Labor from Its Friends," 307–308.

14. Emma Goldman, *Living My Life* (New York: Dover Publications, 1970), 180.

15. Johann Most, "Attentats-Reflexionen," in Candace Falk, ed., *Emma*

Goldman: A Documentary History of the American Years, vol. 1: *Made for America, 1890–1901* (Berkeley: University of California Press, 2003), 119 n. 1.

16. Recalling the escape attempt in her autobiography, Goldman wrote, "The scheme seemed fantastic. . . . Yet I was carried away." Goldman, *Living My Life,* 247. In a letter to Max Nettlau, written in July 1900 while plans were under way, she says she is prepared to meet Berkman in Europe after his escape, obviously hopeful that the attempt will succeed. Falk, *Emma Goldman,* 414. When he wrote his *Prison Memoirs,* Berkman speculated somewhat ruefully that the attempt might have succeeded if Goldman had been in America at the time to lend her organizational skills to the project (395).

17. Emma Goldman, *Nowhere at Home: Letters from Exile of Emma Goldman and Alexander Berkman,* ed. Richard Drinnon and Anna Maria Drinnon (New York: Schocken Books, 1975), 95.

18. "Rare Garden," *Cleveland Press,* July 15, 1930, Alexander Berkman Papers, International Institute of Social History, Amsterdam.

19. Alexander Berkman Papers, The Tamiment Library and Robert F. Wagner Labor Archives, New York University, New York.

20. Alexander Berkman Papers, June 12, 1925, International Institute of Social History, Amsterdam.

21. Alexander Berkman, "Innocent Abroad 2," *Mother Earth* 9, no. 12 (1915): 388.

22. For suggestions that Berkman was involved in the explosion, see Paul Avrich, *Anarchist Voices: An Oral History of Anarchism in America* (Edinburgh and Oakland: AK Press, 2005), 206, 213, 218. On Berkman's denying knowledge of the plan, see Goldman, *Living My Life,* 536.

23. Goldman, *Living My Life,* 698.

24. Ibid., 709.

25. Goldman, *Nowhere at Home,* 97.

26. Ibid., 63.

27. For example, Berkman took note of the failure on the part of the IWW and the Socialist Party to condemn the arrest of labor agitator Frank Tannenbaum, who had led a parade of unemployed workers into a church for refuge. He accused Socialists and the IWW of seeking means "to limit and paralyze the movement of the unemployed." See Alexander Berkman, "The Movement of the Unemployed," *Mother Earth* 9, no. 2 (April 1914), reprinted in *Anarchy! An Anthology of Emma Goldman's Mother Earth,* ed. Peter Glassgold (Washington, D.C.: Counterpoint, 2001), 338–344.

28. Alexander Berkman, "Legal Assassination," *Mother Earth* 11, no. 8 (October 1916), reprinted in *Anarchy! An Anthology of Emma Goldman's Mother Earth,* ed. Peter Glassgold (Washington, D.C.: Counterpoint, 2001), 289.

29. In November 1919 and January 1920, in response to the Bolshevik Revolution and continued labor unrest at home, radicals, particularly anarchists, were deported from the United States under the direction of Attorney General Mitchell Palmer and his appointee, J. Edgar Hoover.

30. Alexander Berkman to Pauline Turkel (March 21, 1935), in Berkman, *Life of an Anarchist: The Alexander Berkman Reader,* ed. Gene Fellner (New York: Seven Stories Press, 2005), 260.

PRISON BLOSSOMS

Even in the strictest prison one can do a lot of underground work. For instance, in the Penna. prison, 40 years ago, one of the most reactionary prisons and very strict, we did publish a little magazine secretly and we got interested in it a number of ordinary prisoners. They even became contributors—some discussing the daily events in and out of prison, others commenting on their cases, their experiences etc. The little magazine (PRISON BLOSSOMS and the JAIL BIRD) was awaited anxiously and read with avidity. It was considered an honor to be admitted to the confidential circle that edited, published and circulated the magazine in Riverside (Western Penitentiary of Pennsylvania).

ALEXANDER BERKMAN
to journalist Henry G. Alsberg, ca. 1933–1935

Remembering Homestead—
The Strike and the Jails

I N T H E S E S E L E C T I O N S the anarchists explain the political work among the Carnegie Steel Company workers that led to their arrests and trials. Carl Nold's vivid narrative "Capital and the Battle on the Monongahela" describes the fateful confrontation between Carnegie's hired Pinkerton army and locked-out workers at Homestead, Pennsylvania. In "A Fateful Leaflet," Henry Bauer captures the volatile and explosive mood at Homestead as he describes his harrowing experience attempting propaganda work. In "Autobiographical Sketches," one of his few self-revelatory accounts in either published or unpublished writings, Alexander Berkman recalls the formative youthful experiences that led him to anarchist work. Insisting that agitation in America will be effective only against economic targets, not political ones, Berkman introduces an argument he will use in other writings to distinguish his attempted assassination of steelworks manager Henry Frick in 1892 from anarchist Leon Czolgosz's assassination of President William McKinley in 1901. Although Berk-man offers a narrative of the moments that preceded and followed his shooting of Frick, he does not describe the attack itself in *Prison Blos-soms*. He does offer a dramatic account of the shooting in his *Prison Memoirs of an Anarchist* that is excerpted in the introduction to this volume.

Charged with the attempt on Frick's life, all three anarchists de-scribe the conditions of the Allegheny County Jail, where they were held while awaiting trial. In their trials, which they called farces, Bauer and Nold used attorneys to mount their defense. Berkman, adher-ing to anarchist principles, refused an attorney's help. He recounts his later frustration in court when he was prevented from presenting his personally prepared statement to the American working class.

Capital and the Battle on the Monongahela

CARL NOLD

. . . THAT'S THE WAY it happens; let mankind go to the dogs, wringing its hands, and conservative leaders of workers and other preachers cite the contents of the Bible, the American Declaration of Independence, the laws of nature and of man, but Capital will only have a scornful laugh to spare, for Right is not Might, but rather Might is Right! That's how it is according to the agenda of Capital, that's how it is done and indeed, things will be done like that until the workers make this agenda their own. The Homestead Strike teaches us the same lesson.

When in June of 1892 the wage contract between the Amalgamated Association of Iron and Steel Workers and the Carnegie Company expired, and the company, under the management of H. C. Frick, refused to sign a new wage contract, thus ceasing to recognize the union of its employees, it was evident that the company was more willing to lose millions than to give their workers—who had made them rich—

3

even the crumbs from their table. Even before the old wage contract had expired, the company had already decided to break the employee union at any cost, yes, even with force, the same force that had already sent thousands of poor devils to prison, but that the Carnegie Company was allowed to wield, just because it is a member of the privileged law-breakers of this land.

A strong, high, wooden fence was built around the company mill, fitted out with barbed wire and firing slits. The well-known outlaw company "Pinkerton" was given the go-ahead to have 300 of their people at the ready, and preparations were made to fill the mill with scabs without delay in case the unionized workers went on strike.[1] Then the workers were told either to comply with the company's terms—low pay and leave the union—or be thrown out onto the street.

And this well thought out and well prepared plot of the Carnegie Company against its workers was completely legal, whereas the later attempts of the workers to persuade the scabs to stop work were damned by the judges as illegal.

The workers did not comply with the company's terms, whereupon the company shut down one part of their mill and threw several hundred employees out into the street. Subsequently, everyone stopped work, nearly 4,000 men. This was how the Homestead Strike, now well-known internationally, began.

In the second week of the strike, the company called up the Pinkertons, who, 300 strong, sailed up the Monongahela River in two boats during the night of July 5–6, in order to secretly enter the Homestead mill abutting the river that the strikers were guarding (and in order to shield a number of scabs). This plan was foiled, however, by the vigilance of the strikers. For as soon as the boats came into sight on the morning of the 6th of July, they were met by the partially armed strikers who had gathered on the bank, and were prevented from landing.

The leader of the Pinkertons gave the order to fire and the workers answered the shots of the enemy. Thus was battle joined and it raged nonstop for the next ten hours. The boats were fired on by two old cannons; logs soaked in oil were set on fire and thrown into the river in order to burn the boats; even dynamite bombs were used. Meanwhile, a spirited volley was maintained on both sides. Among the 300 Pinkertons, fear and despair prevailed. Several Pinkertons chose to commit suicide by jumping into the river rather than fall into the hands of the strikers.

Toward evening the Pinkertons ran up a white flag. They were allowed to land, their weapons were taken from them and, humiliated and disgraced, they were driven out of the city by blows, shoves, and a hail of rocks.

Joy over the victory of the workers was great, but greater still was the jubilation over the defeat that the bloodthirsty dogs of Capital had suffered.

Here, as in the Great Railroad Strike in Pittsburgh in 1877, might was set against the might of Capital and in both cases the workers walked away in victory because of it.[2]

The capitalist press railed against the lawless strikers in special editions; but they found the lawless scheme of the Carnegie Company quite in order. They swore up and down that no one could or would sympathize with workers who resort to violence and tried to stir up public opinion against the strikers using every argument, but in vain. The entire working class in the United States sympathized with the strikers who had successfully given the hated Pinkertons as well as the company a dose of their own medicine.

The Pinkertons were now indeed defeated, but the strike not yet won, because the state, the guardian of all privileged predators and exploiters, then came to the aid of the Carnegie Company. The Pittsburgh Militia, a volunteer military organization largely made up of young, ignorant boys who take foolish pleasure in carrying guns and wearing brightly colored coats, who should be given a nanny rather than a gun to take into the field, and who don't have enough brains to understand that they are merely the trained bears of Capital, were sent off to Homestead to restore holy order. So now, with around 4,000 militia boys at their side, the police—from whom nothing had been heard until then—gained new courage and at the company's behest made new arrests every day until 167 of the strikers found themselves charged with murder, riot, conspiracy, etc.

In the other mills of the Carnegie Company, in Pittsburgh, Beaver Falls, Duquesne, etc., the workers then went on strike and thus showed in a heroic way their sympathy with the Homestead strikers, but to no avail. The Carnegie Company's millions were stronger than the empty fists of the workers; the slew of scabs that showed up, as well as the hunger that slowly crept into the cottages of the brave strikers, had a share in the fact that after struggling for five months, the strike was acknowledged as a lost cause; the union was broken and most of the workers returned to work under the terms of the company.

Andrew Carnegie, flatteringly self-styled multi-millionaire, iron and steel king, philanthropist, organ benefactor, founder of libraries and steel-plate swindler, could now shake the hand of his unscrupulous general manager, the multi-millionaire, coke baron, flayer of workers, H. C. Frick, and congratulate him on his victory.[3]

But the victory of the Homestead workers over the Pinkertons stands as the pinnacle in the history of the American workers' movement and at the same time as a lesson for all workers in solving the social question. One can be for or against the use of force, but the fact that Capital always uses force first and strives with ever more success to wrest from the worker his last legal resources like strike, boycott, petition etc., cannot be denied and teaches us that no means are left to the worker except force; he is in fact driven to use it by Capital.

Five months after these events, justice, now turned prostitute, was raped in the Pittsburgh Criminal Court.

The strikers under arrest were charged first and foremost with murder; there followed charges of riot, conspiracy, disorderly conduct, carrying concealed weapons, etc. The more charges against the strikers, the better, thought Frick and the public prosecutor, and the ridiculous charge of high treason was added on. So, by stringing up a dozen of these strikers on the gallows on these charges and throwing more than a hundred into prison, the Carnegie Company reckoned they'd have their peace—this in return for the strikers' sending the company's bloodthirsty lackeys, the Pinkertons, home with bloody heads.

Although the press had deployed all their means during the five months to stir up sentiment against the strikers, they had not succeeded. The charge of high treason was generally considered crazy. The public prosecutor did everything he could to satisfy the bloodthirsty Carnegie Company, especially Frick, and to help him earn his blood money by sending some of the accused to the gallows. But to his indignation and to the indignation of the press, of the capitalists, and of the judges, his fervent efforts were in vain. Sylvester Critchlow, Jack Clifford, and Hugh O'Donnell—the latter was the leader of the strike—who were charged with murder and put on trial, were acquitted.[4] In view of the public's great sympathy with the strikers, it was well-nigh impossible to find the accused guilty, and the charge of murder against two dozen others had to be dropped; but because of the charges of high treason, riot, etc., all of the prisoners had to be detained on bail for further trial.

The strikers had been charged with every possible crime, but on the other hand not the least effort was made to punish the Pinkertons, those murderers, bought and paid for by Capital, or the Carnegie Company itself, against both of whom the strikers had brought charges of murder and conspiracy.

Capital simply buys itself justice as it needs it, but poor workers have to wait half a year in a cramped jail cell for a murder trial vengefully forced on them, with the gallows before them day and night.

The Pittsburgh public prosecutor, realizing that no jurors would have anything to do with sending the strikers to prison, settled the matter with the lawyers of the strikers and the Carnegie Company as follows: "If the strikers drop the charges against the Carnegie Company, we'll set them free." And so it happened.

But unless the Carnegie Company's thirst for revenge was slaked, it wasn't really conceivable that the whole affair would just sink into oblivion. From time immemorial, those in power have swung a cross in the one hand and a stick in the other over their slaves, so it was a matter of course that this time, too, no exception should be made.

The scabs who had taken over the places of the strikers in the Homestead mill were so hated that they could obtain neither food nor lodgings in the entire city. The company found itself therefore forced to set up kitchens and places to sleep inside the mill. Shortly thereafter, a number of the scabs fell ill and several died. The rumor was circulated that the strikers had poisoned them by mixing poison in their food. On the basis of statements made by Patrick Gallagher and J. M. Davidson, Robert J. Beatty and Hugh F. Dempsey, the latter the District Master Workman of the Knights of Labor, were arrested and all four were put on trial for poisoning.[5] The first two appeared as witnesses for the state against the other two. The evidence for poisoning was highly suspect: even though it was shown that there was reason to doubt the character of the two state witnesses that the Carnegie Company and the Pinkertons were watching over like guardian angels, and even though it was proven that bad water from the Monongahela River, spoiled food of poor quality, as well as extremely dirty conditions in the kitchen were enough to make any healthy person sick, Dempsey and Beatty both received sentences of seven years in the penitentiary, Gallagher five years, and Davidson three years.[6] Another man had already been sentenced to 22 years, and two others were to be presented with five years each—altogether 54 years' imprisonment for seven people. That eased the Carnegie Company's thirst for revenge to some degree.

> "Down with everything that stands in our way; blood and corpses don't scare us. With the state on our one side, with the church on the other, we'll seize power and double our millions. That is our purpose in life."

That is Capital speaking. In contrast, the worker with a wife and children lies in the dust, hungry and bleeding from a hundred wounds, relying on the law and the Bible, giving resolutions and the vote a try, clenching his fists in his pockets and crying out to the gods. Exploited by the state as cannon fodder, by Capital as a drive belt, by the church as a sacrificial lamb, by politicians as a mindless herd of voters, he finally lies down, exhausted, to make way for new, young victims. Not having enjoyed the pleasures of life, having learned nothing from history, having worked his whole life yet without earning enough to be able to pay for his burial, he is at last hastily shoved in the ground. His death means stale bread for another.

And triumphantly the pleasure train of Capital rolls on, spattering the blood of crushed, wretched men to either side. Blinded by the brilliance of gold and diamonds, those inside see nothing. The blood-curdling cries of those who are run over are drowned out by the clink of glasses and the laughter of the travelers. Onward, ever onward, it travels along the track, and yet it must stop eventually. At the end of the line in the years 1789–94, the French revolutionaries had set up not a grand, elegant train station, but—a guillotine.

> "And history repeats itself."

A Fateful Leaflet

HENRY BAUER

TOGETHER WITH A COMRADE by the name of Paul Eckert, Carl Nold lived in the three-story building at 5 Cherry St. in Allegheny.[1] Eckert lived on the first floor, Nold on the second, and on the third, the Allegheny Group I had installed a printing press.[2]

In the first week of the month of July 1892, when the Homestead strike was blazing the most fiercely, several comrades thought it would be useful to issue a leaflet in English for the strikers. A manuscript was soon at hand, and two comrades—of whom Nold was one—set and printed it, and it was then distributed by me and two other comrades in Homestead. The name of the author as well as the names of the two comrades who handed out the leaflets with me cannot, for understandable reasons, be given here.[3]

The leaflet itself is reproduced verbatim in what follows. . . .[4]

Strikers! Brothers! Read and Think! "Resistance to tyranny is obedience to God!" That was the battle-cry of our ancestors at the revolution of 1776 under the leadership of Washington, Payne, Jefferson, Franklin, etc. We strikers are obliged to witness how tyranny is strutting at Homestead; to see how the greatest fraud and hypocrite of Pennsylvania, the "philanthropist" Carnegie, has transformed his factory, created by us workingmen, but robbed from us by the thieves Carnegie, Frick and Co. and by law and privilege, into an armory, and has thus actually declared war against us workers whom he has robbed of their wealth. They ask us to work upon conditions which we can not accept unless we are cowardly curs. None but curs will lick their master's foot after being kicked. Brothers! You all know that Carnegie wants to pay us starvation wages and means to lower us into a condition unworthy of human beings. He wants us to be his obedient, meek servants; his submissive, fawning slaves; and since he is importing into our peaceable community the suspicious tools of the robberclass—murderers, deputy sheriffs and Pinkerton assassins—for the purpose of shooting us down because we are not willing to starve to death, we are obliged to resort to effective methods of defending our lives and our rights.

Carnegie was the first to adopt violent measures against us; he is intent upon starving and suppressing us even if he has to butcher us cold-bloodedly to accomplish it. Are we workingmen who have created all of Carnegie's wealth, to suffer this? No! a thousand times: No! The infamous Carnegies, Fricks and their ilk are forcing revolutionary methods upon the working people and are indeed destroying all hopes of a peaceable solution of the economic problem. Brothers! We have no alternative but to meet force with force. We have seen several of our brothers murdered in cold blood by the Pinkerton assassins. He says we attempted to prevent the landing of his hellish army, but it was a costly attempt. These murderers are armed with Winchester rifles while we have but revolvers and stones. What absurdity! We ought to prepare for war in times of peace. If we have no Winchester rifles like themselves or something superior it would be suicidal to fight the Pinkertons. Remember that, brothers, and do not be killed on account of a trifle. If you wish to fight capitalism you ought to be sure you have superior arms or else yours will be all the dead and wounded. Remember that and act accordingly!

The present system of production, distribution and transportation created Carnegies, Vanderbilts and Jay Goulds, etc. on one side, and poverty stricken wealth-producers, tramps, beggars, prostitutes and criminals on the other, and is the cause of all our troubles.[5] Strikes, boycotts and arbitrations will never bring about a change of system. All peaceable methods are in vain to begin with.

The modern strikes must be carried on in different style from those in the past. The factories, mills, machinery, in short, all of Carnegie's wealth was produced by us and by rights belongs to us. We therefore ought to remain in the mills and factories belonging to us and ought to defend them against all invaders. If we adopt revolutionary methods, we ought to be consistent and change the infamous system of production which is the cause of all of our troubles. Brothers, become Anarchists!

At four in the afternoon on the 8th of July 1892, armed with 5,000 of these leaflets and several hundred anarchist newspapers in English, German, French, Bohemian, and Italian, two comrades and I boarded the train in Pittsburgh that was to bring us to Homestead, seven miles away, where two days before, the power of the workers had revealed itself in so magnificent a way, not to be misunderstood. The leaflets and newspapers were divided into three packages and we each had one under an arm. Various nonsensical reports in the daily newspapers that anarchists among the strikers as well as from other cities were moving to blow up the Homestead steel mill with dynamite may have caused fellow travelers in the train to look at us from all sides and to "smell" dynamite in our suspicious-looking packages. Noticing this, we opened one package and gave everyone present on the train a leaflet. Since we three were as good as strangers in Homestead, our mission seemed to us in fact rather difficult. Luckily, one of my companions remembered that he had an old acquaintance in Homestead and we decided to go look for him first of all. Upon arrival in Homestead, our packages aroused the suspicion of the strikers who were keeping watch over the station, the arriving trains, and the people. They thought we were scabs and questioned us. In answer, we handed out some leaflets and asked about my companion's old acquaintance, whose apartment we soon found and whom we met there. He did not, however, seem very enthusiastic when he heard about our mission and that we wanted to use him as a guide. But he did go with us to the Carnegie steel mill as far as the board fence and showed us where the battle had taken place two days earlier. Since the mill was closely guarded inside by those loyal to the company and on the outside by armed strikers, who marched back and forth in troops, forced entry into the mill was not to be thought of. To these troops of workers as well as to anyone at all whom we met, we distributed the leaflets and saw that they were accepted with pleasure and were being read. We wandered around the plant until we were stopped from going farther; we turned into another street and everywhere the leaflets were received like hotcakes. We provided Bohemians and Italians, who regretted that they couldn't read English, with Bohemian and Italian newspapers; some Frenchmen did not go away emptyhanded either. Everyone was astounded at the number of newspapers in various languages. In one inn, Americans paid our bill and we had to promise to appear at the headquarters of the strikers. There was handshaking and satisfaction on all sides; people seemed to be pleased by our presence. Unsolicited, people offered to distribute the leaflets for us. We gave them the main share and we saw later that they were well distributed, when we went into the streets and saw people everywhere reading them.

Our guide had left us with the excuse that he had to go eat the evening meal. We too entered a restaurant and asked for a simple evening meal. We were asked if we belonged to the strikers or supported them and when that was answered with "yes," we were brought a meal that costs 75¢ in the good hotels in Pittsburgh. That put us in bad spirits, because we couldn't and didn't want to live so high. Our surprise was therefore great when we were told that the meal would cost 20¢ each, with the remark "because you are friends of the strikers." Evidently we had chanced upon a restaurant where scabs either got nothing or had to pay three to four times as much as the strikers and their friends did. As we left the restaurant, we met up with a reporter from the *Pittsburger Volksblatt* on friendly terms with us, who did something stupid the next day and published my name in his report.[6]

Then we headed for the meeting place of the strikers in order to hand out the rest of our leaflets there.

Strikers who were going the same way offered to secure admission to the hall for us, which they succeeded in doing with no trouble. Earlier we had asked about the leader of the strike, Hugh O'Donnell, but we learned that he was out of town.[7] Then we asked about the secretary and the strike committee; the latter was just then in session and since strikers were now quickly filling the hall, we distributed the rest of the leaflets and newspapers without having the committee's permission. So it came about that the whole room full of people soon quieted down little by little, because they were all busy reading. Several came to us, expressed their pleasure over the content of the leaflets and talked with us in the most friendly way. In this way several hours passed in complete harmony until suddenly several men pushed forward and shouted loudly: "Where are the three people who passed out this leaflet?" They were brought to us and even before he reached us, one of them shouted: "Who are you; who gave you the right to hand out leaflets; who sent you here? Frick sent you, you are Pinkertons." The shouter, who was asking all these questions at once, without listening to what we had to say, was a big guy, of strong build, with a very flushed face, puffy like it gets from overindulging in liquor. Hot-headed and insolent, without listening to our explanation, he continued to bellow: "You are Pinkertons sent by Frick and only pose as anarchists and even if you really are anarchists, we have chased off the Pinkertons without your help and will deal with the rest without you." Everyone in the room stood around us in a circle and since we were crowded into the middle of the room like this, we could see that the accusation—that we were Pinkertons in the service of Frick—ran through the hall with lightning speed, and since we couldn't in fact get a word in, it was no surprise that the mood soon turned against us, for even though we answered all questions explicitly, we couldn't be heard everywhere in the hall because of the din. A riot seemed inevitable. One of my companions, no longer listening to anyone, began in a loud voice: "We come from the International Workers Association, an organization fighting against each and every instance of oppression.[8] In your cry of victory over the Pinkertons, you forget that the strike has not yet been won and will in the end be lost if you don't listen to experience." But it was to no avail—tumult, shouting, fists appeared. At this moment one of those standing around shouted: "Take them off to jail (Jail!)!" No sooner said than done. We were taken by the arm and amid curses and shouts, with the whole horde of agitated people following us, it was off to jail we went.

Only those who led us off had remained calm and held back those who were crowding in on us. The way was short. Upon reaching the jail, they packed the three of us into a cell and locked the cell door. For a few minutes we were alone, time we used for a short discussion. Insistent calls penetrated from outside: "Out with the Pinkertons! Hang them up!" We believed our hours were numbered and decided that

we would sell our lives as dearly as possible, if it came to that. Appall-
ingly, we weren't well armed; our only weapons were one dagger and
a revolver. Then a couple of men came to the cell and asked if we had
any friends or acquaintances in Homestead who could prove that we
weren't Pinkertons. Of course, we had to answer with "No," because
we neither could nor wanted to call as our witness the man who had
served as our guide at the beginning, and besides he didn't know two
of us. But we did say that we possessed union cards as well as membership cards for the Pittsburgh Turnverein and showed them.[9] One
of us showed his card for the local union in Pittsburgh which belongs
to the Amalgamated Association, the union to which the strikers also
belonged.[10] We also produced our return train tickets with the remark that it was our intention to leave on the next train. Since we also
answered all the questions they asked to their satisfaction, the men
withdrew for a consultation, as they said. The big shouter, who had
tried to make us out as Pinkertons in the hall, was not among them.

The noise outside got louder with each minute, everything seemed
to have turned wild, several dozen voices shouted: "Out with them!
Hang them!" and because the jail was only a small one-story building made up of one room and a couple of cells, everything at ground
level, it was to be feared that they would simply tear the whole place
down. We were waiting eagerly for the result of the consultation.
They didn't make us wait long, however; soon the men came with our
identification cards, gave them back to us and said in a friendly tone
that they would try to bring us through the crowd of people to the
train station. On the way there we should keep calm, they would protect us; for at the moment, it would be impossible to make it clear to
the angry crowd that we were not Pinkertons, and we couldn't stay
here, because we would surely be hanged in the night.

Shortly thereafter, some others came and said they were ready to escort us to the train station; it was time, the train was due soon. The door of the cell was opened; some 25 men armed with guns and clubs were standing in the anteroom. They took us into their midst and pushed their way through the crowd. It was about 10 o'clock at night. The lights seemed to have been extinguished, but when people noticed that we were to be brought away, the fracas got so huge, that it begs all description, and again the ominous shouts: "Here are some ropes, hang them." Others cried out: "Take the goddamned Pinkertons to the river and sink them!" Amid such cries and crowding, and with our protectors continually beating back those crowding around with their guns and clubs, we finally reached the station. Right away the train came in that was to bring us our painfully awaited salvation; we were pushed in, the engineer got the signal to depart immediately, and we heaved a sigh of relief.

Only now, as the train moved off under full steam, did I look at my two companions in their seats with their pale faces, and I held out my hands to them, congratulating them on our close escape from an undeserved and unwelcome death. For this much I feel I may reveal, my two comrades were young married men with pretty, young wives and beloved children at home, while I was free and single. You can imagine our reflections on the few hours we spent in Homestead. "No, I've never been so close to death as this time," said the one. "And in the middle of such danger, all desire to agitate can die, and you should just let the people rush headlong toward their own undoing," said the other. "And that they will do," I added. "They'll have the opportunity, when the strike has been lost, to think about the content of the leaflets."

On boarding the train, we had noticed that a number of strikers had boarded as well; we suspected therefore that once they arrived in Pittsburgh, they would try to have us arrested; so we jumped off at the first station in South Side Pittsburgh, hurrying along several dark side-streets to a friend who had been waiting for us for several hours in tense anticipation.

His astonishment was great when we reached him at about 11 o'clock in the evening and told him of our adventures.

The leaflets which had turned out to be so fateful for us had been distributed; that they would yet bring down disaster on me and Carl Nold—who hadn't even been present at their distribution—*that* we didn't anticipate when I arrived at the latter's apartment in Allegheny at midnight and brought him our account of handing out the leaflets.

Autobiographical Sketches

ALEXANDER BERKMAN

1. In America

It was November 1887. I was sitting in the public library in Kovna, Russia, reading a newspaper. At that time, I was thinking for the first time in my life about committing deliberate "robbery": stealing myself from "Father State" and emigrating to America. So of course I was following all the news items about my future asylum with great interest. The following note caught my eye: "On November 11, the anarchists Most (as reported in the Russian newspaper), Spies, Parsons, Lingg and their comrades were lawfully hanged in Chicago."[1]

Sitting across from me at the same table was an expelled student from Kiev University, whom I knew. "What are anarchists?" I asked him.

"A political party," the ex-student answered.

"What do they want?"

"I don't know myself."

It fell to America's lot, with red martyrs' blood not yet dried on its soil, to enlighten me about anarchists and their aspirations. And in my case, enlightenment about anarchism meant conversion to it.

There are two kinds of education: school and life. In Russia, as the son of a prosperous *Meschtschanin* [petit bourgeois], I had the benefit of book-knowledge. But America gave me my second education, the real, rational education of the proletariat, acquired in life, in sorrow and in battle.

Well schooled in the hate of tyranny and the love of justice by the Slavic despot, my sympathies belonged to all those who have ever been oppressed and suppressed—and in the anarchists hanged in Chicago I soon recognized the cross bearers of a new civilization in America, persecuted like the pioneers of humanity, who have always been those who prepare the way for progress.

Personally freed from the burden of absolutism, I craved complete freedom; it was my passion, an idée fixe, like Catholicism was in its time and then Protestantism, or science in the Renaissance and revolution in the eighteenth century.

America was bound to disappoint me, disappoint me a thousand times over. For I came searching for freedom, the freedom to live free and be happy,—but what did I find?! . . .

The worship of the republic could inspire me as little as monarchical idolatry. The "sanctity of parliamentary forms" left me as cold as the popish doctrine of the Immaculate Conception—the one a political, the other a theological fable. The arithmetical pantheism of universal suffrage revealed to me the futility of purely political upheavals.

For my eyes were open and I clearly saw that all these republican household gods only served as a pedestal for the throne of the almighty god Zeus, holy Zeus, whose golden calf's head gleamed high over all his divine helpers in the sunshine of republican Olympus. And human sacrifices were brought daily to the insatiable, unmerciful Zeus, just as in Hellenic times. And the incense of human flesh and blood rose up into Zeus's great nostrils and tickled him pleasantly and then spread out again in thick clouds over all of Olympus and threatened to suffocate all the other gods.

"The place of woman in society"—someone has said—"demonstrates the level of civilization." More accurately, one could say that the place of *work* in society would demonstrate the true level of civilization. And in this respect, America, or the United States of North America—this republic is the Eldorado of an industrial despotism the likes of which has not taken such hold in any other land. Nowhere is the discrepancy between rich and poor greater, more obvious, nor exploitation more thorough, than here. America demonstrates most strikingly that political freedom without economic freedom has an empty ring, and that freedom, that is, economic freedom, cannot follow the path of political reform, for political changes arise out of economic changes and not the other way around.

The struggle of the exploited, of the cheated and robbed—if they want to be free, free to rejoice in life—must be conducted on an economic path. Agitation and propaganda, the organization of the working class, must be of an antipolitical, economic character whose purpose must be the destruction of the economic cudgel; it must be the abolition of the barbaric system of slave labor and private property, that institution of legally sanctioned robbery, which is the epitome of every vile act.

At age 18, I buried the old world and set foot on the path to freedom sketched here.

2. *Attentat* Plans (6–22 July 1892)

The 6th of July 1892 found me in Worcester, Mass., where I was working as the manager of a friend's business. I was leading a quiet, secluded life and had taken no active part in the anarchist movement for several months.

The news of the battle in Homestead, Pa., pierced my quiet existence like a bolt out of the blue. The oppression and exploitation of the Homestead workers by the Carnegie Corporation, the continuing systematic wage cuts, the despotism of the corporation, its extensive preparations—made long before the lockout—to massacre the Homestead workers, the planned strike against the life and freedom of the workers—all that enraged me against the brutal directors of the corporation.

The Homestead workers' act of self-defense was a warm ray of hope in my soul, all the more because it was not a chance, spontaneous act, done in the heat of the moment, but a well planned and heroically accomplished defense of life and what is right. It seemed that one was dealing here with Americans—in the best sense of the word—with people in whom a spark of humanity still existed, with intelligent and resolute workers, who were not so cowardly that they would put up with every imperious, despicable act.

And I was glad of it. I saw that the Homesteaders had taken a step in the right direction. Only such resolute behavior is capable of instilling respect—and alarm—in the oppressors. Only when they make the oppressing few feel unsafe can the oppressed many bring about an alleviation of their situation. As I said, the strikers, i.e., the locked-out workers, struck the right note by opposing force with force. It

seemed to me to be an opportune time, first of all to give the Homestead combatants good advice—for only in such moments, in times
of adversity and danger, do the masses heed advice, and when the first
exhilaration of their victory wore off, the strikers themselves seemed
half frightened over their courageous act, and didn't know what to do
next. Second, I didn't want to let this excellent opportunity for the
propagation of sound views go by, for such opportunities are rare.

The eyes of all were on Homestead. Most sympathized with the
workers. I wanted to use the opportunity offered me to demonstrate
the solidarity of the anarchists with the working class—for the first
time in this country—by means of an indisputable *deed* and thus win
the sympathy of the people for anarchists and their endeavors.

My decision was soon made: I would go to Pittsburgh, issue a
call to revolution among the strikers in Homestead, and sweep Mammon's Attila, H. C. Frick, the manager of the Carnegie mill, out of the
way as a lesson for the oppressed, as a warning of what is to come for
the oppressors—a Brutus stab by the tormented, the murdered, and
the tortured—an act of propaganda for social revolution.[2]

I notified my boss and friend that private affairs summoned me
to New York and that I was taking leave "indefinitely," as I told him
blithely. On Saturday evening, the 9th of July, I departed for New
York.

Arriving in New York Sunday morning, I took myself off to my
apartment "up town." It consisted of one room in which several "necessary little things" were stored. Proclamations in English and in German were quickly prepared, and I was ready to have them printed by
a friendly printer.

When I had left Worcester, I had only a few dollars with me, but I
expected to get enough money for my purpose in New York, where
a few friends owed me some money. I needed about 100 dollars, I
thought, for printing and travel costs and other odds and ends. But I

was disappointed in my expectation of drumming up money. Some of my "debtors" were out of work, others were suffering from a chronic lack of money, and so on. It would have been easy for me to raise the necessary sum, if I had told a few friends and comrades of my self-appointed mission.[3] But there was no question of that, because I wanted neither helpers nor confidants. I was forced to lie to my friends, that I had lost my position in Worcester and was now going to look for work in the west. But people thought there was no hurry, I should stay in New York a few weeks, while they scraped together the money I needed.

Two days passed; I spent them in fear and agony that I would not be able to carry out my plan because of a lack of funds. Many a good plan for a good deed was given up or was lost because of a lack of Mammon. The third day came and before it was over, I recovered my good humor. On that day I managed to get some money from a well-to-do nonanarchist friend. I decided to travel immediately to Pittsburgh, in spite of the fact that I possessed only the absolute minimum fare. The idea of a flyer had to be abandoned, of course, first of all because I couldn't spare the printing costs, and second, there was no time to lose. In my opinion, the handbills were no longer absolutely necessary, since I had learned from the latest news from Homestead that a couple of anarchists from Philadelphia (as reported in the New York newspapers) had distributed revolutionary flyers among the Homestead workers. I believed this report, since I knew that Philadelphia rejoiced in a number of able comrades.

With little money in my pocket, but in good spirits, and with a suitcase in hand, I got under way. After my ticket was bought and at 12 midnight on the 12th of July I had boarded the train that was to bring me to Pittsburgh, my entire fortune consisted of just one dollar in silver.

At about 11 o'clock in the evening on the 13th of July, I reached

Pittsburgh—it was a slow milk train—and spent the night in the "Merchants Hotel" next to the B&O depot.

3. In Allegheny, Pa.

Before my departure from New York, a friendly comrade, Claus Timmermann, gave me several addresses and letters of introduction to comrades in various cities in the west, so that the addressees could be of help to me in my travels and my supposed search for work.[4] One of these letters was addressed to the Allegheny comrade, Carl Nold, whose acquaintance Timmermann had made the year before.

On Thursday, July 14, at approximately 10 o'clock in the morning, I set off to find Nold's residence. I did not personally know N., had never seen him before, but since there was, very worryingly, only wind in my pocket, and since Timmermann had recommended Comrade N. to me as a good, hospitable fellow, I decided to stay a few days with N., until my finances would have improved. That is to say, New York friends had promised me to send money to the points along my route that I had specified. Had I known at the time, however, that first of all, N. was married and that second, his home served as a gathering place for Allegheny anarchists, I would never have thought of visiting him. But Timmermann had told me that N. was a bachelor, which, to be sure, was the case at the time that Timmermann had called on N. in 1891.

After searching and asking the way for a long time (this side of the Monongahela, no one seemed ever to have heard of a Cherry Street), I managed to get to 5 Cherry St., N.'s residence. I rang. A young woman of the American type, N.'s wife as it turned out later, opened the door.

"Does Carl Nold live here?" I asked in English.

"Yes."

"Could I speak to him?"

"He's at work in Pittsburgh."

"Then I'd like to wait for him in his room."

The woman seemed somewhat surprised; she glanced questioningly at my traveling clothes and my suitcase, but when I didn't say anything, she stepped into the house and told me to follow.

In the dining room, the woman stopped and said I could wait for C. N. there. Another woman, in dishabille, was in the room, and I wondered what was really up with N. The two women soon began to ask me questions. I answered—with more brevity than gallantry— that my name was A. B., I was a comrade of C. N.'s, and came from New York to look around for work as a typesetter in Pittsburgh and Allegheny. I then immersed myself in reading the latest reports from Homestead and the women left me alone. When I was finished with the newspaper, I asked if N. didn't have a private workroom. I was informed that there was such a room on the third floor that I could have a look at.

I went upstairs. To my astonishment, I found an actual print shop—printers' type, press, forms, etc. I examined several leaflets lying on the table and suddenly it dawned on me. The leaflets were no doubt intended for distribution in Homestead—that much I gathered from the content. And so the distributors, I thought, had been comrades from Pittsburgh or Allegheny, and not from Philadelphia, as the New York newspapers were reporting. I was glad that the leaflets contained a pithy revolutionary message—a good, if unintended, preparation of the masses for my deed, I thought.

Several hours went by, during which I subjected the room to an inspection—not a private room, but the Pittsburgh-Allegheny cell's print shop, as I rightly concluded.

Then I heard steps on the stairs and a young, slight man of barely middling height, wearing glasses, entered the room. The expression on his face, the abstract look in his eyes revealing the idealist—his whole being reminded me vividly of my brother Max, a student in Leipzig, who recently, within the year, had died of the impecunious student malady.[5] (We live in an enlightened era!) I felt instinctively that I could be friends with this young man.

After introducing ourselves, I handed him—it was C. Nold—Timmermann's letter, which he began to read immediately. When he was finished reading, I explained to him that I had come to Pittsburgh to look around for work and that I would like to impose upon his hospitality for a short time because of my lack of money. N. gave no sign of surprise; on the contrary, he seemed to regard it as a matter of course. He was very friendly and soon invited me to supper.

Several days passed. Nold went to work early every day, and we saw very little of each other. I, too, went out every day for several hours, to look for work, as I was accustomed to telling the ladies of the house— Mrs. Nold and Mrs. Eckert.

Since I was an absolute stranger in Pittsburgh, my task was above all to locate Mr. Frick's places of residence and business, as well as to familiarize myself with the physical appearance of the man, for I had never seen him. I was not planning to gather information by asking questions. So I visited several libraries and found the necessary information in a couple of magazines about his residence and business locations, etc. Then I went to several fashionable photographers where I pretended to want to buy pictures of famous stage artists. In the studio of a photographer on Fifth Avenue in Pittsburgh, I found a splendid photograph of H. C. Frick and studied it.

In the meantime, I looked at a furnished room in Pittsburgh and waited for some money from New York in order to rent it. For, when I had found out that Comrade N. was married and his residence was used as a gathering place for Allegheny comrades, I believed that it would be better for N. and Eckert if I left their house—which they occupied together—as soon as possible, without leaving the police any trace of my visit.

Unfortunately, a registered letter addressed to me "in care of C. Nold" arrived from New York the same day.[6] This circumstance vexed me a lot, that is, that the letter was registered. A registered letter in the Allegheny post office was evidence of my stay with N. There was, however, nothing to be done. I couldn't prevent what had happened, since to warn my friends who had promised to send me money not to send registered letters would have attracted notice. I had to resign myself to the situation and remain with C. N., for after other registered letters for me soon followed the first and were delivered and received in his house, there was no point in throwing away my money for a room. And I had to be very sparing with the money. Therefore, I remained in N.'s house and decided to leave a few days before committing the *attentat*.

I spent altogether just eight days with N. In the evenings during this time, two or three comrades usually came by, among them Henry Bauer, whose acquaintance I made on these occasions. The big, strong man with his genial expression appealed to me a great deal, but I soon noticed that he viewed me with suspicion. I wondered at it, because I was not aware that I had said or done anything inappropriate or suspect. My wonder and uneasiness increased when I became aware that Eckert and a few Pittsburgh or Allegheny anarchists who came to call while I was there were also cool toward me. An epidemic of suspicion seemed to have broken out in the house; even the two housewives looked at me with reproachful eyes.

At first, I was very annoyed at such treatment; I brooded over the mystery, but couldn't explain it. Since my thoughts were elsewhere, I paid no more attention to it and acted as if I didn't notice anything. C. N. was the only one who was not infected by the household epidemic; he showed that he had a keener instinct than the others, and his behavior toward me was open and free.

One afternoon, H. B. came by and mentioned in my presence that a comrade by the name of Ch. Diether, who had recently had an accident, was staying at his house. H. B. asked me if I knew Diether. "Yes," I said, "that is, not personally, but from several poems by him that appeared in *Freiheit*." B. asked me then if I would like to go see Comrade Diether. I felt that to refuse would be to contribute to Bauer's suspicions—of whatever nature they were. So I accepted H. B.'s invitation and we went, together with C. N., to 73 Spring Garden Ave., where B.'s residence and office were located. There we found Marcus Albrecht, an old revolutionary who occupied the house together with H. B., and the ailing Diether. We talked about various things: Diether told us his tale of woe, we discussed the movement, the Homestead strike, etc. H. B. then said that he had cancelled his subscription to the New York *Anarchist* because of its personal content. With that, the conversation passed on to the (so-called) autonomous newspapers— the London *Autonomie* and the New York *Anarchist*.[7] B. spoke disparagingly about these publications; I defended them. Bauer then let the remark fall: "One can never know who the spies are; even among us five there could be a spy." This remark cut into my heart more painfully than a knife could have done. Among the five people present in the room, I was the only one not known to B. It was clear that B. meant me, or wanted me, the possible spy, to understand that he was on his guard against me. I bore this insult, for me the greatest of all insults, calmly and said nothing. I had something higher to do than to defend my person against suspicions. I couldn't afford to get into trouble with B. and possibly be stopped.[8] So I was silent, but in my heart there was a storm. So they were suspicious of me, I thought; they insinuate that I am a spy, in the very moment that for the sake of my beliefs I am as good as standing in the shadow of the gallows. Suspicion of me! And that on the eve of my *attentat!*

That evening, when H. B. accompanied me back to Nold's place, we did not revive the subject of his suspicions. I was too proud and considered it absolutely useless to defend myself against such suspicions. H. B. and others like him will soon, very soon, be disabused of their vile mistake, I thought. It only bothered me that B. had not wanted to bring his suspicion and the cause for it out into the open.

Only within the year, when B. and N. were in the penitentiary with me and we had gotten better acquainted and had become friends did I learn the reason for this suspicion. That is to say, when I landed in Allegheny and called on N., several Allegheny anarchists applied to Most, the editor of the New York *Freiheit,* asking who I was. To this day, I don't know what Most's answer was literally. According to H. B., it was a long letter that in essence advised the Allegheny comrades to be wary of me and that in general cast suspicion on me.

It can be attributed to this circumstance that the Allegheny anarchists viewed me with distrust and were prejudiced against me and later to some extent against my deed.

Western Penitentiary of Pa.
July 1895

Jail Experiences

ALEXANDER BERKMAN

TAKING THE PREJUDICES and biases against anarchists into
consideration, it is not surprising that anarchist prisoners are
treated differently than ordinary prisoners. I was to find that out on
my first day of internment in jail. As a rule, prisoners in the Allegheny
County Jail are permitted to receive visits from friends, lawyers, and
reporters, to read daily newspapers at their own expense, as well as to
have friends send in meals. None of that was permitted me. Not even
reporters were let in to me, a fact I did not regret in the least. Here
too, just as in the police station, precautions were taken that not a
hair on my head would be harmed. They even took away the spoon
that was in the cell I was put in: "It would be better that way," said
Warden John McAleese.[1] So that none of my fellow prisoners could
slip me their newspapers or anything else, I was not granted the privilege every other prisoner had of exercising twice a day in the yard.
Two weeks long, all day long, I had to sit in a small airless cell with

nothing to do, nothing to read, neither newspapers nor books. The cell doors of the prisoners remain unsecured the whole day—until four P.M.—shut just by means of a bolt mounted at the top of the door. But my door was always securely bolted and locked.

This shameful treatment lasted two weeks. Ex-detective McAleese made every effort to do the dirty work for the police. He had orders to keep me in the dark about the movements of the police and about anything at all to do with my case. But at the end of two weeks after my arrest, the police saw no more point—for obvious reasons—in keeping me in ignorance about the "discovery of a conspiracy." Then all the rights that I had been deprived of were restored; I could buy newspapers, take exercise, etc. Yet they still treated me more harshly and watched me more closely than the other prisoners. The spoon was not returned to me.

In spite of all the precautionary measures, my fellow prisoners found opportunities to slip me newspaper clippings and the like on the sly. In this way I found out that comrades Carl Nold and Henry Bauer were in custody and that my friends in New York—especially Emma Goldman and Claus Timmermann—were being stalked and harassed by house searches; they tried to catch them out with spies and reporters' tricks, etc.; luckily all with the same success that the Pittsburgh Police Chief O'Mara had with the arrest of Comrade Frank Mollock of New Jersey.[2] When he was passing my cell on his way to receive a visitor, a fellow prisoner surreptitiously whispered the story of O'Mara's coup that I just mentioned, the forcible abduction of Mollock. The news of Mollock's arrest didn't worry me very much; I was sure that with all the will in the world they wouldn't be able to implicate Mollock in my deed. All Mollock had to do to hold on to his freedom was to practice the art of remaining silent. I knew Comrade Mollock and knew that he would be successful at it. And anyway, he couldn't say anything compromising, even if he wanted to. He owed me some money; I wrote him a candid card from Pittsburgh, explaining to him that I found myself in Pittsburgh without work and pressed for money. Mollock then sent me several dollars by registered letter. That was Mollock's "part" in my deed. For the police hero O'Mara, of course, the mere fact that Mollock knew me at all was enough by itself to send him to jail for at least 10–20 years.

That is no mere claim, but fact. A short, true story should be recounted here that characterizes American pillars of social order in their dealings with anarchists.

About a year after my conviction, a man by the name of Eckert was arrested in a house in Allegheny that wasn't his. The man was drunk at the time. He was brought before the police court, accused of having entered a stranger's house with intent to steal. During the preliminary investigation, it was determined that Eckert had neither stolen anything in the house in question, nor had he had intent to steal. Eckert succeeded in convincing the police court judge that he was so drunk that he mistook the house for his own. The policeman who had arrested him testified that Eckert had been very drunk at the time. Then the judge asked the prisoner, "Are you the same Eckert with whom the anarchist Alexander Berkman lived for two weeks?" "No," answered Eckert, "that was a different Eckert, a cousin of mine." "Do you know Alexander Berkman?" "No, I've never seen him." "Well, that's lucky for you," the judge said in conclusion. "If you had been acquainted with Berkman, then I would turn your case over to the magistrate, and in that case, you'd have gotten ten years in prison. As it is, I'll sentence you to six months in the workhouse."

That's the way they think, those law and order scoundrels!

During my detention in jail as well as after my conviction, I received almost daily declarations of sympathy and compassion from every big city in the union. My daily mail in the jail was very heavy; of course, among the letters were some from cranks, that is, people who have windmills in their heads, who wrote a lot of plausible and even more implausible nonsense. Among my letters there was also a number of letters that were quite different in nature and had a quite different purpose than the correspondence from the cranks—namely planted letters sent by the police that were composed as if my alleged fellow conspirators and backers had written them. These letters were written in diverse languages, English, German, Bohemian, etc., almost without exception the same languages of O'Donnell, the leader in Homestead, as if he were the instigator of my deed.[3] This correspondence dealt with "bombs that were at the ready to blow the Homestead mill sky high." A couple of letters—written in different hands!—were signed "O'Donnell" and contained drawings of bombs, the Carnegie works, and Frick. You could see the hand of the police only too well in these miserable epistles. Within two days of my imprisonment, I had already received six or seven of these letters! Then the whole thing got too dumb. I had the Warden brought in and told him in a forceful tone that he should put an end to the delivery of this fictional rubbish. Of course, he acted as if he knew nothing of the whole affair. These letters, he said, most certainly came from my friends! So then for the next two days, I refused to take my mail. Then on the third day I was given several letters (I was forced to open all my letters in the presence of a guard—if they hadn't already been opened by the Warden—to read them and to send them back to the office of the Warden), and on closer inspection—what a surprise!—there were no more planted letters among them. I knew that Warden McAleese had given the police the tip-off that their ruse wasn't working. Great gang, that!

During my imprisonment, I received a number of letters with money from anonymous friends in Pittsburgh, Brooklyn, Chicago, and other places, and I would like to express my heartfelt thanks at this time to these friends as well as to my other anonymous and not anonymous correspondents.

Since no one had had any part in my "conspiracy," it is clear that I received no letters from comrades that were compromising in any way. But such letters were awaited with great impatience in certain quarters. It is telling that all of my letters with a New York postmark were delivered to me already *opened*—in spite of repeated protests on my part. Not for nothing is McAleese an ex-detective. One would, after all, like to climb higher on the social ladder—no better or surer way to do so than in the role of a voluntary spy and police lackey.

When H. B. and C. N. were brought to the jail and got "secure lodgings," I learned the sad news from a friendly fellow prisoner whose feeling of friendship for me was so strong that he gave me his word that he would keep me company in the penitentiary as well. This fellow was good-humored and swore he did not want to be separated from me. He has kept his word, too, and is still keeping me company today. At the time, I was still not allowed any newspapers, but a newspaper report about B.'s and N.'s arrests was slipped to me in secret the same day. My astonishment was great when I found various tales in it—about meetings that "the three Anarchists" were supposed to have held in N.'s house, conferences that had supposedly taken place between us three, about my visit to Diether at 73 Spring Garden Ave., my staying out late that evening and my return with H. B., then about a registered letter that arrived at N.'s when I had already left the house, etc. Who could have handed all these tales—most of them lies—to the newspaper reporters and thus to the police? I asked myself. The newspaper in my hands named Eckert. It appeared extraordinarily suspicious to me that B. and N. were taken into custody, but Eckert was let free, for the house in Allegheny in which I had spent eight days was not B.'s after all, but Eckert's as much as it was N.'s. Comrades B.

and N. were too intelligent, I thought, to let themselves be pumped in this way by reporters or the police. These stories came either out of Eckert's mouth or from the two wives of the house. I thought about it, and since I already knew that Eckert hadn't been hassled by an arrest, I gradually came to the conclusion that Eckert was the guilty party in the matter. I was soon strengthened in this conviction, namely by the fact that B. and N. had been indicted by the grand jury and the newspapers reported that Eckert would appear in B.'s and N.'s trials as a prosecution witness—which then proved to be true.

During the first four to five days of my confinement in jail, the police were busy having me "identified." Dozens of policemen, detectives, and citizens came every day to gawk at me. Usually they put me in a line with five or six other prisoners, who were more or less dressed as I was, and they whispered to the visitor who had come to "identify" me, that Berkman was the one who was wearing glasses. And since I was always the only one among the prisoners who was wearing glasses, the "identifications" were made relatively easy in this way. One day I was taken from my cell and positioned outside the door that led from the prison to the Warden's office. This door is made of fine wire mesh. A young man stood on the other side of the door. Warden McAleese asked me if I knew him. I took a fleeting look at him without really being able to see him—I was already sick of previous identification comedies—and answered the Warden with "No." Then they took me back to my cell. A little while later one of the guards told me that the young man who came to identify me was acquainted with me. "It was Paul Eckert," he said.

A few days after my transfer to the jail, I was asked if I insisted on a preliminary hearing or if I would dispense with it. In the hope of finding an opportunity during the hearing to make a public statement in my case, I answered the first question in the affirmative. The hearing took place in the Warden's office, but I was disappointed in my hopes, because I was not allowed to make any statement at all; I was only to answer the questions put to me by the investigating magistrate. During the hearing, J. G. Leishman, the Assistant Chairman of the Carnegie Co., Limited, swore to it that it was my intention to kill or at least to attack not only H. C. Frick, but also him, J. G. Leishman. He stated that I had aimed at him when I shot the fourth time, but that my weapon had not gone off. I denied emphatically that it was my intention to attack Leishman. Upon questioning by the judge, I stated that when I entered Frick's private room, I had neither known that Mr. Leishman was in the room nor had I any idea who he was. My target was Frick and Frick alone.

"What did you want with Frick?" asked the judge.

I had no intention of hiding my objective. So I answered, "I wanted to kill him." The stenographer on duty almost fell from his chair when I gave my answer in a calm, loud voice.

With that, the hearing ended.

I remained in the custody of Warden McAleese from the 24th of July to the 19th of September (of the same year).[4] During this time, the Warden behaved toward me like the detective that he is: on the outside a citizen, on the inside, a policeman. He constantly endeavored to squeeze information out of me—for the police—with pathetically little success. Under the pretext of having to fill out my personal record, he tried to coax a positive response out of me on whether or not I was married. He pestered me for days with the same question: "Are you married?" and by his behavior forced me to get rude. "But do tell me; I have to fill out your personal information. Are you married and to whom?" That's how I was accosted every day by McAleese. "That depends on the situation," I told him once. "When I'm in the right company, it might happen that I would marry for the length of a sweet night." Such an answer was enough for the Warden to wish with all his heart that Frick would die of his wounds so that they could hang me. Another time, I'd give him the answer, "I'm a married bachelor."

"Should I enter you in the record as married?" he'd ask me.

"Brand me however you want."

"But what is the truth?"

"The truth is that in captivity, I am a bachelor."

McAleese put many another police-spy question to me. For example, Who is the man you got a letter from yesterday? What does he do? Would you give me his address? and more such questions. The insults I gave him instead of answers to such questions appeared to have no effect on his stoolie character.

McAleese also tried to convince me to plead guilty to the charges against me. I was told that he receives a dollar for every prisoner he convinces to plead guilty. In my case, however, his efforts to that effect didn't pay off. He just couldn't understand how I could plead not guilty and at the same time admit to my deed.

About two weeks before my trial, all letters suddenly stopped. In answer to my daily queries, I was given the same answer: "No letters here for you." One day the Warden made the remark: "It may well be that no one wants to write to you any more. You're in trouble and your friends have abandoned you." "Have no fear," I said to him, "there are no Christians among my friends." I wrote to my friends, but no answer came. It wasn't until after my trial, when I was already in the penitentiary, that the matter was cleared up. My friends and comrades besieged me with the question of why I had not answered any of their letters from the last ten days before my trial; they had written to me daily. It turned out that for the ten days before my trial all the letters that were addressed to me, as well as all those that I wrote, were intercepted by Warden John McAleese—an act that according to American law is a felony punishable by penitentiary. But McAleeses are sent to the penitentiary as wardens, not as prisoners.

During my incarceration in the Allegheny County Jail, I came to know Mr. McAleese as a liar, police lackey, spy, and suppressor of U.S. mail.

Western Penitentiary of Pennsylvania, in July 1895

Further Arrests

CARL NOLD

I HAD HEARD NOTHING FROM Berkman since he had left me. It was Saturday, the 23rd of July, about three in the afternoon. I was standing at the forge at Taylor & Dean on Market Street, Pittsburgh, where I had been working for two years, when one of my coworkers called out to me: "That rascal Frick is shot." This news did not especially surprise me, because it was to be expected that sooner or later something like that would happen to that bloody Frick, who had caused so much workers' blood to flow, and even Frick himself cannot have been surprised, if he thought of the two dozen or so Coke workers and of the seven Homestead strikers who had been murdered by his mercenaries.

But that Alexander Berkman, as I found out an hour later, had taken on the role of avenging spirit, that was a surprise for me.

So this young Russian, who told me that he was going to Chicago, turned around and taught the biggest of all oppressors of workers,

H. C. Frick, a lesson that will remain inextinguishable in the history of the battle between Capital and Labor.

Yet I was in doubt about whether it was really the Berkman who had stayed with me or some other Berkman. The more detailed description of the assassin and his picture in the newspapers soon convinced me that it was indeed the man who had spent eight days in my house and whom I had gotten to know as an intelligent, highly sensitive and serious young man.

But greater still was the amazement of the Allegheny anarchists, especially of those who had made Berkman's acquaintance. On the following Sunday morning, the print shop at 5 Cherry Street was crammed full with comrades on whose faces the astonishment over Berkman's unexpected action could still be seen. The antipathy that several comrades had shown toward Berkman had disappeared.

I spent that Sunday afternoon in the circle of Jewish comrades from Pittsburgh, where Berkman was honored as the hero of the day. In the evening, an English gathering (with lecture) was supposed to take place in South Side Pittsburgh, but the meeting hall was closed to anarchists that evening and for the future as well. Several friends voiced the opinion that the police would probably arrest me because I had put Berkman up in my house. I didn't worry about it much; after all, I had nothing to do with the *attentat*.

On Monday, the 25th of July, 12 noon, just as I stepped out of the factory office onto the street to go to a nearby restaurant to eat lunch, two men came in at the door and I just heard the following exchange: "What's his name?" the one asked and the other answered "Carl Nold." That was enough for me. On the way to the restaurant, these thoughts came to me: Detectives, asking specifically for me; should I return to the factory or not? During the meal I came to the decision to return and let myself be arrested, for, I thought, nothing can happen to me; no one can possibly implicate me in the shooting.

Since Berkman stayed with me, they'll ask me a number of questions; it can't get too bad.

I had never before had anything to do with the police and never dreamed that giving room and board to a poor devil for eight days would be enough to get me accused as an accomplice. So I returned to work after finishing my meal and, sure enough, behind the door stood the two upholders of law and order, with their criminal's physiognomy and stinking of schnapps.

"Carl Nold, you are wanted in the town hall."

"Fine," I said, "but I would like to wash first and change out of my dirty work clothes—only five minutes."

"Oh, that's not necessary. You'll only be asked a few questions; you can be back at work in a quarter of an hour."

So then I went along to the old town hall, 10 minutes away. The question that was put to me there was where Berkman, the man who had been in my house, had left his suitcase. "He took it with him to Chicago," was my answer. "Berkman will certainly know where it is."

"That will do," said the questioner, "we're locking you up in the Central Police Station for the time being," and off we went to the Central Station in the patrol wagon. My clothes were searched carefully, I was thrown in a cell, and then the detectives came and asked various questions that seemed suspicious to me. For example: Where is the letter that came after Berkman had left 5 Cherry St.? Where is the suitcase? What did Berkman, Bauer, and Diether discuss when they met at Bauer's? Where is the letter from Timmermann? Realizing from these questions that the police already had information from another source, I explained what was already laid out in the fourth chapter of this book, "Berkman in Allegheny," a faithful account of the facts that could harm neither me nor other comrades.[1] But this explanation didn't satisfy the police, it plainly wasn't enough reason to implicate me in Berkman's *attentat*. I was besieged three times: I should make a complete "confession" and then they'd let me go. They appeared to be after the suitcase in particular. "I don't know more than what I've already said," was my answer. Toward evening I was questioned closely for the fourth time with a coaxing form of address: "Carl, we've found the suitcase, we've arrested H. Bauer and now we know the whole story. We mean you well. Take our advice and make a full confession and then you can go home." Such stupid old police tricks couldn't faze me. "What you all know!" I said. "Then you must also know that Bauer can't confess any more than I can and that neither of us had anything to do with the *attentat*. That is the last thing I have to say in this matter."

The fact was, however, and so I had conjectured correctly, that first of all, Bauer had not been arrested nor had the suitcase been found, and second, that through the registered letters Berkman had received, the police had found out from the postal authorities that Berkman had stayed with me. Accordingly, the police went to my house at 5 Cherry St. and found Paul Eckert there, who was home sick.[2] The police could have received the first bits of information only from him. In any case, Eckert himself told me later that the police had come while I was at work in Pittsburgh, dragged him off to the Pittsburgh Police Headquarters, and offered him 200 dollars if he would confess and act as the main witness.

What Eckert told the police, we know nothing about; certain is that he knew nothing more and could say nothing more than what is reported in the fourth chapter of this book [see note 1]. Significant, however, is that Bauer and I were arrested and charged, while Eckert, who had no more and no less to do with Berkman than we had, was neither taken into custody nor charged.

There was another, who, driven by cowardice when he heard of my arrest, broke faith and went off to the Allegheny police station and confessed that he had been a member of an anarchist singing society a year before, but he had resigned and had nothing more to do with anarchists. The police forgave him his sin and sent him home.

Henry Bauer was sitting in his office at 73 Spring Garden Ave., Allegheny, when people in the street shouted, "Frick is shot." In the special editions of the evening newspapers, he learned with certainty that Berkman, whom he had met at my place, was the assailant. Bauer immediately packed up his address books and other small effects and put them in a safe place. When he heard on Monday of my arrest, he figured very correctly that the police would be interested in him as well, and so stayed away from his office to hear first what I had to say. All of Monday, until 12 midnight, detectives watched his house while some comrades watched the detectives and kept Bauer informed. But he was of the same mind as I had been, he felt and knew himself to be innocent, so when the detectives were gone, he returned to his office Monday evening after 12, fully expecting to be arrested, and lay down to sleep. The next morning, Tuesday, the 26th of July, he took care of a few errands and awaited whatever events were in the offing. Events didn't hold off for long; they came at 9 o'clock in the form of two detectives.

"Are you Henry Bauer?"

"That's right."

"Chief Murphy wants to speak to you."[3]

"Fine," said Bauer, and a third keeper of the peace appeared at the door. The following conversation took place at the Allegheny police station between Bauer and the police chief:

> *Question:* "Where were you yesterday during the day and at night?"
> *Answer:* "In the company of good friends."
> *Qu.:* "Did you distribute leaflets in Homestead?"
> *Ans.:* "Yes, on July 8, two days after the battle."

(Bauer had to admit that right away, since for agitation purposes, his business imprint was printed on the distributed leaflets: H. Bauer, Agent for Labor Literature, 73 Spring Garden Ave., Allegheny.)

> *Qu.:* "Who were the other two who were with you in Homestead; you know them, don't you?"
> *Ans.:* "Yes, of course I know them."
> *Qu.:* "What are their names?"
> *Ans.:* "Well, a lot more people would like to know that; they both have very nice names. That's all."
> *Qu.:* "Do you know Nold and Eckert?"
> *Ans.:* "Yes. I am acquainted with both of them."
> *Qu.:* "Do you know Berkman who shot Frick?"
> *Ans.:* "I can't say for sure; I'd have to see him first."

The big "Chief" went off with his loyal followers and soon after that, Bauer was searched and despite his protests put in a cell. An hour later, they wanted to put handcuffs on him in order to transport him to Pittsburgh more securely. Bauer resisted and lashed out. He was, however, helpless against the dozen policemen who came at a signal; his hands were tied fast and he was thrown into the patrol wagon. When they arrived at the Pittsburgh Central Station, his wrists were so swollen because the handcuffs were fastened too tightly that even the sergeant on duty reprimanded the detectives. Their excuse: "Bauer is a strong man—and an anarchist."

I didn't know that by this time Bauer was there to keep me company. Suddenly I heard someone singing the Marseillaise; I recognized him from the voice and sang along. So each knew where the other was; he was downstairs, I was one flight up. Soon after, Bauer was put in a lineup with five other prisoners, to be identified by a businessman whose business was across from Frick's office and who believed he had seen Bauer in front of the office in the moment before Frick was shot. The police pointed out Bauer, who stood a head taller than the others, but the businessman couldn't and wouldn't state that he had seen him.

In order to let our comrades know where we were, Bauer sent a postcard to 73 Spring Garden Ave.: someone should bring us some handkerchiefs. Two friends came and brought them and were detained for their efforts and stuck in a cell as suspicious characters. The next morning they were let go again.

They wanted to wring confessions and "secrets" out of Bauer in the same way they had tried with me, and since all the old police ruses didn't work, an apparently drunk man was brought into his cell one night at two A.M. Since several empty cells were available, Bauer realized at once that he was again dealing with another police trick. The supposedly drunk man at first acted like he wanted to sleep. Then he started talking and asking questions, and pretended that he knew Bauer and wanted to strike up a friendship with him. Bauer indicated that he should keep quiet and when he didn't pay attention to this warning and started asking questions again, Bauer jumped up and grabbed the fellow by the neck. A guard who had been on the watch for some trouble, opened the door and removed the quaking spy.

On Thursday, the police brought a comrade, Frank Mollock, from Jersey City, New Jersey, a distance of about 450 miles.[4] His crime was that he had owed Berkman several dollars and had sent him the sum by registered letter to Allegheny. Because of that he was branded a co-conspirator and the clever police were pleased with their sharp canine sense of smell in exposing such a widespread conspiracy. They rested on their laurels while we rested on the hard wood bench in an iron cage.

What inanity to lock us up on the unfounded assumption that just because we were acquainted with Berkman we might possibly be co-conspirators!

I had been arrested in my old work clothes, dirty and black from the foundry fire, and I was not allowed to wash in the police station. Just as I was, I was to remain until the newspaper reporters came and were able to write their long, mean articles about the dirty anarchist who never washes himself. "You can wash yourself tomorrow morning," I was told when I called for water to wash with.

Although according to law every prisoner is to be interrogated within 48 hours of his arrest, we had to wait five days until Saturday, July 30, all the same. In the meantime, the habitual layabouts and good-for-nothings, the police officers, court reporters, and other Christians came, accompanied by their prostitutes at all hours, usually at night, at 12, 2, and 3 o'clock. These fools stood there before our cells and gaped at us as if we were exotic animals; the police station seemed to me like a modern menagerie. We were allowed no newspapers, no books; not even our friends were allowed to see us. The guards fed us only when they had time. If there were a lot of prisoners to interrogate, we got our breakfast at noon and our lunch at night. And then the bad, stinking air when a lot of prisoners were there, the cries, the raving, the vomiting drunks, the singing, and then the howling of the prostitutes again, and five nights, lying sleepless on a narrow, hard bunk, no chance to get undressed, without pillow or blanket, nothing at all, and added to that, the lousy, rotten, sporadic meals. It was beastly treatment that a decent person wouldn't wish on his dog.

I had never before seen the inside of a police station, but what I saw and heard there was simply disgusting; scenes that make a mockery of civilization. Young boys 8–10–12 years old, locked in a cell with a couple of drunk men; since only one could lie down on the bunk at a time, the others lay down on the dirty stone floor, which was besmeared with tobacco muck, beery spittle, and schnapps slobber. Two guards dragged in a drunk floozy, one had her by the legs, the other had her by the arms; she was literally thrown into a cell this way. Her forehead was smeared with blood, but no one paid any attention to that. She lay there on the stone floor, beastly drunk, her dress torn across her breast and pulled up way past her thighs. The prisoners in the cells opposite cracked bad jokes about her, sang, whooped it up, and swore. The little street urchins bawled right along with them.

One drunk howled without stop; the guard opened the cell door and hit him on the head with a club so that he fell backward onto the bunk. Another, waking from his drunkenness, was horribly thirsty. A hundred times he called and asked pitifully for water; the guard passed by his cell fifty times and laughed at him. Finally, after an hour of agonizing thirst, after the fellow had yelled and begged himself hoarse, the guard gave him a cup full of that warm tap water that is undrinkable in the summer.

I saw many more such scenes, but enough of that. This is the vaunted order the police keep, this is the morality they strive to up-hold, this is the way the poor victims of a social system turned upside down are treated. And when anarchists argue that such an institution is not worth keeping and should be junked, the sooner the better, the worshippers of false gods—the State, the Church, Capital, the police, and morality—call out with one voice: "Crucify the anarchists!" And the masses who feel comfortable in their ignorance, who don't per-ceive this rule of Caesar, are ready to raise up the crosses and crucify those who call out for radical changes for the better.

"Blessed are the poor in spirit, etc."[5]

As yet only arrests of anarchists had been made and many a sensation-seeking reader of the capitalist newspapers must have wondered where on earth the indispensable dynamite was that was inevitably associated with anarchists. Yes, it was still to come. After the police had Bauer and me in detention, our lodgings were searched. Everything in the room Berkman had slept in was overturned, even the chamber pot was not left undisturbed, but nothing was there to be discovered. In my room they confiscated several old special editions of *Freiheit,* a letter, and a postcard, neither of any importance. Whether the police at that time didn't know or it didn't occur to them that there was a printing press in the third story of the house, I don't know. In any case, they only searched my room and Berkman's. I assume that at that time the police still knew nothing of our printing shop, otherwise they would undoubtedly have stolen the printing press with joy.

From my house, they went to Bauer's at 73 Spring Garden Ave. Western Pennsylvania's oldest comrade, the tried and true Marcus Albrecht, a shoemaker, lived together with Bauer; he had been a pioneer in Germany and France, in Switzerland and New Orleans under the banner of international rebellion. To add to his many battles this trusted soldier was now to experience a little one. The police came with a wagon and without the least embarrassment loaded up two trunks filled with Bauer's most valuable books. Since they weren't able to force open the desk, they loaded that up, too, and in addition, a pile of less valuable books, pamphlets, writings, newspapers, a revolver, a dagger, and a gun. Even medicine bottles were taken away, as well as a couple of the shoemaker's new shoe lasts. And now comes the most important thing, the long looked-for, strongest evidence against anarchists. In a dark corner of the back room, a brown substance in a tin box was found and cautiously loaded onto the wagon: dynamite—. The triumph of the police was complete. Marcus Albrecht was dragged off to the police station together with the wagon full of books and writings that were to serve as further evidence against Bauer. At the station, it turned out that the police, ever over-eager in such a situation, had mistaken the shoemaker's cobbler's wax for dynamite. Marcus Albrecht began to laugh in scorn and was let go.

Our comrades had not been idle in the meantime; they had formed a temporary defense committee and had handed over the matter to the lawyer Joseph Friedman.

On Saturday, 30 July, our interrogation finally took place. The only new thing that came out was an attempt by the police to prove that H. Bauer stood in front of the *Chronicle Telegraph* building while Berkman attacked Frick on the second floor of the building. This attempt failed, because Bauer could prove that he had been in his office in Spring Garden Ave. at the relevant time. In half an hour this judicial farce was over; the magistrate declared that he had to refer the case to criminal court, and that therefore the amount of bail had to be set by a criminal court judge and in the meantime we would have to await events in jail (detention pending trial).

Bauer and I, handcuffed together, boarded the patrol wagon escorted by three policemen, to be driven to the jail 10 minutes away. There was no doubt now that the police wanted to make an example of us anarchists, although there was nothing but ridiculous evidence against us, and I thought to myself that I would have to do six to seven years' time in prison. Even though more order and cleanliness prevailed in the jail than in the Central Station, we were still accorded the same foul treatment here.

While other prisoners were allowed daily newspapers and visits of friends and relatives, we were allowed neither the one nor the other. Our fellow prisoners were even ordered not to let us read their newspapers, but we read them anyway.

In addition to Attorney J. Friedman, our comrades had engaged the well-known attorney Col. W. D. Moore, and only these two were allowed to speak to us.

The food that one gets in jail can only be called dog food. In the morning a loaf of bread and a small cup of warm black water, called coffee. Midday, soup and sometimes a little piece of meat; evenings nothing.

No knife or fork; you tear the meat with your fingers and toes like a savage.

The cells are about five by eight feet; in other words, very small. The bed consists of an iron frame with canvas stretched over it, pillow, and blanket. As privy one has a bucket in the cell that is emptied every morning, but that befouls the air all day and all night. A chair completes the cell furnishings, for a table is also unknown.

On Sunday, for variety, one gets a loaf of bread and black water in the morning, and then nothing more for the rest of the day. In this way the prisoners can be fed for 25 to 30 cents a week. Isn't it amazing how Father State cares for his victims? He doesn't even give them enough to eat.

On Sunday afternoons a parson usually comes with a few shining lights of the church who in travesty offer the hungry prisoners "spiritual" food. Just think of the contrast: on the one hand several hundred hungry prisoners, invariably more than half of whom are innocent of the crimes pinned on them; on the other hand a well-fed parson, who speaks of the love of God, of humility and repentance, of the sanctity and justice of the laws—. The "Church lights" sing a few well-known hymns with organ accompaniment and the parson calls on the prisoners to join in. From thirst and hunger, however, they can barely spit.

The idea of God's justice has never seemed to me so ridiculous as in the face of this spectacle.

Bauer and I were to be released on $3,000 bail. But when the defense committee came, together with the bondsmen and the lawyers, the "wise" judge had changed his mind and demanded $5,000 each.

So for the present, only one could be freed; it was Bauer, who would find the necessary $5,000 for me. When he had managed to do so, the judge had changed his mind yet again; anarchists had risen in price from $5,000 to $7,000. Finally, on August 13, I was freed on $7,000 bail.

In the factory where I had worked for two years, there was no more work for an anarchist. Bauer started up his agency again and we both devoted ourselves to agitation more than before.

The defense committee, now permanent and enlarged, put out a call for financial support to comrades in the entire country that was quickly and generously answered.[6] The two lawyers were sent to Berkman to defend him, but he sent them away with thanks.

Comrade F. Mollock had to be released again because of lack of evidence. But the police did not give up their pet theory that they had uncovered a huge anarchist conspiracy. In New York several anarchists, including Emma Goldman, were pursued and harassed, but to no avail. Then the news came from New York that a certain anarchist and friend of Alexander Berkman's was on his way from New York to Pittsburgh in order to finish off Frick, who had recovered in the meantime.[7] Accordingly, a stranger was arrested in Pittsburgh, but to the ridicule of the zealous police, he was let go again, because he wasn't the one they were looking for.

So Bauer and I were out on $12,000 bail, accused of two crimes: incitement to riot in Homestead and conspiracy with Berkman to murder H. C. Frick. We awaited our trial, though we didn't await justice.

An American Court Farce

ALEXANDER BERKMAN

Truth forever on the scaffold,
Wrong forever on the throne,
But that scaffold sways the future.

Lowell[1]

The merit is determined by the actuating motive.

A. B.

THE "ACT OF '92" WAS the *first* aggressive anarchistic act in the United States, and as such it naturally had to cause a big sensation, even outside the union. The voices of the defenders of the status quo, for whom everything that currently exists is right and proper and who see eye to eye with Hegel in this regard, that "what is, is right," were soon heard. I was accused of brutality, breaking the law, ambition, fanaticism, and, from a certain "friendly" quarter, of failure. To the first accusation—of brutality—I answer with the words of the conquered King of Persia, at whose crude weapons Alexander of Macedonia had sneered: "If you knew how precious freedom is, you would defend it even with a hoe." As to the accusation of breaking the law, I say: I deem natural law higher than obedience to the laws of man; humanity and justice are of greater worth to me than all laws and constitutions.

You accuse me of ambition?! Believe me, ambition chooses smoother paths to fame.

Fanaticism?! Yes, indeed! What were the pioneers of humanity, who kept the world turning in their own time, other than fanatics, criminals, and madmen?! But in their view, it was these very epithets that entitled them to the remembrance and gratitude of generations to come. Fanatics! Because their sympathies were boundless and as deep as the ocean, because their ocean of love for mankind and truth knew no shores, and because enthusiasm was the very life of their souls.

And failure?! It was my comrades' duty to ensure the moral success of my deed—my real objective.[2] For the rest, should a person (or a deed) be judged solely on the degree of its direct success and be valued or condemned accordingly? Was John Brown a scoundrel because he had no immediate, significant success and Lincoln a hero only because he was successful?![3] Would Jefferson, Lafayette, Washington, and other American revolutionaries be condemned if they had been defeated by the superior might of George II?[4] Certainly not! We must be more enlightened, more just, and judge men and deeds according to their actuating motives. We are accountable—if one may speak of accountability—only insofar as our motives and willingness are taken into consideration.

My motives—even my enemies know this—were of the best and most noble kind; and in my willingness to act on my convictions, I knew no fear of death. My deed was an act of conscience, and as such, a noble act; whether right or wrong, such acts epitomize the best of human nature.

I am willing to be judged by world history, the world's Last Judgment.

The Allegheny Defense Committee for Comrades Henry Bauer and Carl Nold sent the lawyers of the two—Col. W. D. Moore and Jos. Friedman—to me to take over my case. But I rejected their offer to defend me with thanks, as I had done with the lawyers who had come to see me during my detention in the Central Police Station and who had offered me their professional services gratis. I could not, if I were to remain consistent, defend myself against the crime with which I was charged in the sense of the law; I did not deny my act, but also did not acknowledge it as a crime. I was accused by the "Commonwealth of the State of Pennsylvania" to have broken the laws of the state and thus to have harmed the Commonwealth itself. But I did *not* do that, that is, I had not harmed the Commonwealth of Pennsylvania and had not intended to do so. On the contrary, it was my intent, it was the purpose of my act to be of use to this Commonwealth—even if indirectly and in my own way.

I did indeed violate the laws of the state but with the best intentions. Then too, not just from a moral standpoint but also from the standpoint of the law, an unlawful act is usually judged according to the motive from which it springs. Admittedly, it is usually everyday motives that the law recognizes; it does not take social-revolutionary motives into consideration.

Therefore, in eyes of the law my act was an unlawful, unjustified, criminal act, but in my eyes it was a good act because it was in a good cause.

These two points of view are irreconcilable. To let myself be represented at court by a legal representative, who would, after all, be compelled to defend me from the viewpoint of the law, would be to deny my own self and recognize the viewpoint of the law as de facto correct and thus to acknowledge my act as a crime. I could not do that. For that reason, I had to reject legal representation.

Yet another circumstance was involved: I granted no mortal the right to sit in judgment over me. For this reason and because I was innocent of the crimes I was charged with and neither expected justice from my enemies nor wanted their mercy, I scorned the idea of defending my act in any way whatsoever in court. I intended solely to use the opportunity of the trial for propaganda purposes.

With this goal in mind and while I was confined to jail, I prepared my "defense," which was about 5,000 words long and was nothing less than a denunciation of the status quo. Unfortunately, I cannot reproduce my "defense" pamphlet here, since the manuscript was confiscated after my trial by District Attorney Burleigh.[5] It comprised a panorama of the crass class differences in the "promised land," then a critique of the status quo with reference to the Homestead lockout, an explanation of the motives, meaning, and goals of my act, and finally a view of a future free society. Using the dock as a tribunal, I wanted to speak freely to the people.

On Monday, the 19th of September, at about nine o'clock in the morning, I was taken from my cell, searched, and brought to the courtroom adjacent to the jail. I was to be tried immediately. I had not expected my trial to be on this day, since according to the trial calendar, it was not scheduled for the week of the 19th to the 24th. The day of my trial was kept strictly secret; even the press, which normally announces the day for each trial a few days in advance, was not informed of the exact date of my trial. That was no doubt a stratagem of the District Attorney's to prevent a crowd in the courtroom and forestall a possible demonstration. A few unimportant trials were scheduled for Monday, September 19, and because of that, only a modest number of people was present in the courtroom. When I arrived in the courtroom, everything was ready for this tragicomedy to begin. Judge McClung and the twelve jurors who were to "try" me were already in their places.[6] District Attorney Burleigh sat at a long table—the counsel-table—and behind him Knox, Mr. Frick's lawyer.[7] H. C. Frick, J. G. Leishman and the witnesses for the prosecution, all—with the exception of a detective—Frick's employees, were also on hand.[8] I took the place I was directed to at the upper end of the table. Judge McClung asked me whether I had a defense lawyer, or if I wanted to have one named by the court. I answered "no" to both questions with the explanation that I had with me a written statement that constituted my defense, which I intended to deliver myself.

I was to be tried according to the so-called king's jury system and therefore, as the District Attorney announced, I could question the choice of only four jurors. I glanced at the faces of the 12 men in the jury box. In the end it doesn't matter who these 12 fools are, I thought. They'll condemn me anyway, that's certain. But I made use of my right and asked four of the jurors whose appearance didn't appeal to me to step down. In their place, the District Attorney called up four other jurors, who took their places in the jury box without further ado. I myself did not examine the jurors.

The District Attorney then began to read out the charges against me to the jury. There were six of them: 1) murderous attack on H. C. Frick; 2) criminal attack on J. G. Leishman; 3) entering a building with criminal intent; 4) ditto; 5) ditto; 6) carrying concealed weapons.

The one offense, the attack on H. C. Frick, was thus multiplied, and out of one charge, six were manufactured in order to secure the maximum sentence for me. At first, the District Attorney had brought seven charges against me, but the grand jury had "only" charged me with the six "crimes" listed above.[9]

When the District Attorney was finished with his opening remarks, H. C. Frick was called as the first witness for the prosecution. He identified me and swore that I had attacked him with weapons with the intention, as he believed, to kill him. He was then handed a bundle by the District Attorney, which he identified as the clothing he had worn at the time of the attack and he then described to the jurors the wounds he had received.

The District Attorney then turned to me with the question: "Do you have a question to ask?"

"Just one," I answered; "whether he saw me shoot at J. G. Leishman?"

"That I can't say," Frick answered.

J. G. Leishman was the second witness. He repeated the testimony he had given during my preliminary interrogation, namely that I would have shot at him but that the gun had not fired.

In the cross-examination, I asked Leishman the question: "Are you sure that I aimed at you?"

> *Leishman:* "Yes."
> *Question:* "Isn't it possible that in the excitement of the moment you mistook my intent?"
> *Answer:* "No."
> *Question:* "Were you wounded?"
> *Answer:* "No, the weapon didn't fire."

After J. Leishman, Dr.———?, H. C. Frick's family doctor, entered the witness stand. He gave a description of his patient's wounds. The District Attorney then posed the question: "Were Frick's wounds dangerous in nature?"

"Each and every one of them," answered the witness.

It would have been relatively easy to refute the testimony of this witness as to the dangerous nature of "each and every one" of Frick's wounds, if the right witnesses had been on hand. It was known that as early as the second week after the attack, two members of the Homestead Advisory Board saw Frick going for a walk in front of his home in Homewood and had chatted with him. "Each and every" wound of Frick's can therefore not have been dangerous in nature.

David Courtney, the elevator operator, testified that he had brought me up to the upper floors of the *Chronicle Telegraph* building three times. He also stated that during my interrogation, I had said that I had not intended to harm anyone except Frick.—After a detective had identified me and my weapons—a revolver and a dagger—the prosecution ended its evidence against me, and Judge McClung asked me if I had anything to say.

I asked for an interpreter with the explanation that I had prepared my defense in writing, in the German language, and meant to read it. The District Attorney raised an objection, saying I should make my defense in English, but the Judge permitted me to read it aloud in German with the help of an interpreter.

The Clerk of Court raised his hand with the words: "I swear—"

"I don't swear," I interrupted him and entered the witness stand without further ado.

I began to read my "defense" when the Judge interrupted me with the words, "You must just state the facts."

But I responded, "I claim the right to present a full defense, since I have neither lawyers nor witnesses." Then I proceeded to read on. I read with a clear, distinct voice, but the interpreter—a small, nervous, blind man who later went crazy—was not capable of interpreting what I read sentence by sentence as I had expected of him. Instead, he translated word for word in such a way that made it impossible for those listening to understand the meaning of the whole.

I was not at all happy with this kind of interpreting, but I continued reading in the hope that among the newspaper reporters, a representative of a German newspaper would be present, who would take down my "defense" in German in shorthand. But as it later turned out, there were only English-language reporters present at my trial, who only wrote down a few sentences and put those together at random.

Here is a sample of what the reporters achieved in this regard— an excerpt from the report of my trial in the *NY World* from September 20, 1892.

Berkman asked for an interpreter. He refused to be sworn in and had a pamphlet ready, from which he began to read, when the court said, "You must just state the facts."

"I demand the right to present a full defense, since I have neither lawyers nor witnesses," said Berkman. "I know that an example will be made of me because of my act, and no one will much care [! my words were: but not much will be gained thereby. A. B.], no more than in the case of John Brown's murder or that of the five men on the gallows in Chicago in 1887.[10] The injustice of the ruling class is responsible for that. They oppress the worker. I belong to those who were murdered in Chicago. That crime made me think. Just as the objective in murdering my Chicago friends was not achieved, so will the objective that one seeks in my case now also fail."

After Berkman had been reading for about an hour, Judge McClung said, "You must finish by one o'clock."

"Well," said Berkman, "I can have as much time for my defense as I want, and I will take as much time as I need."

"We'll teach you different if you think you can lay down the law here," said Judge McClung. "You have until one o'clock; that's twice as much time as we would have given your lawyer, if you had had one."

"A lawyer told me I could have as much time as I need," said Berkman.

"Well, he was very much in the wrong," said the Court.

"This is the beginning of the conclusion," Berkman continued to read. "A battle against the status quo has flared up. The rich are getting richer and the poor poorer, and the end is near. These little strikes will soon end in a big one, and freedom for the workers will follow. And this big strike is not as far off as you think. Preparations for it are being made in every country. And now to my case. What were my motives for this "crime" and what have I achieved? The provocation was great . . ."

At this point, Judge McClung interrupted him. "It is now one o'clock. We will give you five minutes more."

"I can't state my motives in this amount of time."

"Well, you have to," said the Court.

"The reason for my deed was to free the world from the oppressors of the workers. (? A. B.)[11] I wanted to punish him, not kill him. I did not attack Mr. Frick, I attacked the person who had oppressed the workers. I do not name any person by name, but only the cause of the trouble, and this cause was what I wanted to get rid of."

At this point he was interrupted by the Court again: "You have had your time, and you must stop now. We have been too forbearing."

The case was hereupon handed over to the jurors.

After the District Attorney had made a short speech to the jurors, in which he demanded that they find me guilty on all counts, the charge sheets were handed to the foreman of the jury. The jurors stood up from their seats. At the same moment, the District Attorney approached the jurors who were about to leave the jury box and whispered something to them. At that, the jurors took their seats again and after a few seconds of discussion, the foreman of the jury wrote the word "guilty" on each of the six charge sheets.

I was called up at once to receive the verdict. Standing up from my seat I said, "I expected no justice and have received none."

The Judge sentenced me to 22 years—for the first charge of the murderous attack on Frick, I received 7 years; for the charge of the criminal attack on J. Leishman, 5; 3 years each were added for the three charges of unlawful entry, and finally a year in the workhouse for carrying a concealed weapon. In all, 21 years penitentiary and 1 year workhouse.

The court farce was now over. The Judge gave me the maximum sentence for each of the six charges—as was not to be expected otherwise. And the 12 jurors had once again "saved" the state.

But what else could be expected of 12 common houseflies like these jurors, with their hate and prejudice against everything they can't take in or understand!?!

Truth forever on the scaffold,
Wrong forever on the throne,
But that scaffold sways the future . . .

I was condemned. Condemned by people who see matters with their prejudices more than with their eyes. But my conscience was clear, for despite any and all court decisions, "merit is determined by the actuating motive."

At two o'clock in the afternoon on the 19th of September, the Court's guilty verdict was pronounced. By three o'clock I already found myself behind the walls of the Western Penitentiary with these words, unuttered, on my lips:

"all hope abandon ye
who enter here."!

Two Further Court Farces

HENRY BAUER

Before Berkman's trial, anarchists—especially those writing for the *Anarchist* that appears in New York—pointed out that it was an offense against anarchist principles when anarchists engage the help of lawyers in their trials; it would be inconsistent. Maybe. But is it not better in such a case to do something inconsistent than to plummet more deeply, though consistently, into the calamity that threatens the accused man?

But why theorize? Berkman's trial provides the best illustration. Berkman had refused the services of lawyers. What advantage did he or anarchist principles gain thereby? Absolutely none, quite the contrary, and the disadvantages had far-reaching consequences. Berkman shot Frick; that was clear. No lawyer could deny that, but a couple of capable lawyers could have prevented a blackguard district attorney from fabricating six charges out of one and Berkman, therefore, from receiving a 22-year sentence. Lawyers could have—and there is no doubt about this—reduced the six charges to no more than three, which would have meant a shorter sentence for Berkman. Lawyers could have seen to it that Berkman could have given his entire speech in his defense instead of a few words of it. Anarchist principles would not have lost anything by that, and Berkman could only have gained by it.

According to certain comrades, Nold and I brazenly violated anarchist principles; but the fact that anarchism lives and progresses as well today as it did five years ago is not to the credit of those who continually mouth the word "principle" but rather to those "unprincipled" people, those who rid their ideals of dogma in order to keep an eye instead on the practical goal—that is, on a goal appropriate to the moment.

But we can say that by doing something a little inconsistent that caused no harm in any way, we did not receive sentences as long as they would otherwise have been. For while we were out on bail, the public prosecutor added a third charge to the original two, but because of the efforts of our lawyers, the third charge was dropped.

Our trial was supposed to take place on Wednesday, the 15th of February, but it was delayed to the next day, because, as we were told, the district attorney's mother was ill. Would the district attorney have delayed our trial if my mother had been ill? On February 16, Assistant District Attorney Goering replaced District Attorney C. Burleigh and the fraud could begin.[1] The courtroom was full of people who wanted to see the anarchists. Our lawyers had considered it practical to have us tried together, and the first charge, incitement to riot, was to be dealt with first. At nine o'clock the Assistant District Attorney opened the curtain on the comedy "in the name of the people of Pennsylvania." Judge Joseph Slagle presided; Paul Eckert was a witness for the state.[2] Twelve jurors were soon found, for every law-abiding taxpayer could be used to damn the anarchists. And so there were 12 jurors, all rascals who today would still gladly carry the wood to burn a witch at the stake, if only they had the opportunity. (I will not name them here; otherwise these "intelligent souls" would think too much of themselves if they saw their names shining from the pages of a book.)

A detective from Homestead, whom I had never seen in my life, identified me and the leaflet I had distributed in Homestead. The prosecution wanted to prove that the leaflets had incited the citizenry in Homestead to lawlessness and insurrection against the sacred law and order. But the defense gave the prosecution a setback by proving that the battle in Homestead took place on July 6, 1892, and that the leaflets were not distributed there until two days later on July 8, and that after their distribution, not the slightest lawlessness had occurred. What was to be done? If one couldn't get at us this way, then something else had to be tried.

The Assistant District Attorney made a face, ran his hand through his hair, and called Eckert as a witness for the state. Eckert was at first at pains not to do us any harm with his testimony and made out as if he knew nothing about the whole thing. The Assistant District Attorney had soon exhausted his store of absurd questions; he had to run his hand through his disheveled hair again. Then he passed his hand over his high "thinker's forehead" and posed the question: "Who set and printed the leaflets?"

Eckert: I myself with the help of Carl Nold.
Question: Where were they printed?
Answer: In our house, No. 5 Cherry Street, Allegheny.
Question: To whom does the print shop belong?
Answer: To the International Workers Association.[3]

That was a success! The Asst. Dist. Atty. couldn't have asked for anything better. No one had known who had printed the flyers or that we had a printing press. It was even a surprise for the Asst. Dist. Atty.

as well as for the detectives, who admitted that they had not seen a printing press during their search of No. 5 Cherry Street. In point of fact, it was not a crime to print the leaflets or to own a printing press, but since we were known to be anarchists, the Assistant District Attorney was able to capitalize on this with little effort and pull the wool over the eyes of the jurors with anarchist secret presses, revolution, and other horror stories. He succeeded in doing just that in the afternoon. In the meantime, there was an hour's pause, for it was lunchtime.

In the afternoon, Nold took the stand. He did not want to swear by God and the Bible, so he was given the option to give testimony in the name of truth and honor. The usual questions about name, residence, business, and other uninteresting questions are omitted here; only the most important things will be quoted here, as later in my own and Berkman's statements.

Asst. Dist. Atty.: Did you help Paul Eckert prepare the flyers?
Nold: Yes.
Qu.: Why?
Ans.: Because I thought it essential.
Qu.: Who wrote the manuscript?
Ans.: I don't know.
Qu.: You were with H. Bauer in Homestead, weren't you?
Ans.: No. I have never seen Homestead.
Qu.: Who were the two who were with Bauer in Homestead?
Ans.: I don't know them.
Qu.: But you are a good friend of Bauer's?
Ans.: Yes, but I don't concern myself with the affairs of others when they aren't any of my business.
Qu.: Do you believe in the Hereafter?
Ans.: The what?
Qu.: Do you believe in God?

At this point, our lawyer Col. Moore rose to object, but before he could say anything, Nold had answered the question with a forceful "No."

After this, I entered the witness stand after I, like Nold, had promised to give testimony in the name of truth and honor.

> *Asst. Dist. Atty.*, with the flyer in his hand: Did you distribute flyers like this in Homestead?
> *Ans.:* Yes.
> *Qu.:* Who were your two companions?[4]
> *Ans.:* I refuse to answer.
> *Qu.:* Why?
> *Ans.:* Because I don't want to cause two of my friends any trouble.
> *Qu.:* Who are these friends?
> *Ans.:* I refuse to answer.
> *Asst. Dist. Atty.* to the Judge: Your Honor, the accused refuses to answer; he is in contempt of court.

"Must I answer the question?" I then asked the Judge.

> *Judge:* Yes, you must answer.
> *Asst. Dist. Atty.:* Who were the two people who distributed the flyers with you in Homestead?
> *Ans.:* I refuse to answer this question.

At this point our lawyer Col. Moore jumped up in agitation and said: "You no doubt do not understand the consequences that will result from your refusal. Answer the question."

> *Judge:* If you don't answer, I'll declare you in contempt of court and sentence you to 60 days' confinement.
> *Asst. Dist. Atty.:* Who were the two who were with you in Homestead?
> *Ans.:* I refuse to answer.

Judge: At the end of this trial I'll show you how we deal with people like you.

Asst. Dist. Atty.: Are you an anarchist?

Ans.: Yes.

Asst. Dist. Atty., with a picture of a bomb in his hand: Did you
draw this?

Ans. No.

Qu.: Do you know what this drawing depicts?

Ans. It seems to be a closed tin box.

Our lawyers protested, questioning the admissibility of such evidence, and were sustained by the Judge. (The police had found this
drawing in my office in a suitcase containing the writings of the late
Joseph Frick that he had left to the International Workers Association.[5]) After our lawyers had established with several questions put
to me that I had distributed the flyers in Homestead not on the 6th
of July 1892 but on the 8th of July, I was allowed to leave the witness
stand.

Given the fact that absolutely nothing had been proven against us,
Col. Moore moved that the charges be dropped. The Judge disagreed,
and Col. Moore then gave his speech for the defense in which he
showed that the charges against us were unfounded and ridiculous.
But his efforts were in vain. Then the Asst. Dist. Atty. rose to speak.
His speech was one long horror story—he had no case after all—a
story of lawless anarchists, conspiracy, secret presses, the breakdown
of law and order, the state in peril, etc. During all this, he stuck the
flyer under the noses of the jury every few minutes, pointing to the
words: "Force must be met by force." The jury retired and in half an
hour brought in their verdict: "Guilty." We had expected it. The first
act of the tragicomedy was over.

Nold went home. I didn't hear that we were found "guilty" until
the next morning, because right after the trial, I was brought before

Judge Slagle, who outlined to me the magnitude of my crime, that is, not answering the question and thus being in contempt of court, and suggested that foreigners must be taught a lesson, and so on, and sentenced me to 60 days in the county jail. In the cell to which I was then led, I had the opportunity to think about the trial. It is not enough that they will find us guilty, but they want to force me to turn traitor as well, just so they can throw two more comrades into prison. Here is where the Beast of Law and Order reveals itself in all its barbarity. Not satisfied with two victims, no! They wanted four and in order to get them, I was supposed to become the most contemptible, the most ignoble of all men—a traitor. All in the name of the "High Court." Though all traitors are hated and held in contempt, the Court exerts itself to force a man into an act of betrayal, and if he does not stoop so low, he is punished. On the other hand, if he does sink so low by turning traitor in court, he will always benefit from it: in exchange for his treachery he will receive a lighter sentence or even come off entirely free, as often happens. How depraved, how base, how Christian must such a judge, such a district attorney be! The traitor is rewarded, the steadfast man is punished.—

But they are Christians and that explains the whole hoax, for Christians are always capable of such dirty deeds. The shouts of the newspaper boys intruded into my cell: "Extra! All about the anarchists!" I lay down to sleep.

At nine o'clock the next morning, Friday, February 17, the trial was continued; the charge of conspiracy with Berkman was to be dealt with. Due to the newspaper reports, it had become known that Berkman would be brought from prison, and as a result, the courtroom was packed with the curious. Many couldn't find any room and filled the entrance to the hall. The "wise" Judge Slagle again took the presiding chair. On his face, you could see the Assistant District Attorney's joy over his victory from the preceding trial; Eckert played his role as witness for the state again. When Nold took his seat next to me, his first words were: "There's no point to this play of fools; they'll find us guilty again." Then suddenly all eyes turned to the door. Alexander Berkman was led in by three men, one to his right, one to his left, and one behind him. He took his seat next to Nold, who whispered to him: "We'll soon be keeping you company."

Twelve jurors were soon chosen; they were of the same caliber as those in the first trial. They knew we had been found guilty on the first charge, so it was self-evident that they held it to be their duty to find the anarchists guilty again. Books and writings of mine, seized by the police, lay on a table as evidence against me. After the police and the detectives had "conscientiously" related the course of events in our arrest, one of them reported that two trunks of *anarchist* literature had been found in my office in 73 Spring Garden Ave. Col. Moore grabbed a book by Darwin as well as a history of the French Revolution, both in German, and asked the witness, "What kind of books are these?"

> *Witness:* I don't know.
> *Moore:* Do you understand German?
> *Witness:* No.
> *Moore:* Then how can you claim that you'd found anarchist litera-
> ture?
> *Witness:* I'm not claiming that; I just thought it was.

The rest of the witnesses made similar fools of themselves.

The fact that Nold had shown Berkman various newspaper offices—among them the office of the *Chronicle Telegraph*—was misrepresented and the claim made that Nold had knowingly shown Berkman not the relevant newspaper office but Frick's office, which was in the same building; as if the police could read from Nold's eyes what his intentions had been half a year ago! Are we to believe that any court of law would view such evidence, based only on supposition, as admissible? No! But in Criminal Court in Pittsburgh with Judge Slagle presiding, this is what happened. There was a recess at this point; it was 12 o'clock.

Berkman caused a sensation in the afternoon when he took the witness stand. Before that, prosecution witness Eckert had done his "best" to give himself the appearance of an unwilling witness. He answered every question with "I don't know" and repeated this "I don't know" so often that the reporters called him the "I-don't-know-witness" in the next issues of the daily newspapers. Berkman was questioned for half an hour about his stay with Nold, his acquaintance with me, with Diether, etc., without anything new being brought to light than what the readers already know from the fourth chapter: that Berkman told Nold and me that he had come to Pittsburgh to look for work as a typesetter, that he had not taken Nold and me into his confidence, had held no secret meetings with us, and had finally left Nold's residence on 22 July '92, ostensibly to travel on to Chicago.[6] Then the Asst. Dist. Atty. posed the following questions.

> *Asst. Dist. Atty.:* Where did you send your suitcase?
> *Berkman:* To Chicago.
> *Qu.:* To what person in Chicago?
> *Ans.:* I refuse to answer.

At this, the Asst. Dist. Atty. appealed to the Judge to force an answer, like the day before in my case, but the Judge answered: "Berkman is already a condemned prisoner, in other words, a convict, and the court can therefore not force him to answer." The Asst. Dist. Atty. grimaced, brushed his long hair out of his face and—

> *Qu.:* Why did you shoot at Frick?
> *Ans.:* Because he is an enemy of the workers.

Qu.: Who are your co-conspirators?
Ans.: I didn't need any.

In the course of the examination, Berkman declared emphatically that neither Nold nor I nor anyone else had had anything to do with the *attentat,* nor had anyone else known of his plans.

Qu.: Do you believe in God?
Ans.: What kind of thing is that?
Qu.: Answer my question.
Ans.: You answer mine.
Judge: You understand the question very well; answer it.
Berkman: The Asst. Dist. Atty. should kindly explain what he means by 'God,' then I'll answer.
The Judge then got angry and asked: Do you believe in the Hereafter?
Berkman: I believe only in nature and common sense.

The Asst. Dist. Atty. didn't know where to go from there. Our lawyer Col. Moore began his speech in our defense after he had moved that the charges be dropped, which the Judge did not allow. He described the efforts of anarchists in positive terms and worked himself up at the end to cry out: "No decent human being can have sympathy for Frick! I would be ashamed even to shake his hand!"

The Asst. Dist. Atty., as was to be expected, made the same speech again as the day before: anarchists, murderers, bunch of criminals, don't believe in God, want to tear down the state of Pennsylvania with its exalted laws and institutions, every law-abiding citizen in danger. Men of the jury, save the state and society; it is your duty; find the anarchists guilty!

The jurors retired, and while we waited for the answer from these 12 "wise men," Col. Moore made this trenchant observation: "The

Judge and the Asst. Dist. Atty. know no more about anarchism than the chair I am sitting on."

Nold advised the newspaper reporters, who were also waiting for the pronouncement from the oracle, to go home and to report that the anarchists had been found guilty, because that would surely be the outcome. That morning I had already given the reporters an article about anarchism that I had written earlier in my cell.

When the jurors had still not reached agreement after half an hour, I was taken off to my cell, Berkman to the prison, and Nold went home for the last time. Not until nine o'clock in the evening did the jurors deliver a sealed verdict, which was opened the next morning. It read: "Guilty."

Nold's release on bail was therefore at an end, and he, too, was taken into custody. Evidently one or more of the 12 jurors realized that we were innocent but in the end agreed to the guilty verdict so that they wouldn't have to remain locked in the jury room overnight.

If I had not experienced it myself, I would never have believed what folly and disgrace such a court trial is and how easy it is to find innocent people guilty. How much worse must it be in most cases where poor defendants don't have the means to engage lawyers! Just like those who were taken off to the slaughterhouse in chains during the Inquisition, these people, once the pro forma "guilty" verdict has been pronounced, are dispatched to the prison. Everything as fast as possible. No trace of justice, no inkling of humanity; better to send 99 innocent people to prison than to let one guilty person go—that's the rallying cry. You can't talk of impartiality here, because the jurors, who really should be impartial, are afflicted with the authority disease like all their fellow human beings. Judges and district attorneys are always regarded as authorities by everyone, and therefore their influence on the jurors is a matter of course. How rarely a defendant is freed in criminal court provides the best proof that jurors are always influenced by the authorities. A Christian believes in and swears by his authorities like he believes in and swears by his God.

Our lawyers called for a new trial, which was, however, denied us. At the behest of the defense committee and against our will, the lawyers appealed the case to the Pennsylvania State Supreme Court. And if that doesn't work, they told us, then the board of pardons still offers us a spark of hope. But our experiences during the two days of our trial had extinguished in us every spark of hope for justice, and Nold remarked dryly: "The main thing now is that we go to prison as soon as possible; the sooner the better."

We spent the days from the 17th to the 25th of February in jail, which Nold gave an account of in an earlier article.[7] I was put in a row of cells together with the Homestead strikers H. O'Donnell and Critchlow, who were waiting for their trial that would take place in the next few days.[8] Nold was in another row of cells with H. Dempsey, whose trial had taken place before ours and who was now, like us, waiting for his sentence.[9] Several anarchist newspapers, *The Freedom* and *Commonweal* from London, which I had been able to smuggle in, were read by the Homestead strikers with pleasure.[10]

On Saturday morning, February 25, the verdicts were read. I had anticipated the full penalty, two years for the first charge, seven years for the second. Nold reckoned he'd serve six to seven years. To our surprise, we each got one year for the first and four years for the second charge. That wasn't so bad as expected; in fact, we could count ourselves lucky. It is no idle statement if I say that we would surely have been hanged together with Berkman if Frick had died from his wounds. That same day, the 25th of February, 1893, we were handcuffed to each other, Nold to my right, a prominent businessman sentenced to six years for sexual abuse of a little girl to my left, and transported to the prison in Allegheny, to keep comrade Berkman company for the next five years.

[Note appended[11]]

. . . We are sending numbers 10 to 18. The booklets don't belong together the way they are numbered. Some of them don't belong to *Prison Blossoms* at all, while others that do belong haven't been written yet. What we're sending here is what is on hand to date. Answer right away; then read the booklets through and let us know what you think of each number. Numbers 10 and 11 make up the conclusion of the first part of *Prison Blossoms*.

    K. G.

Debating the Act—Assassination
and Propaganda by Deed

D ENIED THE PUBLIC ARENA of the courtroom to defend his
attack on Frick, Berkman uses the secret prison magazine to
plead for the higher morality and political importance of his act.
Appealing to a native-born readership, he presents his deed as consistent with the tradition of American revolutionary heroes. When he
turns to the immigrant anarchist population, Berkman writes regret-
fully of anarchist leader Johann Most's condemnation of his attack on
Henry Frick. In their turn, Carl Nold and Henry Bauer defend Berkman, suggesting sympathy for his act was widespread among working people. Nold and Bauer deplore the fracturing of the anarchist
community that had resulted from the dispute with Most, while their
endorsement of Berkman notably defends his character and motive
more than the soundness of his revolutionary strategy.

A Few Words as to My Deed

ALEXANDER BERKMAN

F EW REVOLUTIONISTS, I think, have enjoyed—under conditions similar to ours—the opportunity of saying an explanatory word concerning their deeds, free from the auspices of censorship. We have been favored by the gods—though with great difficulty, the anarchist convict-trio has succeeded in creating such an opportunity, and I am now about to take advantage of the same.

Much has been said from diverse quarters, regarding me and my deed, yet I myself have not as yet—for obvious reasons—been heard.

For several days succeeding my arrest I remained in ignorance concerning the physical condition of Mr. Frick. But when it transpired that Mr. Frick would recover, it seemed to me that this circumstance, purely accidental as it was, would not tend to produce any minimizing effect on the signification and importance of my act; for a deed, such as mine, that in its meaning does in no way depend upon the physical consequences (to the parties concerned) incidental to that act, must have for its criterion the purpose underlying the deed and should be estimated according to the moral effect—called propaganda—produced by such an act. As far as my purpose and aims were concerned, it mattered very little whether my shots were fatal or not; indeed viewed from the true anarchistic standpoint, it did not make the slightest difference what the outcome, the physical results of my attempt were. I had, as already stated, no private axes to grind, no personal wrongs to avenge, no private feelings to satisfy. Whether Frick was among the living or the dead was a matter comparatively indifferent to me. It might popularly be supposed that the object of my attempt was to remove an obnoxious person. Yet nothing could be further from my real purpose. It was my aim, first and last, to express, by my deed, my sentiment toward the existing system of legal oppression and industrial despotism; to attack the institution of wage-slavery in the person of one of its most prominent representatives, to give it a blow—rather morally than physically—this was the real purpose and signification of my act.

There is much talk nowadays about Anarchists, yet very few people have a correct idea regarding their aims and purposes. They are misrepresented, libeled, and caricatured—and very little understood. They are represented as archenemies of society, murderers, and lunatics. But did it ever occur to the believing public to inquire why these enemies of society should, of their own free will, subject themselves to all the inconveniences and dangers as arising from unfavorable public sentiments, why they should willfully and willingly risk their liberty and enjoyment of life and even sacrifice their very lives, as they often do, in pursuance of—what?

Insane fancies, utopias, phantasmagoria?

Is it lunacy to wish to make the world better? Insane fancy to hope for a more just and rational condition of affairs? Is it utopian to desire freedom and the enjoyment of life for every human being? Are

Socialists and Anarchists enemies of society because they think the world could be improved upon and every man, woman, and child made free and happy?

If this is lunacy and a sign of enmity toward society, then Anarchists are indeed criminal lunatics.

But is it?

The History of Darkness records the names of men whose genius devastated whole countries, ruined its people, and caused the death of thousands upon thousands of human beings in order to demonstrate their right to a disputed claim of a hole in the ground; it immortalizes the names and records of men who waged war upon their neighbors because they were weak or because they were strong; it tells us of other men who unsparingly sacrificed human life while trying to convince the world that one is three and three contained in one; or that bread is flesh and wine is blood and many other disputed questions of equal "importance." These are the deeds of the great men of the History of Darkness and Despotism.

The History of Light, on the other hand, tells us of men whose lives' sole ambition was to make the world better, to dissipate the shadows of ignorance and disseminate the seeds of Knowledge, to raise the curtain of darkness and let the beautiful rays of light carry its vivifying warmth into the human heart. They were men of genius and they, too, waged war; war against Darkness and Despotism, against Ignorance and Slavery. And when human life was sacrificed in these wars, it was only out of necessity, to ensure the happiness of the many at the costs of the few. And because humanity was dearer to these men than their princes, because they thought more of the people, their rights and liberties, than of the strength of the throne, they were persecuted and punished. They were proclaimed enemies of the nation, traitors to their country and its interests, murderers and brigands, and were treated accordingly—until they had gathered strength enough to come out of the struggle as victors. And with success came recognition and now the names of the lunatics of 1793 and of the traitors of 1776 are held in sacred memory, and the men that had fallen under the hoofs of tyranny are regarded as martyrs to humanity.[1]

And who shall say that the lunatics and social enemies of our day will not, in time, be successful and prove themselves pioneers of light and freedom?

But, you say, it is lunacy to hope to revolutionize the world by an individual revolutionary deed. So it is. And what is more, no revolutionist of modern times—be he Anarchist, Socialist, or so-called Nihilist—ever expected the reconstruction of society to follow upon the heels of his deed.

It is by means of a primary *intellectual revolution,* to take place in the heads of the masses, that the Radicals of modern times hope to bring about a change in the social, political, and economical status quo. The propagandists by deed are at the same time agitators by word. They believe in and work for the education and enlightenment of the masses, the means they regard as the surest and absolute[ly] necessary qualification for the social revolution.

Now as to the purpose and signification of individual revolutionary deeds in general and of the act of '92 in particular.

A revolutionary deed has for its purpose either the removal—by forcible means—of a tyrant, a dangerous spy, and so forth, with or without the intent of making—at the same time by means of the deed—propaganda for the ideas of the removing intelligence; or the forcible direction of public attention to certain social conditions and to the attacking party (not, however, to the person, but rather to the motives and intentions of the same) with the view of reforming the former and making propaganda for the ideas of the latter. This holds true in the cases of almost all the revolutionary deeds of the last 25 years, as could easily be demonstrated in every instance. But two examples shall suffice.

The sentence passed upon Alexander II by Young-Russia had for its object the punishment and removal of a tyrant; the terrorizing of Absolutism into granting more liberty, probably a constitution; the enlightenment of the Russian peasant concerning the true source of his misery, Tsarism, supposedly sacred and enjoying divine protection;[2] the punishment of the tyrant, the strangler of free thought and speech; revenge for the almost Siberiaized fatherland; the calling of the attention of West Europe to the shameful conditions existing in the land of the barbaric autocrat; etc.

The deed of Vaillant (1893), on the other hand, was an act of propaganda pure and simple.[3] It could have no other purpose but that of forcibly drawing public attention to the unendurable social conditions, to point out the fountainhead of national corruption; in fine, it was a protest against the existing state of affairs, a voice raised against modern slavery, in the cause of freedom.

Vaillant was too intelligent a man to expect the liberation of mankind, or of his own country, to result from his attempted annihilation of the French Parliament. He knew, as every enlightened revolutionist knows, that the problem of freedom is much more difficult of solution; he knew that ignorance, servility, and lack of spirit comprise the strongest links in the chains that hold the masses in bondage. But Vaillant wanted to give a healthy stimulus to rational thought—he struck at the very heart of corruption. He did not believe that his deed would revolutionize the world, nor were his motives those of personal revenge. It was an act of propaganda, having, as deeds of this nature do, that hatred which is love for its background.

And now as to the act of '92.

My views concerning propaganda were at the time of the Homestead trouble precise and radical. Though the ideas of Anarchy have for years been propagated in this country, the native-born population still remain indifferent, I thought. Why? Because, first, they entertain perverted views as to Anarchism, and second, because they do not earnestly believe in our sincerity of purpose and solidarity with the working classes. The American is of a practical turn of mind, he puts little faith in phrases; to convince him, solid facts are necessary. "In the beginning was the deed."[4] If we wish that the American working-man should listen to our words, we must primarily demonstrate to him by deed that we mean well with him, that we are his friends. We must prove to him that our sympathy for and interest in him is not a mere empty sound, but that his cause is also our cause and that we do not stand idle by, indifferent to his misery and struggles; but that we feel, suffer, and fight with him, for him.

To demonstrate this and thus win the sympathy, the heart, and ear of the American workmen, there is no better way, or rather there is but one way (I thought)—to wit, to sacrifice our blood, our very life, on the altar of his liberation.

But such a demonstration should not be given in this country on the heads of political life—as is so often the case in European countries; for the American—(and by American is meant the citizen of the United States) believes himself to be politically sovereign and would consequently have neither sympathy for, nor a fine understanding of a so-called political deed. The proof to be given, which, if successful as such, would be a propaganda deed par excellence, must be acted out in the industrial arena.

Such were my views in 1890–93. And as to myself, I was, I must say, but too willing to sacrifice my liberty, even my life, for the benefit of the cause—to hasten the approach of the social revolution, to serve as the dead timber under the feet of humanity, marching onward.

The Homestead lockout seemed to me to offer the long expected opportunity of translating my ideas from theory into practice. The circumstance that it was a lockout, that is to say a forced discontinuation of work, the extent of the same, the despotism of the Carnegie Company, the sentiments of the Nation, favorable as they were to the workmen and condemnatory of the oppression and tyranny on the part of the employers, and, further, the glorious battle with the myrmidons of capital, that memorable event which proved the Homestead workmen still to possess something of the spirit of their progenitors—all these circumstances crystallized in my mind in the conviction that the strike of Homestead offered me the opportunity of a lifetime.

To give the American people the above-mentioned proof of our sincerity, friendship, and solidarity, to enlighten it as to the true aims of Anarchists, to point out the primary cause of their misery—wage slavery, as an institution—to impart a miniature lesson with regard to ways and means of liberation—the collective deed as preface to the social revolution—in fine, to make propaganda in the interest of Anarchy, that was the object of my act. And my motives had their roots in my great hunger to do something—according to my own standards—in the interest of my cause.

It is in the nature of the thing that when an *Attentat** is committed, even those who as a rule take no interest in social problems, or have no time to reflect upon them, are stimulated by such a deed to thought. Everyone desires to know "who the man is," what were his motives; his purpose and so forth. And when it transpires that the man is an Anarchist, then the public interest grows still more inten-

---

* A. B.: *The German word* Attentat *signified, when applied to a radical, a revolutionary deed.*

sive; they wish to know who those Anarchists are, what they are after etc. At such moments the public offers an attentive ear, eager to learn everything concerning Anarchists, their ideas and purposes, and Anarchy can but profit by such conditions.

This circumstance I had taken in consideration when laying my plans, and I hoped much from the same.

The Anarchist movement in this country was rather low at the time of my attempt; I believed that my deed would prove a healthy stimulus, and I hoped that my comrades would not fail to exploit my act in the interests of propaganda.[5]

But what an awful, cruel disappointment [awaited] me! What a disillusion had been reserved for me! The persons or rather the person whose duty it was and in whose power it lay to call out a demonstration in behalf of my deed—with the object of propaganda—this person was pleased instead to theorize over "propaganda by deed," to criticize the personality of the Attentäter,* to satirize and cast insinuations concerning the physical results of the attempt. Unfortunately (for my deed and myself) this person, John Most, editor of the New York *Freiheit,* possessed at the time great influence over the German-speaking comrades, so much so, that his word was law to many an anarchist-believer.[6] In consequence of the above-mentioned attitude of Most with regard to my case, the Anarchist camp divided itself into two factions: the one whose mouthpiece was Most and the New York *Freiheit,* against me and my deed, the other, with comrades S. Merlino and E. Goldman in the lead, whose sympathies were with me.[7] A newspaper controversy soon developed between the leaders of the two factions, which contention was of a forcible and personal nature and consumed much energy and time, which should have been employed in the interest of propaganda.

---

* A. B.: *A person committing a revolutionary deed by force.*

My friends used their best efforts to propagandistically exploit my deed; they arranged mass-meetings in which my deed was ably expounded and endorsed; they neglected no opportunity of working on my behalf; their efforts, however, were unfortunately comparatively too insignificant to produce a marked influence on public opinion.

But what circumstance caused Most to take his position as against me?

It was his opinion—Most wrote in the *Freiheit*—that the propaganda by deed in general and in America in particular, is useless, nay, even harmful since the masses do not as yet understand us and our motives. Granted, for the present, this alleged conversion of Most to peaceful means to have been real, was Most's outspoken inimical attitude toward my deed and myself justifiable? By no means. Even the individualistic Anarchists, those by principle enemies of all force, treated my case with more integrity than Most did.[8] Moreover, there was nothing to hinder Most from exploiting my deed in an agitatorical way, no matter whether he concurred with me in regard to matters of tactics or not; yet Most never even attempted anything of the kind; on the reverse, he endeavored to paralyze by his attitude every movement in behalf of my deed; thus, for instance he expressed himself in the *Freiheit* in a way as to make it appear as if he doubted the sincerity of my attempt; he refused to recognize the genuineness of my deed by invariably using the words *Attentat* and *Attentäter* enclosed with the marks of quotation, when their usage had reference to my deed; he even attempted to insinuate the existence of some personal motives by inscribing the following notice regarding my case in the letter box of the *Freiheit* (literal translation): "The cuckoo may know why and how."[9]

I have referred to Most's "conversion" to peaceful and lawful means. Neither was this conversion real nor did it represent the true cause of the stand taken by Most in my case. Everyone acquainted with Most's views regarding the propaganda by deed as expounded by himself in his brochures: "The Science of Revolutionary Warfare" and "Reinsdorf and the Propaganda by Deed" knows full well his sentiment concerning anarchist tactics.[10] Most himself demonstrated his conversion to have been fictitious by glorifying publicly in the *Freiheit* the acts of Pallas, Vaillant, and Henry, all of which deeds have taken place after Most's alleged conversion.[11]

The explanation for the extraordinary behavior of Most in my case is to be found in a different direction.

Apprehending, on account of my deed, probable difficulties from his reputation as leader of the American Anarchists, which position was aggravated by the well known fact of his (Most's) previous friendship with the writer, Most believed himself in danger of being accused by the police as *particeps criminis,* eventually indicted and convicted as one of the "conspiracy." Heroic measures, it is evident (thought Most) must be used as a way out of this dilemma; accordingly, he boldly took his stand—officially and publicly—against my deed and myself. His avowal in the *Freiheit,* the discountenancing of my deed, carried in itself his safety.

Most himself has since actually confirmed the truth of this view. Thus he had written in a subsequent edition of the *Freiheit* concerning his position in my case: "We got the best of the police by the use of a little cunning."

It may be mentioned also that Most has borne me and my friends ill will since the rupture of our friendship on account of my sympathy with the Autonomists; this circumstance may have influenced Most with regard to my case.[12]

Behind the bars and consequently unable to defend myself against the journalistic attacks and insults of my anarchistic and other enemies, I soon came to realize that the propagandistic effect of my deed will, to a large extent, be wasted owing to the unsympathetic position taken by the principal Anarchist paper of the country, the *Freiheit,* and the sequent indifference of the great mass of Anarchists.

What a crushing realization this was! I felt terribly disillusioned . . .

The Red Bugbear

CARL NOLD AND HENRY BAUER

I T ALWAYS AFFORDS THE CAPITALISTIC press special pleasure to exercise the privilege of the ass-fraternity of kicking its
hoofs into the chained lion. It is a great joy to the press to fall over the
Anarchists and empty over their heads tons of literary dirt, since
it can be done with immunity, aye, even with profit. It is therefore
natural that the most despicable of the capitalist tools—the press-
myrmidons—are for the above named reason, the most "courageous"
of all in heaping abuse and throwing stones at anarchists. They have
given a fair specimen of their ability in this direction at the time of
the Haymarket affair, during the trial of A. Spies and comrades and
again, later, they have excelled themselves in building veritable mountains of filth and throwing denunciations at a man whose admirable
moral courage and beneficial sincerity no honest man can doubt, and
all because this man—P. Altgeld, Governor of Illinois—sought, by an

act of simple justice to remedy, as far as lay in his power, the atrocious legal man-sacrifices made to Mammon in Chicago on the 11th of November 1887.[1]

It is a notorious fact that editors and reporters of newspapers are mere tools in the hands of their employers, doing the bidding of the latter in all matters of opinion. Parading as the representatives of public opinion, these Knights of the pen strive to press public sentiment into the forms cast by the hand of Mammon. The burning social question of the day, and all phenomena produced by the contrast of unearned riches on one hand and appalling and undeserved misery and poverty on the other, are treated by these brainless and conscienceless hirelings of the press as the red bugbear of anarchy, with a view of instilling terror into the public mind. But thanks to the fact that the intelligent public gradually grows cognizant of the false colors under which the capitalistic press of all sublunar waters is sailing, the attempts of the press to form and press public opinion to suit its own devices are not always successful.

This was demonstrated by the deed of Alexander Berkman. Public opinion, or better the opinion of the working classes, was on the side of A. B., voicing the very opposite of those sentiments which the capitalistic press pretended to "represent." In this case, the bugaboo tactics of the press failed to terrorize the people.

What was the feeling of the people with regard to A. B. and his deed?

From the general sentiments called to life by Berkman's deed, those are of chief importance to us which manifested themselves among the working classes and in their organizations and also among those in sympathy with them. For capitalistic papers, Gorgons of the strongbox, and all those belonging by "divine right" to the classes which professionally rob and deceive the people could naturally have nothing but words of damnation and rage against anarchy in general and Berkman in particular. But in the circles of working men, the general sentiment was: "That's good for Frick. We hope he is done for."

The working classes felt that whoever the man was who shot Frick, he had done the right thing to the right person at the proper time; and many a man, who, for some reason or other did not wish to give public expressions to his sentiments as to the deed, has nevertheless shown that he had no sympathy whatever for Frick. . . . We have visited on the evening of Berkman's deed popular resorts in Pittsburgh where we found Americans drinking the health of B. We have heard street-car drivers greet each other, on meeting on their trips, with the words: "It's good for Frick."

Thousands of such little scenes were enacted all over the country, for there is hardly a village in America but that knows Frick as an exploiter and oppressor of workmen.

Homestead received the news of the attempt on Frick's life with undisguised signs of joy. Among other incidents which have taken place in Homestead the most notable was that of W. L. Iams, a private of the Militia then stationed in Homestead, who called for three cheers for "the man that shot Frick." For this evidence of heart-felt sentiment poor Iams was brutally disciplined. By the order of Lieutenant Colonel J. Streator, Iams was hung up by the thumbs, which inhuman punishment lasted for half an hour, inflicting great pain on the private. Iams was, in addition, drummed out of the camp and excluded from membership in the Pennsylvania militia. Streator's barbarity toward Iams had its epilogue in the courts, but the Lieutenant Colonel Silver-Spoon came out victorious.*

---

* *Streator had several months after the above mentioned court trial, in a beastly intoxicated condition, stolen silver spoons from different saloons in Wheeling, W. Va.* [Bauer and Nold crossed this note out in their manuscript, perhaps feeling it was redundant.]

It is quite superfluous to mention that B's deed was greeted almost unanimously by the Anarchists of the country [with favor] and B himself unqualifiedly approved of. But a great surprise awaited the comrades, which produced a change in the flow of their sentiments. The surprise came from John Most. We have already alluded to the fact that John Most, for many years editor of the New York *Freiheit*, was an intimate friend of Alexander Berkman's and that the two friends had subsequently fallen out on account of some autonomistic matter; later on during Alexander Berkman's presence in Allegheny, the comrades of Allegheny had applied to J. M. for information concerning A. B. and Most advised them, in essence, not to have anything to do with Berkman.[2] J. Most had from the beginning very unfavorably discoursed in the columns of the *Freiheit* on the deed of Berkman and on Berkman himself. His stand against Berkman naturally created much comment and wonder among the anarchists. An article headed "Attentats-Reflexionen" (Reflexions on B's deed), which John M. had written and submitted to the Group I of New York, was not approved of by the latter; as a result the article failed to get into print for some time.[3] J. Most sent this manuscript article to the comrades of Pittsburgh and Allegheny; it was read there in a specially arranged meeting, approved of after a short deliberation, and sent back to Most. On the strength of this approval Most published the article in the *Freiheit* on the 24th of August 1892, a whole month after B's deed.

This article proved to be the alluded-to surprise to the comrades. It contained some arguments against the "propaganda by deed" with special reference to America as well as sideblows for Berkman. For the better understanding of the matter we give space to the article referred to, faithfully translated into English:

(Here follows the article in English.)[4]

As a consequence of this stand on the part of John Most, the sentiments of the anarchists were soon divided. The views of those who seconded Most and his opinions, to which number the anarchists of Pittsburgh and Allegheny belonged, were against Berkman as shown in the article above; while those who took the part of Berkman, with Emma Goldman in the lead, used the then in New York printed paper *The Anarchist* as their mouthpiece and tried all the means in their power to exploit the deed of A. B. for the benefit of anarchistic propaganda; but the dispute of the two factions, having unfortunately developed into personal quarrels, prevented either side in succeeding to any marked degree in propagating their respective views.

Robert Reitzel, the genial and ingenious editor of *Der Arme Teufel* of Detroit, Mich., to whom the blue and red party flaglets are as little sacred as the gold and silver embroidered flags of State and Church, gave Berkman the credit he deserved for his courage and well-meant act.[5]

Every one, it is true, has a perfect right to view and criticize (according to his own standard) an act such as Alexander Berkman dared to do; anarchists however should never forget themselves so far as to calumniate and libel the man himself.

The reader will naturally expect us to state at this juncture our personal opinions concerning Berkman's deed as well as our views with relation to Most's stand in the *Freiheit,* seeing that we have had to keep Berkman company for five years, though innocent. Well then:

In brief—We have nothing to say against Berkman's deed, as such, nor anything against the motives underlying the deed and its object. As to Berkman himself, we know that he was animated by the purest and best motives, as noble as those of a revolutionist ever were.

Concerning the stand of the *Freiheit,* i.e. of John Most, we believe that his words against the propaganda by deed concerning America especially constituted his sincere opinion; however his personal criticism of Berkman we find unjustified. Moreover we must say that we could never befriend the tactics which the *Freiheit* has for years pursued with regard to all those (anarchists and revolutionists) whose ideas are more or less at variance—in principle or tactics—with those championed and propagated by the *Freiheit.*

To throw all those who do not absolutely concur with us into the waste-basket, so to speak, is bad policy, to say the least.

In the interest of justice and of true progress, all factions should be given a hearing, for justice means toleration. It is, moreover, quite impossible as well as undesirable that in the great anarchistic movement all feet should beat time to the same tune. In such matters, dissimilitude, which is desirable, will, when necessity demands it, strive for and reach complete unison, if but the hearts and brains reach out for the same great goal.

Tolstoi or Bakunin?

CARL NOLD

When a deed is done for Freedom
Through the broad earth's aching breast
Runs a trill of joy prophetic
Travelling on from East to West.[1]

WITHOUT ANY "STOP OVER" the head of the Russian Police was sent straight to heaven through the medium of a bomb.[2]

Thou shalt not kill!

Tolstoi, the second Christ, has repeated it over and over: do not kill! I agree with him. It is wrong to kill, no matter whether the killing is done by an individual or in the name of a government; no matter whether a human being or an animal is killed; it is murder and wrong beyond question. A murder is always murder even if sanctified by Church, Pope, Government, or Law. As I cannot give life, I have no right to take life; and as I do not like to be killed, I feel that others don't want to be killed. I imagine that the smallest worm enjoys life and am therefore careful not to step on it. For the very same reason I am against hunting and fishing, unless self-preservation compels me to destroy animal life in order to live. It is then a question of self-defense and the "survival of the fittest." If a mad dog is after me, I shall certainly try to get out of his way, and if this is not possible I shall send him to dogheaven if I can do it.[3]

Such a mad dog was roaming through Russia during the last five years. His name was Von Plehve; he did not do the biting himself, he had a host of other mad dogs at his command who did the dirty work for him—thousands were sent to Siberia, thousands are still in prisons, thousands had been murdered, this blood-thirsty dog could never get enough human blood. Then came a man who had also learned that self-preservation is the first law, and he concluded that to preserve himself and others, the dog must be killed. And so he did it, knowing full well that the best dog is a dead dog.[4]

But what is the use of it, says Tolstoi. Von Plehve was a misguided man, a victim of circumstances and most probably we would do the same in his place. All right, grand old man, if we in his place are just as mad, I say, then we ought to be killed also—that is all there is to it. When a man kills in self-defense, in a passion of heat, in a moment in which he lost control over himself, I am not in favor of killing this man also because he committed a murder. I am not in favor of applying the brutal Christian law, "an eye for an eye etc. etc." But when a man for years made it his business and highest ambition to destroy human life, when a single man was guilty of the "massacres of the Jews, the banishment of the Finns, the spoliation of the Armenians, the persecution of the Poles, the exile of Russia's noblest men and women, the flogging of peasants, the imprisonment and butchery of Russian workmen, the establishment of a terrible system of espionage and the abolition of the very last spark of Liberty," then I rejoice at the news of such a monster's death and all glory to the Knight who fearless killed the dragon.[5]

Surviving Western Pennsylvania Penitentiary

T HE ESSAYS, NARRATIVES, character sketches, and dialogues
that provide this description of prison life recall the range of
writing in the early days of the authors' growing prison correspondence, though most of their first writings were ultimately lost or destroyed. In the first few years, while the select community of "subscribers" to the clandestine booklets grew, each reader was invited to
add his own commentary to the collection as it made its way from cell
to cell, producing a variety of genres that appealed to the editors.

In "Our Prison Life," Henry Bauer recalls this early history and the
inception of a plan for a volume of prison writings to be published
outside the penitentiary gates. With a more mainstream audience in
mind, Bauer writes lengthily of prison abuses in "Penitentiary Administration and Treatment of Prisoners," an essay that acquired
notes of wry or exasperated disagreement when it reached Berkman.
The depiction of corruption, starvation, and beatings in prison is

made more graphic and immediate in the anonymously written account of "Prisoner A-444," who also writes of sexual liaisons between older prisoners and "kids." As Berkman says later in "Prisons and Crime: Influence of Prisons on Morals," these practices were tolerated by prison administrators, who were both powerless to intervene and wary of public scandal.

In two character sketches, "The Shop-Screw" and "The Trusted Prisoner," Carl Nold depicts familiar prison types, describing in some detail the unsavory and unhygienic practice of chewing and spitting tobacco that contributed to the widespread epidemic of tuberculosis among prisoners. Two brief dialogues, "Dialogue between Two Prisoners" and "A Morning Conversation between Dutch and Mike (Two Prisoners)," both recorded by Nold, were in all likelihood included not only to entertain subscribers but also to record the ignorance and political naïveté among prisoners that appalled the editors as they made their accommodation to prison life.

Our Prison Life: Second Half
(February 1895–May 1897)

HENRY BAUER

THE FIRST TWO YEARS HAD gone by quickly without our ever feeling bored. Alexander Berkman had successfully taken up a thorough study of the English language. Nold could now count playing the guitar among his achievements and I had strained my eyes by reading so much that I needed glasses. We all enjoyed good health. We made very little use of the doctor and never got acquainted with the hospital at all. It was now a question of getting through the second half of our prison term.[1] Nold and Schulz were in the new wing of the penitentiary, Berkman, Friend H, and I were in the old wing.[2] It was already the third month since Berkman had been locked up in solitary, but we had gained a little more peace and quiet for, first of all, the Warden was pleased because he had succeeded in separating us, and second, "Jim" had been sick for several months.[3] When the Chaplain soon thereafter announced in church in an emotional voice that "Jim" had bid this world farewell, his devout prisoner listeners would have liked nothing better than to turn somersaults for joy, while the Chaplain's eyes almost filled with tears.[4] This Jim was universally hated among the prisoners, because his main ambition was to convince them that they were simply dogs in his power that he treated as the mood struck him. Twenty years of dealings with prisoners had turned him into a heartless and callous beast. Once, when the guard under whose supervision Nold worked had sent Nold and another prisoner to another department to fetch something, Jim, who had seen that, had nothing better to do than to run to Nold's supervisor and order him not to let Nold out of his sight or let him out of his department any more, because you couldn't trust anarchists. This fool was so afraid of us that the anarchist phobia seized the Warden and the Chaplain down to the very core, too. That became obvious later.

Jim's successor was an old guard who answered to the name of "Benny."[5] The appointment of this man as assistant administrator was greeted with joy among the prisoners, because his ignorance was proverbial. I often heard prisoners jokingly say to each other: "You are as ignorant as Benny." In only one respect was he similar to "Jim," namely in chewing tobacco. Whenever you saw the man, you thought you had a goat in front of you that was chewing its fodder. His first great act as deputy warden consisted in procuring even more spittoons. The next was a little encounter with me. He saw me coming out of the school and gave the order that I shouldn't be allowed in the school any more, because there were "others" here who needed it more. This time I agreed with him, because it was clear to me that he belonged to these "others" first and foremost.

Berkman had gotten work in the cell block; they didn't want to let him in the workshop any more, because as Jim once said, he had an "undesirable effect" on the prisoners.

In the workshop where I worked, a strike broke out. The prisoners wanted good pump water during the hot summer months instead of foul, dirty tap water. I made the suggestion that they should strike for beer instead of for water, but they didn't listen to me. The result was that half a dozen of them ended up in the "hole" [also called the dungeon]. Then, when the hospital was overrun with men ill with fever, the doctor gave the order to give the prisoners good pump water instead of bad tap water.

A third springtime came over the land and seemed three times as beautiful as before.

As already reported: since the suspension of the *Zuchthausblüthen* and *Prison Bird,* Berkman and Nold wrote each other weekly letters in which I also had a voice and in this way we first got to know each other properly.[6] These letters—5-10-15 pages long—all passed though my hands and I read them with the greatest pleasure. I destroyed them only very reluctantly. I wanted to preserve them, but it was impossible. There was no place to hide them; our cells were searched for every trifling reason, and besides that, I had a bundle of written material that Friend D had made over to me.[7] Around that time, our friends in Allegheny had almost forgotten how to write, but we didn't miss their letters much; our own correspondence was much more interesting, and besides, we were kept up to date by Berkman's friends.

It was in such circumstances that I got the idea that the three of us should write a book about our "adventures" in court and in prison. I passed my idea on to Nold, and Nold passed it on to Berkman, and the matter was soon subjected to debate with the result that we decided to put my idea into practice. How we were to send the manuscripts to our friends we didn't know ourselves yet. Our friend H, to whom we turned in this dilemma, as we had with so many other needs, said: Well, just go ahead and write; I'll have found a way out by the time you're ready to send things off. Knowing that we could rely on him, we got down to work. Berkman and Nold mapped out a plan and on the first of May, 1895, after we had accumulated a tidy supply of paper, Nold sharpened his pencil and wrote the first article. Inspired in this way, first Berkman and then I got to work.

In New York in the meantime, Berkman's friends had launched a little campaign to reduce his sentence. Miss Emma Desmond, an American, came from New York to Pittsburgh that summer for this reason, to take the matter in hand with the help of the Pittsburgh and Allegheny comrades.[8] Since prisoners are allowed to receive a half hour visit every three months, and since Berkman was certainly corresponding with Miss Desmond, though he could not speak to her otherwise, it was self-evident that the two wanted to see each other. Berkman had already had visits twice before, so he told the Chaplain, who sent out the visiting cards, to send one to Miss Desmond. "I cannot do it; you must see the Warden," was his answer. Berkman spoke with the Warden, who had this evasion, "You must see an inspector." At first, the latter refused most decidedly with the words, "We don't want anarchists to visit here." Berkman firmly demanded the same treatment others received and told him, "Miss Desmond is not an anarchist as you understand the term," by which he meant that Miss E. Desmond would not come to visit with a dagger in one hand and a bomb in the other in order to commit murder and blow up the prison if she could. He was satisfied by this, and Miss Desmond received a visiting card. In the meantime, the daily newspapers noted that Miss E. Desmond was "an anarchist of international repute" and the brave prison inspector dithered again. Miss E. Desmond came, but wasn't able to see Berkman, because, as the Warden told her politely but decidedly, the inspector had taken back his permission by telephone. "What have I done that I am not allowed visits?" Berkman asked the Warden. The latter gave several lame excuses and left Berkman in the dark. Berkman wrote to Miss Desmond again, advising her to contact a Pittsburgh judge to get permission to visit him. The next day the

Chaplain came with the letter in his hand and said he couldn't send the letter because of its contents: "Not so rash my boy, not so rash. Wait and I will see what I can do when I come back." Our Mr. Chaplain went away for several weeks and Berkman has not received a visitor down to the present day. Even though during every visit a guard is present who hears every word said, even though the Warden himself or the Chaplain can be present (for Berkman's second and last visitor, "Jim" himself was there), these "gentlemen" think it opportune to let their childish fear of a possible or impossible conspiracy or bomb attack come to light. What big babies!

I received the following postcard (copied verbatim) at about this time:[9]

Philadelphia, August 9, 1895
Dear Mr. Bauer
Have just read your article in "Freiheit." Tell you as a worker next to you at one time that I am sorry that you have let yourself be carried away with that crazy anarchism. Think back to your early years and how good you had it then, these years would certainly not have got you into prison if you had held to them but [would have been] the best years and if you continue like this, prison will not be enough but the gallows will conquer so in conclusion I want to express my wish that you should look to yourself and come out of prison and turn your back on anarchism forever, because [they're all] big mouths and slackers
Ge B

Nold, to whom I had given the postcard to read, made an apt comment: "Better to be stuck in a prison cell than in this slave's hide!"

Shortly after these incidents, a comrade from Allegheny paid a call on Nold, telling him that the comrades in Allegheny and Pittsburgh were willing to make the attempt to petition for a pardon for him and me and that they had already taken the necessary steps to do so. Nold replied that he didn't want a pardon: "I have gotten through 30 months and I'll deal with the remaining 21 months, too."

The next morning, Nold reported the matter to me and Berkman in great detail. I thought the whole matter through and soon came to the conclusion that it would be of great interest and advantage to the comrades in Allegheny County, indeed for Berkman and me too, if Nold could be freed now. Until I was released, Berkman and I could finish up the book, while Nold could agitate from the outside, raise money, intercede for Berkman and see to other things that can't be mentioned here. I told Nold my opinion, which wasn't to his liking. "Do you think it's a pleasure for me to labor away at the hot forge in the factory ten hours a day for lousy wages?" he asked me. A debate ensued that Berkman took part in as well. For a week daily letters flew back and forth and after a time, Nold agreed to give the plan a try. Soon thereafter the same comrade who had visited Nold paid me a visit, too, and I told him the results of our deliberations. Two days later Nold and I wrote to the Allegheny comrades and three weeks later it was thought advisable to tell us that the comrades had hoaxed us. That is the story of the pardon attempt that in addition to everything else brought down on us a flood of ridiculous criticism from comrades who make the mistake of clinging to anarchism theoretically like they used to cling doggedly to the Bible.[10]

The third summer and fall had passed and miraculously we had been left undisturbed, so that in the fall we successfully had Part I of the projected book, entitled *Prison Blossoms,* ready to send out. Our friend H, to whom we entrusted it, had done his part masterfully. We would never have dared to undertake something like this if, first of all, all the prisoners hadn't put their complete trust in us and, second, if we hadn't had cash at our disposal.

I was thinking with surprise at how it could be that the three of us had been left undisturbed for so long, when Berkman sent the message: "I have been locked up again; on what grounds I still have to find out." He asked the Warden for the cause, whether perhaps a complaint about him had come in. The former answered: "There are no charges against you whatever."

One morning a key had been found broken off in the lock of the cell next to Berkman's. The neighboring cells and prisoners were immediately searched and Berkman, who had been writing several small sketches in the hours devoted to study, was robbed of what he had written. At the same time, Nold's and my cells were searched but nothing "unlawful" was found. If any suspicion fell on any one of us three so that his cell or clothing was searched, then the other two could always count on having to suffer too. Eventually we were so used to it that we just laughed about it.

The following incident illustrates what kind of guard was in charge of Nold (for example). Nold had a number of books on the table in his cell and his guard, who had seen that, came into his cell one evening with the words: "Would you lend me a good book?" "Certainly," said Nold and handed him "Uncle Benjamin" and he took it off with him.[11] Five minutes later he brought the book back, shaking his head: "Nold, you are incorrigible. No! I won't read a book like this."

The guard had seen right on the first page of the book that God and preachers were criticized disparagingly and his religion raised its hackles. A juicy whorehouse story would have been more to his taste and would have been in better tune with his religious scruples.

(This account covers the time until December 1895)

Penitentiary Administration and Treatment of Prisoners

HENRY BAUER

A NUMBER OF YEARS AGO two thick volumes appeared by the American George Kennan on Siberia, Siberian prisons, the life of the prisoners there, their treatment, the cruelties they are subjected to, etc.[1] That work caused a general sensation; but whoever has read it and has been in an American prison cannot avoid thinking that American prisons, their administration, and the treatment of prisoners would make a good companion piece to the Russian system. A Kennan who made such a journey through American prisons in order to study them and their workings would soon discover that it is much harder to gather the material for such a work in America than it would be in Siberia. He would have no opportunity to speak for hours or whole evenings with a number of intelligent prisoners, as he was able to do in Siberia. The administrators of the prisons (wardens) would conduct him through the best parts of the prison so that he would be able to take only a cursory look at the whole. He would have no opportunity to speak with the prisoners in private and would have to be satisfied with the information the warden provided, which consists largely of the crassest lies, since every warden strives to present the prison under his supervision in the best light possible. (Just think of Warden Brockway of the Elmira Reformatory.[2]) Intelligent prisoners—so long as they are not anarchists—always receive the best positions in the penal institutions, the easiest work, the best treatment, so that when they are freed, they either have no reason to complain or don't want to do it out of consideration for the warden, with whom they have had a close "friendship" and who allowed them various things that the rest had not been allowed.

So a Kennan would have to position himself at the gate of the penitentiary and wait until an ordinary prisoner, ignorant, without much power of observation (like the average prisoner), was released, in order to get information in this way, though in this case it would be of no substantive value.

If I try here to make the uninitiated a little better acquainted with prison and highlight the main points, it is certainly not intended to bring about a state investigation of the place. That would be too ridiculous, since as soon as it were known that a public investigation into a prison or whatever is to take place, the result is known in advance: that is, as Barnum says, "Humbug." Just think of the investigation into the steel-plate swindle of the Carnegie Co., or the investigation of the Berkman committee in New York or the Reform Institute of Elmira (Brockway).[3] Don't forget that the prison in Allegheny was investigated ten years ago. And what was the result of all these investigations? A lot of fuss and humbug. And although in the last two cases the gravest charges were brought against the wardens of the institutions in Allegheny and Elmira, both are still in office and neither had the decency to resign.

Old, experienced prison brothers who have become more or less familiar with several of the American prisons are of the opinion that this prison (the Western Penitentiary of Allegheny, Pennsylvania) is the best prison in terms of the quality and quantity of work. But they are all agreed that it is the worst prison when you consider the food and the meals, and as far as the administration is concerned, it leaves a lot to be desired. The appraisal of these old prison brothers, who cannot (with exceptions) be called dummies, is more important, more important and reliable than that of a dozen wardens (even if each of them had been in office 25 years like, e.g., E. S. Wright of the Western Penitentiary) for the following reasons.[4] Those who have the management of a prison in their charge simply cannot empathize with the feelings and sensibilities of the prisoners, in spite of many years of experience.* They do not understand each other;† they make up two different classes in two different atmospheres. Moreover, years of experience in the management of prisoners is still no proof that the person in question has really made the right observations and now knows the right approach to choose. Much more often, exactly the opposite is the case, that is, that many years of experience and dealings with prisoners makes the person heartless and cruel and thus a beast. The person in charge will never get to know a prisoner well, for no prisoner will completely trust someone who has control over him. He will never speak to him from the heart nor talk about his feelings as he would to his trusted friends and fellow prisoners. Thus, those who oversee the prisoners have no way of studying the true psychological state of a prisoner, as, for example, a fellow prisoner does. In most cases, those in command—especially the guards—have no idea what psychology is. (Benny, the Assistant Warden, most certainly

* A. B.: *"In spite of many years of experience, etc."* It's precisely those many years of experience that make them uncaring.

† A. B.: *The two of them don't understand each other? You really believe that? They understand only too well.* [In Bauer's hand, a retort: *Not true.*]

has no idea.⁵) The overseers do not work or eat with the prisoners, in most cases they wouldn't even look at the food that is set before the convicts, let alone try it. They do not view the prisoners as their equals, but as something *lowlier* than they, something over which they have command, something they can order about and that has to obey them, otherwise "it" earns their disfavor. It is the same old thing: if you give one person power over a second person, then the second person suffers under the first. Where is there a ruler, an emperor, king, or president who has understood his subjects and treated them right? Hardly one among a hundred.

So the claim that the appraisal of an old jail bird is more reliable than the appraisal of a dozen wardens holds true.* That the Western Penitentiary is better in several respects than, for example, the workhouse can also be seen in the fact that it not infrequently happens that before they are sentenced, people convicted in court ask the judge that they be sent to the penitentiary rather than to the workhouse. Those who are familiar with both institutions would rather take 15 months in the penitentiary over 12 months in the workhouse. These facts, however, are far from praise of the penitentiary. If some experienced prisoners prefer this place in some respects and others would rather go to prison than to the workhouse, that's just a choice of the lesser of two evils; they are choosing between hell and purgatory. There's still enough to deplore in both cases.†

The Western Penitentiary is under the command of five inspectors, one warden, a deputy warden, a chaplain, a business manager, two doctors, and some 75–100 guards. Each has a say and that they often disagree goes without saying.

The inspectors are big businessmen from Pittsburgh and Alle-

---

* A. B.: *Lacks connection to the last paragraph.*
† A. B.: *What nonsense. Are you expecting a first class hotel? Even there one can "complain."*

gheny and thus have little time to devote to the prison and the prisoners and therefore have no understanding of them. They meet once a month to take care of the matters that the Warden lays before them as a formality.[6] To be sure, the Warden is subordinate to these five inspectors, but the Warden is the central figure. He is in the happy time of life when one feels young again. He is moody, yes, even arbitrary. He loves to talk about himself and his wisdom and for that purpose has a newspaper reporter question him about the penitentiary every few months or so in order to present to the marveling reading public—lies. For example, in the fall of 1895 an article on "Justice in the Penitentiary" with a picture of the Warden appeared in most of the Pittsburgh newspapers. The article described how prisoners whom guards report for breaking prison rules do not need to submit to the verdict or decision of the Assistant Warden if they think his verdict is unjust. They can appeal to the Warden. Then they get a real mini-trial, and if they are not articulate enough, they can choose an intelligent fellow prisoner to serve as their advocate, etc. etc. If they are then not satisfied with the Warden's decision, they can lay their case before the inspectors, etc. etc.

What the reading public didn't know, of course, was that the whole article was a dirty lie, from beginning to end, and had been arranged by the Warden just so he wouldn't be entirely forgotten by the public.

Let one more case be reported here, where the well-being of the prisoners is dear to his heart* (though only in the columns of the newspapers): During the summer a great many of the prisoners try to save up as many of the candles they receive as possible and hide them in their cells and in the workshops for the winter, when they don't get enough candles for the long evenings. The Warden knows that and

---

* A. B.: *Why should the well-being of the prisoners be dear to their hearts? This is a penal institute, not some recreational facility.*

from time to time he orders the whole prison to be searched for candles. Once it happened that the day after over 1,000 candles had been found, or rather had been stolen from the prisoners, the Warden had himself be "questioned" by a reporter and disclosed to him that the poor prisoners didn't have enough light, especially in winter, and that he would gladly hang an electric light in every cell, if the state would appropriate the money, etc. But that the day before he had stolen more than 1,000 candles from these same poor prisoners—he didn't tell that to the reporter!

Warden Wright mainly likes to command and to invent rules (a flaw all power-hungry people have). The most ridiculous, the most witless orders are the result. Suddenly it occurs to him to teach the guards how to drill so that they can drill the prisoners. For this purpose, the guards were drilled under his command for ten minutes a day for quite a number of days—until it just got to be too stupid for them and they protested. Then he dictated to them how they were to get from the prison to their homes.

Then came the order not to give the prisoners warm water in the mornings any more. Whoever wants warm water has to get permission from the doctor. With that, the warm water that the prisoners had received in the mornings for years for drinking, rinsing out their mouths, or washing dishes, was prescribed like the medicine that prisoners needed for their ailments. Then no one was allowed to carry a newspaper in his pocket; after that, he saw that the moustaches of some of the prisoners were too long and the order came: No prisoners whose numbers were over A-1200 could have whiskers any more, and those whose numbers were under 1200 had to have their whiskers trimmed, etc. That is the man under whose leadership some 1,100 prisoners find themselves.

The Deputy or Assistant Warden, usually just called "Benny," is proud of his 20 years' experience as guard in the prison. He is a tool of the Warden's and has neither an opinion nor a will of his own. It is not possible to discuss anything with him. He does not believe any of the prisoners (the result of his long experience). If a prisoner nevertheless goes to him to be heard, his answer is always "Mmph, mmph, mmph." He cannot speak clearly, because he always has a piece of chewing tobacco as big as his fist in his mouth. From a distance of 15 paces, he can hit every spittoon. The older the man gets, the less he understands of the treatment of prisoners.

Most of the guards, usually called screws by the prisoners, are simply like the majority of ordinary workers, that is, they have little understanding. They are more afraid of the Warden than the prisoners. They know his moods and know that their good jobs—eight hours of light work, $2.50 a day—are on the line if they don't turn a blind eye to "certain things." Most are people you can get along with.* There are several among them who are hardly able to write English, though they are Americans. As proof that this claim is not exaggerated, let us cite what the prison schoolteacher, himself a guard, had to say about his colleagues: In the school one day, he asked a Negro for the answer to an arithmetic problem. The Negro, who couldn't solve the problem, was ashamed, and the teacher noticed that and encouraged him with the words: "Oh you need not be ashamed of that; there are officers in here who cannot count to three." "Is that so?" I asked. He looked at me intently and held his tongue. There are others who are first-class scoundrels, always trying to uncover additional crimes† from unsuspecting and ignorant prisoners and then they run to the Pittsburgh police to report them so that a prisoner being released im-

---

* A. B.: *Where is the connection between the two sentences: "one can get along with most of the guards," and "many of them can hardly write English"? No connection at all. And that's the way the whole article is put together.*

† A. B.: *To uncover additional crimes? What in hell does that mean? Is that German?* [Written in a different hand: *Yes.*]

mediately finds himself again in the hands of the police. Admittedly, the prison chaplain managed to put a stop to the dirty work of these guys several years ago, but one of them with the nickname "Holy Christ" is still at it and is the Warden's pet. He is only too eager to play detective, but was too ignorant for that in our case. He came to my cell several times and also to Nold's and started talking about Berkman, praising him, and said he regretted that Berkman had not killed Frick. Once he asked totally innocently if I didn't know where Berkman had sent his suitcase before the *attentat*. I had to laugh at the guy, because in the very first week of my prison life, prisoners had warned us about him and had described his character. He also smuggles letters out of the prison for certain prisoners, for a dollar apiece. He manages this and other shady dealings all the more easily since he has the trust of the Warden. The same can be said of several prisoners whom the Warden considers his first-class prisoner "trusties."

Some guards are horribly addicted to schnapps, and not infrequently start work half drunk. For others, the prison is like a pantry; what they need, they haul home. The one sticks a herring under his vest, another a piece of meat under his hat, etc. etc.* But it's useless to talk about that, because every politician, every state employee steals what he can. From the ordinary prison guard or policeman right on up to the president, everybody steals. That's the only reason anyone wants to be a state employee. That is the ultimate purpose of all politics. Right, Mr. Warden?

The best of the entire prison staff, because he's the most sensible, is the prison clergyman, usually called Chaplain.[7] He's no saint, but you can talk with him and he knows how best to deal with the prisoners.

That is the prison staff. They are joined by two doctors, an older

---

* A. B.: *Now you say the guards steal the prisoners' food, and earlier you said the guards wouldn't even look at the bad food, much less make use of it.*

one who examines sick prisoners at the rate of "one man per second," and a young one who is practicing on the sick prisoners. A business manager with a couple of assistants finish off the list. Of the last mentioned, there are a couple of fine specimens who understand schnapps better than their work.

There's no real dentist. One comes from Allegheny every other month to be at the disposal of the prisoners provided that they are able to pay: 50 cents to pull a tooth and $2.00 to fill a tooth with the normal filling (platinum). The man has frequently extracted $100 to $150 from the poor prisoners in a couple of hours in this way. There have repeatedly been protests against these exorbitantly high prices, but there's just no one who does anything about it, or it is not in the "interest" of the Warden to do anything about it.

It is as if the Warden downright intentionally seeks out only those prisoners to work in the kitchen who chew tobacco and don't much care whether they spit in the saucepan, on the floor, or in the spittoon. All the food is cooked by the prisoners. In the whole prison there is not a single properly trained cook who could at least give the prisoners in the kitchen some advice. The prison administration has hired people on a monthly salary, such as a trained gardener, as well as people who understand something of the doormat and carpet business, the hosiery business, and broom-making. There are also paid carpenters, machinists, firemen, and a clergyman paid to feed the souls of the prisoners, but to hire a trained cook to feed 1,100 prisoners good food—that is a necessity the prison administration, especially the Warden with his 25 years of experience, has not yet understood, or he does not want to understand it. The reader can just imagine what is cooked up by the prisoners and what the stuff tastes like.

Of course, you can't present every prisoner with a menu and serve him his favorite dish on a platter every day. No prisoner is so stupid to demand such a thing, but each one of them can indeed ask for a piece of meat cooked so that he can bite into it instead of a bone or a piece of fat, good potatoes instead of frozen and rotten ones, and bean soup with tender beans instead of stone-hard beans. The same with tender peas, lentils, etc. All these soups are as a rule only partially cooked, and on Saturdays half the baked potatoes are thrown away because they are half raw. Instead of dirty black chicory water, decent coffee, and instead of the terrible, dirty drinking water that the taxpayers of the city of Allegheny give them, the prisoners want good, healthy drinking water. Such water is available, but the prisoners didn't get it until the hospital was full of sick people and some of the prisoners went on strike. Even then, the Warden with his 25 years of experience would not have relented, if the doctors hadn't had more sense. In fact, good meat is usually delivered to the prison, but the prisoners don't get it. What isn't stolen by the guards is sold by the prisoners who work in the kitchen to their friends and to those who can pay for it. A few years ago, a freed prisoner made the claim in the Pittsburgh newspapers that a certain head cook made several hundred dollars in this way. Warden Wright countered that that was a lie; he had searched the cook and had found no money on him. (As if anyone were dumb enough to carry money like that around here, kept nicely in his pocket until it occurred to the Warden to search his pockets, etc.) Nevertheless, Warden Wright knows that this is still happening in the kitchen.

The food is presented to the prisoners in dirty, rusty, unappetizing tin bowls, from which no one can eat without disgust. This coarse, half cooked fodder means that as a result, many of the prisoners suffer from stomach and digestion problems. Very few leave the prison after four to five years with a good, healthy stomach.

Although the laws of the state of Pennsylvania stipulate that the warden provide the prisoners with good, healthy food,* this law-abiding old gentleman with his 25 years of experience is in this respect as bad as the anarchists, who, as he once told Nold, are "on the wrong side of the fence." He thumbs his nose at any law that doesn't suit him.†

It's the same with the school; schooling is also prescribed for those prisoners who cannot read and write. But can you call it schooling if they are only schooled for one and a half hours a week? That is ridiculous, because what they learn this week they have forgotten again by next week. So it happens that prisoners go to school three to four years and don't even learn how to read. Instead of giving them a couple of hours of schooling per day, it is considered more important to force these ignorant men to work every day.[8] Work is their lot, but not learning.‡

Reading, writing, and a little arithmetic is all the teacher, a guard, tries to teach his big pupils. This teacher also takes care of the monthly provisioning for the prisoners with things like milk, lemons, oranges, soap, handkerchiefs, towels, suspenders, mirrors, etc. Mr. Teacher knows very well how to figure out his profit and earns five or ten cents on every transaction. The wise prison authorities with their experience of many years have also not found it practical to put an end to

---

* A. B.: *So every county pays 28 or 23 cents for the support of each and every prisoner! And that above and beyond the monies that are specially appropriated every year by the state for the guards and other prison expenditures. 23 cents! The daily food for a prisoner costs the prison administration less than 7 cents a person.*

† A. B.: *What nonsense: "As bad as the anarchists etc." Anarchists don't spit on the laws in order to get rich as the Warden does. An idiotic comparison.*

‡ A. B.: *Now you want them to make universities out of the prisons. Everyone in prison should certainly only work, not learn—that would be logical from the viewpoint of the status quo.*

this kind of exploitation. Why not? Only the gods, the Warden, and the Schoolteacher know.

The church, which was newly built—and built too small at the same time—in January 1893, is a stall about 75 by 125 feet. Into this cramped room the little sheep are led every Sunday, in the mornings the Catholics and in the afternoons, the Protestants. In all, there are about 1,000. In the beginning, 16 men were wedged into a pew in which only 10 men could sit. The heat and the stench of so many prisoners so crowded together is intolerable, summer and winter. Luckily, the Warden cannot force the prisoners to attend church, although he has tried to do so several times with threats and other old tactics. A choir made up of a dozen prisoners with rough voices sings several "appropriate" songs and everyone present can bellow along. Sometimes a church choir or musical club from outside comes and sings and plays to entice the prisoners to church, but the pleasure of listening is spoiled by the bad air and the uncomfortable seating. In general, attending church doesn't mean anything to the majority of prisoners, and if the majority *do* go to church, it happens because they are locked in their cells the whole day on Sundays, and by this means they are let out for an hour. In addition, the Chaplain often jokes around a little during the sermon and then there's something to laugh about. Finally, many prisoners think one *must* go to church. It would make more sense if instead of the Chaplain explaining the Bible to the prisoners, a doctor would explain to them the terrible consequences of abusing their genitals.

Fortunately, my companions, Berkman and Nold, and I have not personally become acquainted with the hospital. Some prisoners who have been there say it is a regular slaughterhouse. Others, on the other hand, find it pretty good: that in some cases, [though,] the doctors are more interested in studying and practicing medicine than in curing patients. There is no doubt about that and the doctors don't worry about how long a prisoner is in prison. The fact is that both doctors act according to the watchword: "Go to work and work until the last minute, and when you break down, we'll haul you off to the hospital." Prisoners with less serious maladies like headache, sore fingers, swollen limbs, and who otherwise feel sick, etc. are rarely released from work. Work, always work hard—that is the rule. It often happens that people have to be taken to the hospital from work, or in worse cases, when they are excused from work and left lying in their cells, they are often left there until they have to be carried to the hospital.

The main occupation of the prisoners consists of the production of doormats, hosiery, and brooms. Fifty to 75 men normally work together in one room under the supervision of a guard.[9] Each has a certain amount of work to accomplish per day, and whoever is fairly hardworking and has got the hang of things can easily finish the required amount (called a "task").

An exception is the task in the hosiery department, where only young prisoners between the ages of 16 and 24 work; many of them are too weak to carry out the required work. A strike broke out in this department in the summer of 1893; the prisoners demanded that the task be reduced. As his answer, the Warden sent some 25 workers into the "hole."[10]

One normally works seven hours a day, from eight o'clock to eleven-thirty and from one o'clock to four-thirty. The rest of the day is spent in the cell. On the whole, the work can be described as light and clean. Prisoners who have a long sentence and have already served several years are usually assigned the lightest work. In this matter, however, the Warden himself and the guards often make exceptions. Frequently the prisoners who only have a short time to serve and who know how to curry favor with the Warden or with a guard get the good positions, while older prisoners are intentionally overlooked.

There are cases where a prisoner has hardly arrived in prison and gets the best position. That is usually the case if the convict is a prominent person, a doctor, a professor, or even a French "count." Even a common post-office robber who has already done 12 years' time for murder can ingratiate himself with the Warden to such an extent that his sentence is reduced with the help of the Warden and the Pittsburgh police.

How it comes about that the prisoners in the repairs department as well as those in the cell block run around and do nothing to speak of and in the evenings get an extra portion of pork and potatoes—that's something all those in the mat, hosiery, and broom departments are surprised at; they work more and yet must be satisfied with water-coffee and bread for their evening meal. They have to laugh when the Warden lies to the newspaper readers that he treats one prisoner just like another.

In addition to the jobs already mentioned, there is a tailor and shoemaker department, as well as a bakery. Prisoners who are trained as mechanics, locksmiths, or other metalworkers, or as carpenters or other woodworkers, produce here mats, hosiery, etc., while tailors and shoemakers work in the repairs workshop that deals with metal and woodwork. Bakers work as shoemakers and people who have never seen an oven or a baking tray bake the bread for the prisoners; however, you soon get used to getting sour bread three or four times a week.

Every prisoner is assigned work; no one asks whether he likes it, understands it, or has any inclination for it or concept of it. After a month he has to be practiced enough to produce the required amount of work. If he cannot do so, "Benny" comes and threatens him with solitary confinement. In spite of his 20 years of service in the penitentiary, this ignorant man appears not to have learned that there are people who are not capable of meeting the quota of work—even with the best will in the world—since they have never worked before or are just by nature terribly slow. In the penitentiary, though, there is no consideration in such cases. After "Benny" has warned these sinners once or twice, he sends them to the "hole" for several days and in this way makes a bad situation worse, not better. Under this treatment, the prisoner grows surly and finally refuses to do any work at all. He is sent to the "hole" again, locked in a cross-barred cell (called the "basket cell"), given too little to eat, and beaten frequently. In prison, that is the way you make a good man out of a convict. When such a poor devil is driven insane or is driven to commit suicide by such harsh treatment, as sometimes happens, the Warden always has a good excuse for the newspapers. He is always the innocent one and is surprised that a prisoner under his care could come to such an end.

At the time of the Elmira Reformatory investigation, the *New York World* asked the wardens of diverse American prisons about their respective treatment of prisoners. In a telegraph answer to the *New York World* in the fall of 1894, Captain E. S. Wright, Warden of the Western Penitentiary of Pennsylvania, wrote that he was against corporal punishment and harsh treatment of the prisoners. The following cases will prove the opposite.

In March 1893, an Italian, who was undoubtedly mentally disturbed, was housed in the old cell block. As soon as his cell was opened, he would try to leap out and would call for his wife and children. On one such occasion, two guards worked him over so much that blood spurted from his mouth and nose. They put him in the hole in this condition. Two prisoners had to clean up the blood.

In 1895 a prisoner was literally driven to suicide. It was "Sammy," Number 9521, a young man from Altoona. From time to time he had fits of depression; prison life weighed visibly too heavily on him. In such fits, which normally lasted a couple of days, he refused to work; he sat there without moving and stared straight ahead. Instead of showing consideration for him, especially since he was also weak and sickly, they tried to force him to work by locking him first in the hole and then in the basket and finally in his cell. This treatment played a part in making life unbearable. One evening during the music hour, about three months before his sentence was to end, he cut his throat. The next day the Warden lied to the newspaper reporters that they had let Sammy run around without restraint because he was a crank. On this occasion, he found an old knife and cut his throat. Anything else is unthinkable.

For some reason or other, prisoner Number A-557 called the Chaplain a liar. For that he went into the hole, where he suffered for 17 days with insufficient water and two ounces of bread per day. Think of it! Seventeen days and nights on bread and water, and not even enough bread and water. Without a bed, lying on the hard, damp stone floor of a cell in the cellar. No tobacco, no book, no newspaper, absolutely nothing with which to pass the time. On the twelfth day he was ill; on the eighteenth the doctor ordered him to be taken out of the hole and carried to the hospital, since he could no longer walk. There he lay a long time between life and death. When the doctor believed that his last hour had come, he permitted him to have whatever his heart desired. He asked for schnapps and got well again, though he was as emaciated as a skeleton.

In November 1894, a prisoner by the name of "Dutch Adams" broke up the "furniture" of his cell and was clubbed (worked over with a club) because of it. On the same day, prisoner Number A-428 suffered the same beating because he made too much noise in his cell. Both got thrown in the hole for 14 days and then in the basket, called the basket or the basket cell, a cell on ground level that is brighter than the hole and where the prisoner usually gets soup twice a week in addition to bread and water. The door of the basket is covered with thick, strong, wire mesh so that other prisoners cannot reach anything through to the prisoner inside. Number A-428 had already been clubbed before and in October 1894 he was beaten because he wouldn't allow the doctor to use the stomach pump on him.

A crazy prisoner, Number A-1025, was mercilessly clubbed and had to be brought to the Dixmont Insane Asylum 30 days later.[11]

William Smith has 25 years to serve; that alone is enough to drive a person insane. He was once kept in the hole for 36 ½ days on bread and water, was clubbed four to five times, and as a rule was held in the hole one or two times a month. The man had been held locked in his cell for years and then went crazy. In this condition, he couldn't possibly follow the prison rules. But the Warden doesn't acknowledge insanity of any kind and Smith was punished with the hole for every infraction of the rules. Since he usually refused to leave his cell, he was constantly being beaten. At the beginning of the year 1895, after he had been locked in for more than three years, he attacked a guard when he was to be shaved, and was shot by the latter in the throat. Only after this incident did the Warden admit that the man was crazy. But then, when he was released from the hospital, he was locked in his cell again and since then has been clubbed and put in the hole several times. Finally they brought him to Dixmont.*

In the spring of 1894, that same Smith was clubbed for a trifle and thrown into the hole. One morning, after he had spent ten days there, he threw a full bucket (used in the hole as a privy) at the guard who brought him his drinking water and his two ounces of bread. On that account, he was horribly beaten *twice* that same day. Then no one wanted to put the cup into Smith's hand, because they were afraid

---

*A. B.: G. [i.e., Bauer, *der Grosse*] *you don't seem to know what's happening in the prison. You say about Smith: "finally they brought him to Dixmont." Like hell. He's here today in 10A. Then you say Joe Zappe was also brought to Dixmont. Where are you, anyway? On the moon? Joe is here and remains here and is beaten like always and is in 9K, my neighbor.*

that he'd throw the water at them. "Benny" held the tin cup in his own hand and told Smith to drink. Smith refused point blank and for that got *ten days* in the hole *without bread and water.* (This happened while Berkman was in the hole and is based wholly on the truth.) When they saw that they couldn't break Smith's resolve, they gave in and let Smith take the cup in his own hand. For ten days they came every morning with the water and each time Smith refused to drink from Benny's hand. "You son of a bitch! I will not drink out of your hand!" Smith would say every time. That was the way it was until Smith was victorious. He was held another ten days in the hole.

Joe Zappe, Number A-581, was worked over with fists for disorderly conduct in the evenings. He is an Italian, is in for life, is most likely innocent, and is mentally unbalanced. Zappe was taken to Dixmont in the fall of 1895.*

Spencer, Number A-302, was clubbed and brutalized such that 35 days after he came out of the basket cell, his eyes were still black and blue. Even today he has headaches that stem from that brutal clubbing.

Lancaster, Number 8523, tried to commit suicide twice. Once he cut himself in the throat; the second time, he set his clothes on fire.

Prisoner Number A-452 hanged himself. In both these cases, harsh treatment was the cause.

The above-named prisoner, Lancaster, Number 8523, is a Negro and inflicted a slight neck wound on a guard with a knife; for that they dragged him off to court, where a beast of a judge added seven years to his sentence. That was in the year 1894. He has been kept locked up in the basket cell since then and is now totally insane.

A prisoner named Tom Coslett tried to commit suicide, was caught at it in time, was beaten and carried off to hospital.

---

* A. B.: *Like hell! He's still here today—in 9K.*

Number A-754 is an Italian who has 15 years' time to do. He refused to work in the hosiery department. They wanted to cure him in the following way: 15 days in the hole, two months in the basket, then another ten days in the hole and another month in the basket. To put an end to such a life, he tried to hang himself, but was discovered by the guard in time. The guard cut the rope and in doing so wounded the poor devil in the neck with his knife. He was in hospital for two days, then for two days in the hole, two weeks in the basket, and finally they'd got him to the point that the man went crazy.

A Finn by the name of Hall died in December 1895 in the hospital. He had worked in the hosiery department, then went insane, and was kept locked in his cell. In this state, he often talked loudly with himself and because of that was put in the hole several times.

A prisoner called Patsy refused to work in the hosiery department. The consequence was 15 days hole, two months basket, another 19 days hole, and then they gave him a different work assignment.

A Negro, Number A-845, had taken some wool from a wastebasket in the mat department, intending to use it to sew designs on his towels and handkerchiefs. This wool, not worth even a half a cent, was found in his cell and he was put in the hole for three days.

Jim Burns, also crazy and condemned to 25 years, drinks his own urine and licks out spittoons. But the Warden claims he is sane and is only putting on an act.*

The reader may find the case of prisoner Number A-444, who was brutally mistreated, in another place in this book, where he tells his own story.

Prisoner Number A-34, a Negro with 12 years' prison, worked in the mat department. Although he protested against it, he was trans-

---

* A. B.: *Jim Burns—W. Smith's partner—a Committee of the State Board of Charity later judged him crazy and he was sent to Dixmont.*

ferred into the hosiery department. The old Deputy Warden, Jim, demanded that he report anyone he saw stealing socks.[12] Number A-34 answered that he hadn't been sent to prison to make things difficult for his fellow prisoners. For this answer, he got seven days in the hole. When he was released from the hole, they put him on a hosiery machine, and, not able to deliver the required amount of work per day, he was put in the hole for a further five days. In the next three months, he landed in the hole seven more times. He earnestly tried to comply with the regulations, but without success. He couldn't finish enough work and landed for a tenth time in the hole for ten days. By this time, he was so weak physically that he couldn't work at all and the doctor had him rest in his cell for a week. After that, they sent him back to work, but by now he was bound and determined to get out of the hosiery department, come what may. In a fight with two prisoners, the guard hit him on the head and said: "I'll break your black head." Number A-34 turned around and knocked his hat from his head. That got him 12 days in the hole and then six months locked in his cell. Finally they gave him his old work in the mat department.

"Snakes" Wilson, so called because he thought he saw snakes in his cell, was retarded when he came here. He used to shriek in the night and so on. They tried to cure him by holding him in the hole for *seven months*. The man is a complete mental wreck now.[13]

Those are just a few cases, but they are absolutely not to be considered exceptions. To cite all the cases would fill up a whole book by itself.

When a prisoner refuses to work or asks for other work without the doctor's approval for reasons of health, he has to endure on average 10 to 20 days in the hole and two to three months in the basket.

Consider the fact that in the hole one *never* gets more than two ounces of bread per day and twice a day a drink of water. In the basket you only get a Pennsylvania diet, i.e., bread and water-coffee and once or twice a week a little soup without meat. Prisoners are sometimes kept on this diet for three to four months.[14]

The "straitjacket" and "chaining-up" are typical punishments, in addition to the hole, beatings, and basket-starvation. The two former punishments are extremely inhumane practices that break the prisoner physically as well as psychologically. Several hours spent in a straitjacket are enough to make the prisoner numb all over. Sometimes a prisoner is kept in this instrument of torture for three to seven days. The same applies to "chaining-up" a prisoner. He is chained high on the bars of his cell by his wrists, his feet on the ground, his arms pulled up high, in which position his blood circulation is made difficult. The prisoner is held in this position from six A.M. to four P.M. daily, sometimes for eight or nine days, on two ounces of bread and a drink of dirty water twice daily. This happens in the hole, where the prisoner has on only his undershirt and underpants. Sometimes access to fresh air is blocked in the hole for 10–15 minutes or half an hour until the prisoner almost suffocates.

There are cases here where prisoners are not let out of their cells for one, two, or three years. Without work, without a chance for recovery in fresh air, held normally in a dim cell, they go more or less crazy and no longer know how to follow the rules. Then they are beaten and subjected to the starvation cure in the hole and the basket. When they then go totally mad, the Warden, with his 25 years of experience, says that these prisoners are only putting on an act so that they can leave the penitentiary and go to the insane asylum. Insanity is not acknowledged by the Warden at all; no allowance is made for it. Even harmless madmen are kept locked up until, as often happens, they succumb to raving madness.

When released, prisoners often go to the offices of Pittsburgh newspapers and complain about the vile treatment meted out to them and their fellow prisoners. If one or the other newspaper actually publishes the information, it is done in such a way that the whole thing seems like a joke. And at the same time, a reporter goes to the Warden to find out the "truth." His main argument always consists in the pronouncement that the released prisoner is a liar and an ex-convict and therefore is not to be believed. Then he tells the reporter how badly and shamefully the prisoner conducted himself. As proof of his allegations, he calls in a couple of guards, who already know through experience what they have to say to support the Warden's claims. In other words, they have to help the Warden lie to the reporter. If they were to refuse and tell the truth, they risk losing their jobs.

Many released prisoners have not dared to complain about the treatment they received for fear of being treated even worse in case they should return to prison—something that happens very frequently. Two-thirds of those who have been in prison once return there a second and third time. Other prisoners, who the Warden fears would like to make public statements about the penitentiary [when released], [know they] won't get time off for [good] behavior [if they return to prison],[15] so they will keep quiet.*

Prison rules stipulate that a prisoner with any grievance may appeal to the inspectors, who wish to treat everyone humanely: "The prisoner may appeal to the Inspectors for redress of any grievances. The Inspectors desire to treat every prisoner under their charge with humanity and kindness, etc."[16] But when the Warden lies to the inspectors that a prisoner is a liar and has no reason to complain, etc., they believe the Warden, not the prisoner. Dozens of prisoners complain that they wrote to the inspectors five, eight, ten months ago but have never been called to state their cases.

Brutal treatment and bad food are largely responsible for eroding

---

* A. B.: *Keep their traps shut.*

the physical and mental health of the prisoners, thus making them susceptible to every kind of illness. Once they become ill, their constitution is then too weak to fight off the illness.

However badly the prisoners may behave, these unhappy victims of today's cursed social system have surely not deserved treatment that drives them to insanity and suicide.

When state committees from charity organizations, etc., come to inspect the penitentiary, these people are herded in a great hurry through the various departments like a herd of oxen, so that of course no one has an opportunity to speak with a prisoner.

When a prisoner is released, he is given five dollars if he comes from Allegheny County and ten dollars if he comes from a different county. This is in most cases not enough to pay for a train ride home.[17] With these five or ten dollars, the freed prisoner is supposed to start a new, "honest" life! Apart from these few paltry dollars, he has as a rule nothing—no home, no friends, not even any acquaintances, because those who knew him before now want nothing more to do with the ex-convict. What is he to do? As a rule, not a trained worker, the newly released prisoner can find no work, even when he is genuinely intent on beginning a new life and has not been crippled by prison discipline. He goes looking for work, a few days pass, his few dollars are gone, and he is effectively forced to get what he needs as he did before—he steals, robs, and is thrown again into prison.

Among the printed penitentiary regulations one can read the following: "The aim of all prison discipline is by enforcing the law to restrain the evil and to protect the innocent from further harm; to so apply the law upon the criminal as to produce a cure from his moral infirmities, by calling out the better principles of his nature."[18]

It is obvious that incarceration in prison and mistreatment of the unfortunate prisoner accomplish exactly the opposite. Every prisoner understands that; only so-called prison authorities, the fabricators of laws, Bible thumpers, and other moral heroes can't or won't grasp it, even when criminals and crimes proliferate dismayingly before their very eyes.

Not in prison and slavery, but only in full freedom can man better himself and grow.

The Treatment of Prisoner A-444, in His Own Words

PRISONER A-444

A FEW WEEKS BEFORE THE HOLIDAYS (Christmas and New Year's) of the year 1894, I was in possession of a manmade waste-paper basket and two elegant toothpicks made of bone, together worth three dollars. At this time, I was working in Department No. 2 under the supervision of a guard named Hughes. Prisoner No. A-161 worked in the same department.[1] He asked me for the objects mentioned above so that he could send them to his girl as a Christmas gift. I entrusted them to him. He had no money in the prison office, but Prisoner No. 8931 promised to pay for them.

The latter is a special friend of Warden Wright's, since he has served several sentences under him. He is a fellow who is known throughout the prison as "the kid-man" (a man who likes to go after young men in order to commit pederasty with them).[2] I had expected no trouble as far as payment for my things was concerned, because I knew that No. 8931 receives a monthly pension from the state, but I also knew what vice this man had given himself over to. I had found that out in the summer of 1894 when he had the cell row "M" in his charge. Prisoner No. A-161 was located in cell No. 34 on that row. No one paid attention when a group of prisoners went from work to their cells at three P.M. Every day at three P.M. for three weeks in the month of May 1894, No. A-161 came from work to the cell block and instead of going to his own cell, he went into the cell of No. 8931 and hid under the bed. As soon as the guard who had escorted the prisoners in at three P.M. left the cell block to fetch other prisoners at four P.M., No. 161 came out from under the bed and No. 8931 committed his usual crime (pederasty) on his young victim. At that time the prison was a breeding place for fornication, much worse than it is today.

When No. 8931 did not pay me, I brought his young accomplice to Guard Hughes and the young man confessed his crime to him. I asked Guard Hughes to keep the affair secret and he promised me to do so, since this had not happened on his watch and besides, other guards might get into trouble. For three weeks he went home every night with the secret in his heart. As soon as my business was taken care of and I could see my way clear, I wanted to use Guard Hughes's statements as evidence in order to put a stop to the crime (pederasty) or, if nothing else, at least to get my money.

When No. 8931 discovered that his accomplice had made a confession to Guard Hughes, he wrote him (his young victim, No. 161) a note in which he reproached him for having acted so strangely. I read the note and gave it to Guard Hughes, who took it into the department's privy #2 to read it. When he came back, I asked him for the note, since I wanted to prove with its contents that the two of them (8931 and 161) were guilty. Instead of giving the note to Warden Wright, as was his duty, Guard Hughes told me he had destroyed the note. Finally, I wrote to Johnnie Robinson (a prisoner) to whom A-161 was, as he said, related. He then gave my note to Warden Wright.

He could just as well have put it in the hands of the devil, since the Warden knew every line of my evidence was based on the truth, but to bring his habitually criminal friend to court in Pittsburgh on such a serious charge would have put the mismanagement of the penitentiary in an even worse light.

On March 8, 1895, the Warden sent for me and all those that I had implicated in the affair. When we were all gathered in his office, he asked me how much I was asking to consider the matter settled. At the same time, he offered to pay everything out of his own pocket. I refused to take his money. Then he asked me if I would keep my mouth shut so that the affair would not spread throughout the whole prison, and in order to save myself from a convict's grave, I promised him to be as silent as the grave. He asked further if I wanted to bring shame to the parents of the boy. I answered: No. Then he gave orders to lock me down in my cell.

On March 10, which fell on a Sunday, I attended the prayer meeting in the afternoon. It was customary for the prisoners to settle their disputes there. I was the first prisoner on this fatal Sunday to get up on the platform in the church to speak with the Warden. I asked him for what reason was I locked down. He grabbed my right arm and, pushing me away from him, he answered in a dismissive way, that we would talk about the matter again. I saw the hostility in his face and acting on the impulse of the moment, I hit him on the nose with my fist. Guard Wheeler retaliated in kind by knocking me off the platform with his fist. The Warden then told the onlookers that I had fallen off on my own. The other guards ran over to me and were just starting to kick me with their boots when the prisoners present stood up and protested any violent attack by the guards. Guard Hughes and Guard Edwards hauled me off to the slaughterhouse, a place that was given its name by the prisoners because they are beaten there.

I was stripped of my clothes except for shirt and underpants and I was put into a cell (called the dungeon or the "hole"). After the prisoners had left the church and were locked in their cells, a pack of brutal guards came down to the slaughterhouse and demanded that the Assistant Warden (Benny) unlock the cell in which I was held. He obeyed and Jack Griffin from the hosiery department was the first who came at me and asked why I had hit the Warden. Even before I could answer, he hit me so hard on the mouth with his fist that I fell down on the ground. Then he fell on me like a lion that sees its enemy and wrenched me out of the cell, at which point a number of the other brutal guards worked me over without mercy, chopping, punching, and slugging me from head to foot while I lay there helpless, trying to protect my face with my arms. Guards Edwards and Griffin knelt next to me and hit me in the face, while Guards Dick Geyer, Hughes, Wheeler, and other uncivilized, brutal guards worked over the other parts of my body with dogged determination. It seemed as if they wore heavier shoes on Sundays than on work days, because every time they jumped on me, on my body or naked feet, the pain penetrated every nerve in my system. The Assistant Warden finally gave orders to stop this brutal mistreatment for now. The guards went off to wash my blood from their hands.

Half an hour later, the same gang of devilish creatures was even more bloodthirsty than before. They came again and while I suffered the most extreme pain in my nerves, they began to beat me in the same vicious way. From that day on, down to the present day (written January 1, 1896), I have felt completely broken, in body and in spirit. While the guards took revenge on me in the cellar, the prisoners were screaming bloody murder upstairs in their cells.

Evenings at seven o'clock, both prison doctors are gone, but I believe that both were notified by dispatch to come examine me. Naked, I had to submit to an examination. The doctors determined that no bones were broken, but they gave orders to two prisoners to bind up my wounds and to rub in salve twice a day. I was held for 10 days in the hole on half an ounce of bread and one cup of water per 24 hours. Then I was put in the basket for another 21 days but was given no more to eat. The basket serves the same purpose as the hole except that the prisoner is held there longer, in which case they give him a bed. That was the situation in which I found myself. Toward the end of the 21 days, I began to spit up blood.

(On the 21st day, released from the basket, No. A-444 was locked in his cell and held there until his release from prison in May 1896, that is, about 14 months.)

The Shop-Screw

CARL NOLD

To be in prison and write about prisoners only would be partial, for any person who has "done time" knows that a prison contains besides prisoners other wretched, yet interesting, specimens of humanity.

The shop-screw is one of them.

In the picturesque language of the convicts a shop-screw is an officer who has charge of a shop during working hours. During eight hours per day, he has neither physical nor mental work to do that is worth mentioning, yet he always succeeds in spending the time very pleasantly according to his standard of thinking. To describe the way he does so will include the best possible characterization of the man himself.

Every morning at eight o'clock his "work" commences; he reports for duty. Five minutes later he leads a squad of prisoners from the cell-house to the shop which is a three minutes' march. Having arrived there, the screw looks at the thermometer, gives orders to the "janitor" to turn on or shut off the steam, to open or close the windows according to weather, temperature, or to his own taste. Then he unlocks some doors, cupboards, etc. Having done this task, he is badly in need for a spittoon, then for a cup of water and again for a fresh piece of tobacco. Having produced his plug and properly placed a certain quantity of it in his mouth he takes with three fingers a pinch of scrap tobacco* from his pocket, throws his head well back a little to one side like a goose swallowing a worm, and sprinkles the scrap on top of the plug-tobacco already in his mouth; a performance which he repeats every half hour. This most important preparation done, he is ready to take a seat but not without having previously placed a spittoon in front of his seat which is a big table. Now his real work commences. Sitting on the table he looks around in the shop to see if there is anywhere a prisoner holding up his hand—indicating by this action that he—the prisoner—wishes to go to the water-closet or to take a drink of water, which is not permitted to do without obtaining the permission of the shop-screw. If he sees somewhere a hand up, he raises his hand also or in case he is too tired to do this he just nods with his head which means that the prisoner is permitted to leave his place to satisfy nature.

As there are from 50 to 75 prisoners in every shop and the most of them on account of chewing tobacco desire a drink of water nearly every hour, the shop-screw is constantly nodding his head. After half an hour, he spits out the juiceless tobacco, takes a drink of water, fills up again with tobacco in the manner described above, walks a few

---

* C. N.: *The dust and dirt swept up from the floor and worktables of a cigar-factory; too fine to be used for the filling of the even cheapest quality of cigars, it is made up in packages and sold under the name of scrap. It is this kind of tobacco the prisoners are supplied with.*

yards, and takes his seat on a pile of mats, the inevitable spittoon near him. Half an hour later, a cup of water and fresh tobacco have again become a necessity. Having reloaded, he goes to exchange a few words with one of his collegians in the adjoining shop. They crack a few old jokes, exchange the latest news and then he comes back to take his seat in an old arm-chair. That there is a spittoon near the chair is self-evident. Woe to the janitor if there is not. The screw would immediately call him and remind him of his sacred duty. Having rested in the old armchair for half an hour he takes the necessary supply of water and tobacco and his seat on the table. If he is in good humor he will have a chat with one of his favorite prisoners. Sometimes a trusted prisoner comes into the shop to pay his visits (every shop-screw has his trusted prisoner); then a more serious theme is discussed, as for instance politics or little private affairs. These private affairs are most important when the month is nearing its end. The shop-screw is paid monthly and sometimes he can not make the ends meet. As an employee of the state, dressed in a blue uniform, ornamented with brass buttons, he has credit at the butcher's, grocer's, etc., yet as money is still necessary for many other things, his favored trusty lends a helping hand in any pecuniary embarrassment. Perchance his colleague in the next-door shop is coming to visit him and both tell each other the often told story of the pay-days they have lost when absent from duty in months gone by, while a Warden, Deputy Warden, and other superior officers always draw their full pay even when delinquent for weeks. On such occasions they apply to the Warden and other "dignitaries" epithets such as old crank, scoundrel, scamp, etc. Should the Warden unexpectedly enter the shop, both shop-screws would play the role of humble servants in a manner of which the lowest convict would be ashamed of.

Having in this manner labored all morning, the shop-screw consults his watch; it is half past eleven, the time to get ready for dinner. The shop-screw takes another chew, washes his hands, brushes his hat and clothes, locks the doors, cupboards, etc., blows his whistle, and leads the prisoners back to the cell-house, past the dinner-table into their cells, locks the cell-doors, and is now ready to take his dinner in order to strengthen himself for his afternoon work.

At one o'clock he leads the gang back to the shop. There the same scenes take place as in the morning. Sometimes he takes the trouble of measuring a mat, speaks a few words about the work, and is every time theoretically right and practically wrong. If visitors from the outside are coming, the screw places himself where every visitor can get a full view of him, that they may see the man upon whom is resting so much authority and responsibility.

For a life-protector the shop screw carries a revolver; some of his colleagues less courageous carry revolver and club.

At half past four o'clock the screw leads the squad back to the cells again, locks the cell doors, and his day's work is over, he has earned $2.50.

Thus the shop-screw toils day by day, week by week, month after month. Sitting, chewing, spitting, and drinking is his sole occupation. Chewing for ten cents' worth of tobacco every day, he sometimes complains of his digestive organs. In such cases he brings a bottle of medicine with him to the shop. He then takes a mouth full of medicine, then a cup of water, then the tobacco. Should he run short of the latter, he despises not the tobacco of the prisoners. There are prisoners who do neither smoke—nor chew. In many cases they give their tobacco to the shop-screw; these prisoners are of course his favorites.

In the first morning and afternoon hour, the breath of the shop-screw smells unpleasantly of bad whiskey. Slowly it passes away and in the next hour the stench of tobacco becomes almost overwhelming for any person not using tobacco. Without tobacco he could not live;

tobacco is his first food in the morning, and the last in the evening. If he cannot be seen, he can be smelt, yet he himself cannot smell this odious air about him which reminds one of a dung-pit.

How pleasant this must be for the woman of such a man; what a fine example for the children!

The Trusted Prisoner

CARL NOLD

T HERE IS ONLY ONE BEING to which the trusted prisoner
could be compared and that being is the well-known shopsucker.
Both have much in common and the former is [as] despised [by] fellow prisoners as the latter is by his fellow workmen.

In order to become a trusted prisoner it is as a rule not sufficient to
have been in prison but once. The trusted prisoner is in most cases he
who can truly sing with the vaudeville poet: "We have been there before many a time," i.e. in prison. If he has already "done" two or three
terms in prison; if he has acted as a state witness against his partners
in crime; if he has been accused of perjury and treachery etc., he has
the best chances of becoming a trusted prisoner.

Strange as it may sound, it is nevertheless true that prison authorities put their greatest confidence in such a debased prisoner, because
the more debased the criminal is, the less character he has, the more
willing and precious is he in their hands, while a prisoner with a good
character, serving for the first time, will very seldom become a trusted

prisoner, just as a workman of character and principle can never play the damnable role of a shopsucker.

Enjoying the confidence of the prison authorities, the trusted prisoner has more liberty than other prisoners and he certainly considers himself better than the rest of the convicts. He has the "freedom of the institution," holds the best position in the shop or in the cell-house, does not walk with the rest of the prisoners to and from the shop and is generally freer than the rest. While other prisoners are working, he is reading the newspaper which is brought to him early in the morning by a Keeper. He knows everything that is going on in the prison; he is the friend of the Keepers, does little jobs for them, and they in return try to please him. He smokes good tobacco or cigars, luxuries which are not permitted to other prisoners. He carries a knife, a pocket-book with money in it, a bunch of small keys and other things which, if found on any ordinary prisoner would be declared as against the prison rules and punishable. He receives better food and extra rations of everything that prisoners receive. The Keepers bring him in from the outside whatever he desires and is able to pay for. He sends out letters secretly, receives his mail by the same route, lends money to the Keepers, makes high bets during election time, gambles on base-ball, prize-fights etc. and is a genuine all-around sport. Keepers must do him many favors, else they are in danger of getting reported by him to their superiors. Many a Keeper who had underestimated the importance of being good friends with a trusted prisoner had to suffer for his mistake by losing his position.

When Keepers receive orders to search the cells of the prisoners or to search the prisoners themselves, the trusted prisoner is always informed of this dangerous event in due time to enable him to remove from his pockets or his cell objectionable matters of contraband. If he is reported having money in his possession and is in danger of being searched, he hands his money to a friendly Keeper, steps boldly in front of the Warden and indignant of being suspected he turns out his pockets and of course as no money is found on his person, he is declared as innocent as a new born baby.

The favorite pastime of the trusted prisoner is playing and "fooling" with the youngest prisoners, boys of 16, 17, and 18 years of age. He teaches them everything they do not know about vice, opium-joints, prostitutes, dives, homosexuality etc. His main theme is about the sexes. He is proud of the many adventures and experiences he has had in this particular line and he never gets tired of repeating them.

He is easily offended; to be contradicted by a prisoner he considers an insult for in his opinion all prisoners are his inferiors. If he hates a prisoner or if he knows that he is hated and despised by one, he does everything in his power to render life for him unbearable, he reports him for the slightest violation of prison rules, often even without cause.

If he is not fooling with young prisoners, he can be found talking, jesting, and laughing with a Keeper. He never gets through talking. Even when locked up in his cell, he is in the habit of addressing every officer passing his cell.

It is almost superfluous to mention that the trusted prisoner is always (or pretends to be) a good Christian, a regular church-goer—while in prison—and not seldom a member of the choir, although when free he had rarely seen the inside of a church and he never will enter one after his release.

Having been many years in prison, he is familiar with everything in the institution and knows to behave himself in such a way as not to be easily detected in his wrongdoing. He is a model prisoner in the eyes of the authorities who come to the conclusion that he has at last reformed . . . But as it is impossible for the prison authorities to watch him as close as a fellow prisoner can, the latter knows that a trusted prisoner is a hypocrite in the fullest sense of the word.

Dialogue between Two Prisoners

CARL NOLD

Shorty (speaking to Bill about a fellow prisoner): He will be released in the twentieth century.

Bill: What! That would be in about a hundred and five years from
now.

Shorty: What are you talking about? We live in the nineteenth century now, and after four years we are in the twentieth.

Bill: Well, I'll be d. . . if I ever heard anything like that. Do we not
write "eighteen ninety-five"?

Shorty: I know we do.

Bill: Consequently we live in the eighteenth century. It is as plain
as daylight.

Shorty: I tell you Bill, you are wrong. Although we write eighteen
hundred, we call this century the nineteenth.

Bill: Now Shorty, don't take me for a fool. You can't tell me anything like that, why don't you prove it to me?

Shorty: I don't know how it is, yet I am certain that this century is called the nineteenth.

Bill: I don't believe it. You can't prove it, but I will see in the *World's Almanac.* I'll let you know this afternoon.

Shorty: Yes, do that, you will find that I am right.

Bill: Why don't you prove it to me? See here Shorty. I am forty years old. According to your way of counting the years I must say that I am forty-one years of age.

Shorty: Not at all. You don't count the centuries the same way as you count the years of a man's age; nevertheless you can say that you are in your forty-first year.

Bill: I'll be d...

At this moment Bill saw Mr. G., the schoolteacher of the prison, and he asked him: Mr. G., how is this? I have reached my fortieth year a few weeks ago. Would it be correct to say that I am forty-one?

Mr. G.: If you have been forty years old, you are certainly in your forty-first year now.

Shorty: You see. I told you so.

Bill (angry): Go to hell. I'll be d... if I can understand such nonsense. I'll see in the *World's Almanac.*

Shorty: I hardly think you will find it in the *Almanac.*

Bill (hotly): In the name of Jesus Christ, why don't you prove it to me?

(Deep silence on both sides.)

(This dialogue has actually taken place as it is here recorded in October 1895 during working hours.)*

* A. B. to K. [Carl Nold]: *K: I don't believe the last part is necessary. You can instead write under the title: Dialogue etc. (recorded stenographically).*

A Morning Conversation between Dutch and Mike (Two Prisoners)

CARL NOLD

Mike, to his neighbor in the shop, working on a loom: Good morning, my friend Dutch. How are you on this fine winter morning? You're making such a sour face, as if something were wrong.

Dutch: Thank you, dear friend! I am fine and if I had finished my work, I'd be in excellent shape. Will you help me today?

Mike: No, sir! I have to struggle with work, myself. Have you read the newspapers? What's the latest?

Dutch: Do you know John Bull?

Mike: John Bull? No, who's that?

Dutch: Haven't you ever read about John Bull in the newspapers? He lives in England, in London, I think.

Mike: Oh, yeah. Now I understand. Yes, I know him. What's up with him?

Dutch: Who is he? Is he Queen Victoria's husband?

Mike: Knock it off! Man, you've got silly ideas in your head this morning.

Dutch: What?! I just want to know who he is. Is he her Premier or something?

Mike: Don't talk to me so stupid so early in the morning. Give me a chance to digest the fish I had for breakfast. That's the only thing I can eat in the morning and God knows we don't get enough of it.

Dutch: I don't think you know John Bull any better than I do, otherwise you'd tell me who he is.

Mike: Sooo, Dutchie, do you think you know Uncle Sam?

Dutch: Of course I know him, that's Grover Cleveland, our president.

Mike: Yeah, this time you got it right. And John Bull is exactly the same thing. Do you understand now?

Dutch: I see.

Mike: You're making progress in American politics.

Dutch (smiling): No wonder! I read the newspaper every day.

(This dialogue took place during work in December 1895.)

Defending Anarchy—The Case
against Church and State

T HIS SELECTION OF ESSAYS, allegorical narratives, and poetry explores the repressive nature of church and state, remind-
ing the reader that an anarchist conception of human freedom re-
quires the dissolution of both institutions. With "Prisons and Crime,"
their most intellectually ambitious writings from prison, Alexander
Berkman and Carl Nold undertake a three-part study of the futility of the reformatory project of prisons and the pernicious effects
of prison life on those who are confined. In the first and third parts
of their study, Berkman and Nold blame an increase in crime on the
growing number of laws designed to protect the wealthy, arguing
that capitalist greed creates conditions of poverty and ignorance that
transform men into criminals. Both church and state, in this argument, collude to produce social injustice, with the church sanctifying
state laws that both protect the wealthy and enforce repressive con-

ventions of sexual morality, such as those that constrain free love and inhibit divorce.

The progressive nature of Berkman's and Nold's writing on the sources of criminality is made more evident against comments written at the same time in the 1892 annual report of Western Pennsylvania Penitentiary's chaplain, J. Linn Milligan, a man Berkman found personally compassionate and generous. Representing the more conventional view of the making of a criminal, the chaplain cites the probable cause of criminal behavior as "heredity" or the "want of proper home training," and describes a "dark horde of temptation which comes from the open or half-concealed dens of degradation" to make "the false and alluring fascination of a free and easy life" appealing (J. L. Milligan, *Annual Report to Western Pennsylvania Penitentiary,* December 31, 1892, Pennsylvania Historical and Museum Commission, Bureau of Archives and History, Harrisburg). In response to such theories and the query "What is society to do?" Carl Nold suggests we offer the criminal at the bar a term in college, not a term in prison.

In the second essay in the study on the failure of prisons as social institutions, "Prisons and Crime: Influence of Prisons on Morals," Berkman writes about the effect of sexual repression on the behavior of male and female prisoners prevented from having contact with members of the opposite sex. Taking on a subject long considered taboo, Berkman uses a variety of terms to refer to homosexual behavior, no consensus having yet been formed for appropriate language among those writing about human sexuality. Indeed Berkman apologizes in a footnote to this essay for any medical ignorance on his part that might be owing to his limited access to publications on the subject. He may have been familiar, however, with the argument for the biological foundation of homosexuality in the pathbreaking work of Austro-German psychiatrist Richard von Krafft-Ebing, whose *Psy-*

chopathia Sexualis, published in 1886, was available at the time Berkman was writing. Krafft-Ebing's work and the later work of Havelock
Ellis, who produced *Studies in the Psychology of Sex* in seven volumes
from 1897 to 1928, set the terms during this period for understanding
a range of human sexual practice, while preserving notions of homosexuality as aberrant behavior. A dissociation between homosexuality
and perversity was not made until Edward Carpenter's work *The In-
termediate Sex: A Study of Some Transitional Types of Men and Women*
in 1910.

Bound, then, not only by the time in which he wrote and lived but
also by the isolation of prison life, some of Berkman's commentary
will strike today's reader as naive, particularly his comments on female sexuality, which are at odds with his progressive opinions on
other social issues of the day. Certainly his unequivocal assignment
of homosexuality to the category of "moral crime" seems to deviate
from the anarchist intolerance of any moral policing of the private
lives of men and women. Writing about sex between men in prison in
1896, Berkman places himself in the less radical tradition of his Russian anarchist mentor Peter Kropotkin, another chronicler of prison
life, who wrote in 1887 about "revolting" "breaches of moral law" en-
couraged by prison conditions, in his *In Russian and French Prisons*
(New York: Schocken Books, 1971, 336). In the spirit of Kropotkin's
condemnation of prison repression and its dire outcome, Berkman
describes a fateful transformation of most prisoners from heterosex-
uality to experiencing homosexual attraction.

Years later, having spent almost another decade inside Western
Pennsylvania Penitentiary, Berkman is significantly more compassionate and understanding of men loving men inside prison walls. In
Prison Memoirs of an Anarchist (1912), replying to a fellow prisoner's
account of the love he felt for a young boy, Berkman tells his friend, "I
think it is a wonderful thing," adding that once he had felt horror and

disgust at these things. "But now I think quite differently about them
. . . I think it a very beautiful emotion. Just as beautiful as love for a
woman" (*Memoirs,* 443–445). While *Prison Memoirs* notably and
movingly describes homosexual love, some of Berkman's later toler-
ance is anticipated in this *Prison Blossoms* essay when he insists on the
noble dimensions of human love, a love that accompanies sexual desire and a love for which the prisoner yearns amid his unrelievedly
brutal, degrading, or indifferent treatment in prison. In *Prison Memoirs,* Berkman suggests that when such love occurs between men, its
redemptive, life-enhancing mutuality is a form of resistance against
the psychic annihilation of prison life. (For an interesting discussion
of Berkman's place among anarchists as attitudes toward homosexuality were formed, see Terence Kissack, *Free Comrades: Anarchism and
Homosexuality in the United States, 1895–1917* [Oakland: AK Press,
2008], 97–125.)

Less incendiary than the three-part study on prison life, "Libertas," a fanciful celebration of the fundamental human value of liberty, is, along with some other *Prison Blossoms* offerings, the harmless
product "of an evening's leisure," calculated, if discovered in a sudden search of the cell, not to raise alarms in the prison warden's office (*Memoirs,* 370). Neither, perhaps, would Berkman's "The Sinking
Ship" have raised alarms, a parable in which he mocks the failure of
the working class to understand threats to its own welfare and the
more culpable self-absorption of the intellectual, who might have
helped workers. The heroic efforts of the "Enthusiast," in whom Berkman may have seen a reflection of himself, seem sadly inadequate to
the gravity of the task at hand.

Carl Nold's "The Vision in the Penitentiary Cell" assails the hand-
maiden institutions of church and state in an imagined scene at Cal-
vary, with Homestead workers crucified next to Christ while the
grateful wealthy praise the "gods" who protect their capital. The trio

of church, state, and "money bag," or capital, reappears in Nold's poem "Night of November 11," an elegiac reminiscence of heroic revolutionaries in the history of European political struggle, culminating in the martyrdom of the anarchist Haymarket heroes. The other poems by Carl Nold in "Winter Sun for My Prison Colleagues M & G" continue the themes of opposition to religious oppression and resistance to the imposition of civil law in private lives, particularly in marriage laws, and celebrate the sustaining power of hope within prison walls. The mix of genres in this section evokes the early assemblage of the prison magazine, in which—to the satisfaction of the editors—poems, essays, and narratives appeared alongside one another.

Prisons and Crime

Punishment—Its Nature and Effects

ALEXANDER BERKMAN

DOUBTLESS THERE EXISTS NO other institution among the diversified "achievements" of modern society, which, while assuming to wield a most potent factor in the destinies of mankind, has proven a more reprehensible failure in its attainment, than the Penal Institutions. Millions of dollars are annually expended throughout the civilized world for the maintenance of these institutions and, notwithstanding, each successive year witnesses additional appropriations in furtherance of their improvement; yet the result tends to retrograde rather than advance the purports of their founding.

In the United States these institutions, embracing penitentiaries, reformatories, workhouses, and homes of refuge and industry, are numerically second to the churches. It would seem that these two institutions grow up spontaneously: one impressive feature of their uselessness being that while the generality of churches possess a fluctuating attendance, the penal institutions, per contra, are taxed to

155

their limit of capacity. Yet the Church and Prison are more closely allied than the superficial observer is cognizant. I do not allude to the fact that a certain element of the Sunday school is prominently represented in the prison population, but to economical causes to which I shall refer later.

The accredited "necessity" of penal institutions embodies three distinctive purports, viz: penal, reformative, and protective; two of which, it is construed, tend in the furtherance of the prisoner's welfare, while the third seeks to promote the safety of society. Hence, three objects are sought by means of enforced physical restraint, the corporal imprisonment of the offender—by incarceration of a more or less solitary character, for a specific or indefinite period.

Society seeks to protect itself from its internal enemies, as recognized by their criminal depredation of life and unlawful appropriation of property, by debarring such elements from participation in social life, through the temporary deprivation of their rights of liberty and citizenship, in fine, by means of imprisonment. Upon conviction and commitment, the offender becomes a public charge upon the county, state, or government; then begins the *protective* role of the penal institution. The criminal is removed, and his isolation within the confines of the prison walls assuages the public fear of one less menacing evil to the morals of society. By the employment of this negative means of protection society reaps its sole benefit from the penal institution. But does this prove a substantial benefit to society? Temporarily so; but in the long run? Let us study some of its results.

Let us investigate the penal and reformative phases of the prison question. The penal character of prisons is designed to mete out *punishment* to the offender in lieu of the committal of a crime. Punishment, as a social institution, has its origin from two sources; first, in the assumption that man is a free moral agent and consequently re sponsible for his demeanor, as far as he is supposed to be compos mentis; and second, in the spirit of revenge, the retaliation of injury. Waiving, for the present, the debatable question as to man's free agency, let us analyze the second source.

The spirit of revenge is a purely animal proclivity, primarily manifesting itself where comparative physical development is combined with a certain degree of intelligence. Primitive man is compelled by the conditions of his environment to take the law into his own hands, so to speak, in furtherance of his instinctive desire of self-assertion, or protection, in coping with the animal or human aggressor, who is wont to injure or jeopardize his person or his interests, or even wound his vanity. This proclivity, born of the instinct of self-preservation and developed in the battle for existence and supremacy, has become, with uncivilized man, a second instinct, almost as potent in its vitality as the source it primarily developed from, and occasionally even transcending the same in its ferocity and conquering, for the moment, the dictates of self-preservation.

Even animals possess the spirit of revenge. The ingenious methods, frequently adopted by elephants in captivity, in avenging themselves of the act of some particularly hectoring spectator are well known. Dogs, too, occasionally manifest the spirit of revenge. But it is with man at certain stages of his intellectual development that the spirit of revenge reaches the most pronounced character. Among barbaric and semi-civilized nations, the practice of personally avenging one's wrongs—either existing or imaginary—plays an all-important role in the life of the individual. With them revenge is a most vital matter attaining almost a phase of religion, the holy duty of avenging a particularly flagrant injury descending from father to son, from generation to generation until the insult is extirpated with the blood of the offender or of his progeny. Whole tribes have often combined in assisting one of its members to avenge the death of a relative upon a hostile neighbor, and it is always the special privilege of the wronged to give the death-blow to the offender.

Even in certain European countries the old spirit of blood-revenge is still very strong. The semi-barbarians of Caucasus, the semi-civilized savages of Corsica and Sicily, the brutal and ignorant peasants of Southern Italy still practice it, the former—the Tsherkessy—for instance, quite openly, the latter seeking safety in secrecy.[1] And even in our so-called enlightened countries the spirit of personal revenge, of sworn eternal enmity still exists. What are the secret organizations of the Mafia type, so common in South-European countries, other than the products of this spirit?! What is the underlying principle of dueling in its various forms—from the armed combat to the fistic encounter—but this spirit of direct vengeance, the desire to personally avenge an insult or an injury, to wipe out the same even with the blood of the antagonist. It is this spirit that actuates the enraged husband in taking the life of the "robber of his honor and happiness"; it is this spirit that lies at the bottom of all Lynch-law atrocities, the frenzied mob burning with the desire to avenge the bereaved parent, the young widow, or the outraged child.

But in so-called well-governed civilized communities the individual does not, as a rule, personally avenge his wrongs. He has delegated his "rights" in that direction to the state—the government—and it is one of the duties of the latter to avenge the wrongs of its citizens by punishing the guilty parties. Thus we see, that punishment, as a social institution, is but another form of revenge, with the State in the role of the sole legal avenger of the citizen, in the individual and collective sense—the same defined spirit of barbarism in disguise. The penal powers of the State rest on the principle that, in organized society, "an injury to one is the concern of all"; in the wronged citizen, society as a whole is attacked. The culprit must be punished in order to avenge outraged society, that "the majesty of the law be vindicated." The principle, that the punishment must be adequate to the crime, still further proves the real character of the institution of punishment; it reveals the Old Testamental spirit of "an eye for an eye, a tooth for a tooth," a spirit still alive in almost all so-called civilized countries, as witness capital punishment: a life for a life. The criminal is not punished for his offense, as such, but rather according to the nature, circumstances, and character of the same, as viewed by society, in other words, the penalty is of a nature calculated to balance the intensity of the local spirit of revenge, aroused by the particular crime.

This is, then, the nature of punishment. But strange to say, or naturally, perhaps, the results attained by penal institutions are the very opposite of the ends sought. The modern form of "civilized" revenge kills—figuratively speaking—the enemy of the individual citizen, but breeds in his place the enemy of society. The prisoner of the State no longer regards the party he had wronged as his particular enemy, as the barbarian does, fearing the wrath and revenge of the wronged one. Instead he looks upon the State as his direct punisher, and his hate turns to the law and its representatives, whom he holds responsible for his misfortune; he nurtures in his heart his wrath, and wild thoughts of revenge fill his mind; ultimately he becomes the enemy of society as a whole. Thus while the penal institutions, on the one hand, protect society from the prisoner as long as the latter remains one, they cultivate, on the other hand, the enemy of society. Deprived of his liberty, his rights, and the enjoyment of life, all his natural impulses, good and bad alike suppressed, subjected to indignities, and disciplined by harsh and often inhumanely severe methods and generally maltreated and abused by official brutes whom he despises and hates, the young prisoner, utterly miserable, comes to curse the day he was born on and the woman who bore him and all those responsible—in his eyes—for his misery. He is brutalized by the treatment he receives and by the revolting sights he is often forced to witness in prison; what little manhood he may have possessed is annihilated by the "discipline"; his impotent rage turns into hatred toward everybody and everything, growing in intensity as the years of misery come and go; he broods over his troubles, and the desire to revenge himself grows on him; his until then perhaps undefined inclination to do wrong is turned into a strong desire, which gradually becomes a fixed determination; society had made him an outcast, and he regards it as his natural enemy; nobody had shown him any mercy, and he resolves to be as bad as he was made out to be.

Then he is released. His former friends spurn him; he is no more recognized by his acquaintances; Society points its finger at the ex-convict; he is looked upon with scorn, derision, and unmitigated disgust; he is scoffed and abused; he possesses no money, and there is no charity for the moral leper. He finds himself a social Ishmael with everybody's hand turned against him—and he turns his hand against everybody else.

But why dilate upon this subject? Turn to the pages of *Les Misérables* by Victor Hugo and there you will find revealed one of the greatest sermons ever preached against "man's inhumanity to man."[2] The life and experiences of that failed Hercules, Jean, the convict-hero, vividly disclose the brutality of society in dealing with the criminal elements of its own creation; this book will teach you to appreciate the incalculable good a kind look, a kind word, one kind action can do.

How true the poetess sings:

"So many gods, so many creeds—
So many paths that wind and wind,
While just the art of being kind
Is all the sad world needs."[3]

The penal and protective functions of penal institutions involve a combination, whose labors are more disastrous, though no less absurd, than the efforts of the imbecile who, desiring to build a house for himself, was piling up bricks one upon another with his right hand, while his left was engaged in demolishing the work as fast as constructed. But society, in tearing apart with its left hand what its right had accomplished, drops the bricks with such violence that they are broken. Thus, while the work of the imbecile is merely unprofitable, that of the prison is worse than useless; it is positively and absolutely detrimental to the common good.

It is no better with the reformative phase of penal institutions. Relating to that function of the latter I could, with justice, devote a chapter to its "reformative" work as telling and complete by its absence as the proverbial paragraph on "Snakes in Ireland." The penal character of penitentiaries, State prisons, and workhouses excludes all possibility of a reformative nature on the part of these institutions. The promiscuous mingling of prisoners in the same institution, without regard to the relative depravity and criminality of the inmates, converts prisons into veritable schools of crime and immorality. The same is true of reformatories. These institutions, specifically designed to reform, do as a rule degenerate the inmate and the reason is obvious. Reformatories, as do prisons, use physical restraint and are in a large measure penal institutions—the very idea of punishment precludes true reformation. Reformation that does not emanate from the voluntary impulse of the inmate, one which is the result of fear— the fear of consequences and of probable punishment—is no real reformation; it lacks the very essentials of the latter, and as soon as the fear has been conquered or temporarily emancipated from, the influence of the pseudo-reformation will vanish like smoke. *Kindness alone is truly reformative,* but this quality is an unknown quantity in the treatment of prisoners, both young and old.

But a few days past I observed in the papers the account of a boy of 13 years of age, who had been confined in chains night and day for three consecutive weeks, his particular offense being the awful crime of an attempted escape from the Westchester New York Home for Indigent Children (Weeks case, Superintendent Pierce, Christmas '95) and this was by no means an exceptional instance of that institution's treatment.[4] There is not a prison in the United States where either clubbing, flogging, the straitjacket, chaining-up, the underground dungeon, solitary confinement, and reduced diet (semi-starvation) are not practiced upon the unfortunate inmates. And though the Reformatories do not, as a rule, use the "means of persuasion" of the notorious Brockway of Elmira, New York, yet flogging is practiced in some and the dungeon is a permanent institution in most of them.[5]

But even aside from the penal character of reformatories and the derogatory influence the deprivation of liberty and enjoyment exercise on the youthful mind, the associations of these institutions, above all, preclude, in the most cases, all reformation. In neither penitentiary nor reformatory is there the slightest attempt to classify the inmates according [to] the comparative gravity of their offenses, necessitating different modes of treatment and suitable companionship. In Reformatories children of all ages from 5 to 25 are kept in the same institution congregated for the several purposes of labor, learning, and religious service and allowed to mingle together on the playing-grounds and to associate in the dormitory, the inmates being sometimes distributed according to age or stature, but no attention being paid to the relative depravity of the members.

The absurdity of such methods is simply astounding. Pause and consider. The youthful culprit, who is admittedly such chiefly in consequence of bad associations, is put among the choicest assortment of depravity and is expected to reform!! And the fathers and mothers of the Nation calmly look on and either directly further this species of insanity, or with their silence approve and encourage the work of breeding criminals. But such is human nature—to swear it's day-time though it be pitch-dark, the old spirit of *credo quia absurdum est* (I believe because it is absurd). But it is unnecessary to enlarge further upon the derogatory and degenerating influences those more steeped in crime exert over their more innocent companions. The fact that fully 60 percent of the male prison population are graduates of "Reformatories" conclusively proves the reformative claims of the latter absolutely groundless. For rare cases of youthful prisoners having really reformed are in no sense due to the "beneficial" influences of imprisonment and of penal restraint, but rather to the innate powers of the individual himself.

I am happily (!) enabled to speak upon this subject from observation and personal experience, and it is my firm conviction that prisons are a curse to society. The millions of dollars annually expended for the maintenance of penal institutions could be invested, with as much profit and less injury, in government bonds of the planet Mars, or sunk in the Atlantic. No amount of punishment can obviate crime so long as existing social conditions drive man to it.

Feb. 96

Prisons and Crime

Influence of Prisons on Morals

ALEXANDER BERKMAN

T HE AIM OF ALL PRISON discipline is"—we are informed by
the "Rules for the internal government of the Western Penitentiary of Pennsylvania"—"by enforcing the law to restrain the evil and
to protect the innocent from further harm; to so apply the law upon
the criminal as to produce a cure from his moral infirmities by calling
out the better principles of his nature."

We have seen in the preceding chapter how "the evil are restrained,"
and we know how prisons "protect the innocent from further harm"
by letting loose upon society full-fledged criminals, embittered and
brutalized by their experience in prison; and we know further how
"the moral infirmities" of the prisoner are being "cured"; and the
means employed to "call out the better principles of the prisoner's
nature." The basis and nature of all prison discipline is penal. By what
miracles such methods could "cure moral infirmities" the wise Rules

neglect to state. Probably they expect the skeptical to solve the enigma by personal experience and trial.

I have sketched in the foregoing chapter the character of punishment and its results. Penal discipline acts and reacts in the same way: the procedure of "calling out the better principles of the prisoner's nature" by applications of club and black-jack, by underground dungeon and semi-starvation brutalizes both alike, jailer and prisoner. There is not one single feature in all the methods and forms of prison discipline that is worth a moment's consideration as to its claims of "curing moral infirmities," or in other words, of being reformatory in any way whatever. All claims of this nature are preposterous pretensions, absolutely groundless in fact.

But what I have stated thus far of the positively harmful influences of penal institutions does not comprise the whole field of their pernicious activity. Incarceration as a means of curing moral infirmities is undoubtedly fallacious; solitary confinement inhumane; the use of physical force, unquestionably brutalizing; the whole scope of prison discipline injurious, degrading, and debasing. But worst of all is the bearing of prisons on sexual matters. The pernicious influence of prison life and environments in this direction can hardly be overestimated; its demoralizing and degenerating effects are so certain and thorough, its results so terrible and far-reaching as to make this subject almost too fearful for contemplation. It is the knowledge of it and the sincere desire to call public attention to the real character and work of prisons, that forces me to broach the subject.

The Erotic instincts of man are not physiological merely; stronger, perhaps, than the purely physiological function are the psychic needs of sex. Even with the psychically uneducated—the comparatively undeveloped as to thinking, feeling, and wishing—the Erotic wants are not exclusively physiological. The opposite sexes are instinctively

drawn to each other; the want of company of the opposite sex, the
thirst for an object to place one's affections on, are forms of Erotic desire at least as strong, and by far of a more constant and ever-present
nature than the mere animal expression of the same. With the cultivated, the more platonic needs of love play a very important role in
the life of the individual; and though the physiological function be
the primary motor factor of all inter-sex relations, yet it is the inner
affinity of two beings, the psychic relation of kindred Egos and their
consequent interdependence and intercompletion that hold the true
elements of real happiness.

Both the physiological and psychological sexual needs of the prisoner are alike ignored by society; in prison wants of this nature are
absolutely suppressed. The results are obvious. The very circumstance
that the prisoner is deprived of the society of the opposite sex, deprived even of the sight of them, save for an occasional glimpse of
visitors, tends to intensify his or her longings in that direction, which,
necessarily remaining unsatisfied, show the primary effects of their
suppression on the imagination of the incarcerated. Just as existing
false relations of the sexes in society has given rise to weak, unnatural,
and mawkish sentiments on the one hand and to nervous hysteria on
the other, just so the total deprivation of the prisoner of all sexual
intercourse tends to produce perverted desires, by inflaming the
imagination and keeping the system in a constant state of unnatural
tension.

Nothing has a worse effect on the mind, creating morbid fancies,
promoting immorality and perverted erotic practices and causing insanity, as complete sexual isolation and abstinence. This truth is recognized by progressive physicians and all those familiar with the subject. Nature never intended the sexes to be isolated or her functions
suppressed, and we must obey the decrees of Nature; we cannot neglect her laws with immunity; *she must have her own and she will.* We

have all of us read the biographies of the early Christian ascetics, those religious fanatics whose "saintliness" seems to have consisted chiefly in their professional defiance of all laws of Nature. We know how they have fared—*they* had not conquered Nature, rather Nature them. Later on and in modern times we see, after the example of the ancient "saints," voluntary self-denial and abnegation perfected in the institutions of monasteries and nunneries. As a fact, it is well known that these institutions of religious retirement are menaces to society in more than one sense. Though irresponsible to secular authorities and protected by secrecy, as these institutions are, yet intelligent men know that they are breeding places of immoral and perverted practices. Things of this nature rarely become public, but occasionally instances leak out that are so terrible in their nature, so pernicious and immoral, and so revolting in their details as to arouse the unqualified indignation and condemnation of monastic institutions on the part of laymen. Only a short time ago, the papers published the partial confession of a young girl, an inmate of a cloister in Ohio (?), whom the Mother Superior of the Institution brought to one of the city Hospitals of Columbus, Ohio. The girl complained of severe rheumatic pains in the limbs, but the attending physicians soon discovered the real nature of the complaint. The patient's limbs were swollen to thrice their natural size, and the cause was discovered when the Doctors had extracted about two dozens of pins and needles from different parts of the girl's body. The patient at first persistently refused to vouchsafe any explanation, but finally relented and made a confession, according to which she and another inmate of the convent, nearly driven mad by sexual desire, had become victims of homosexual practices, "had acted to each other"—in the very words of the confessed girl—"as lovers." Accused by her conscience, the distracted girl would, after every "performance" insert a needle or a pin into her limbs as penalty and penance.

Such are the horrible and hair-raising results of suppressing the legitimate wants of Nature. But self-imposed, voluntary abnegation is by far easier to bear and, consequently, less disastrous as to results, than forced renunciation. Thus it is, that involuntary prisoners suffer much more under the unwilling restraint than those of convents or others whose denial is self-imposed, voluntary. The natural wants of the prisoner are bound to manifest themselves during the time of the subject's incarceration and forced abstinence; the natural means of satisfying his (or her) needs are denied the prisoner; thus, he (or she) is literally forced into immoral and unnatural practices.

There are three distinct forms of Immorality practiced in prisons: Onany (male) or Masturbation (female), Homosexuality, and Erotic Perversion.*

A. Onany

From the several forms of Immorality met with in prisons, the practice of Onany or Masturbation is fraught with the greatest danger to its victims; its effects are of a most terrible nature, disastrous to both body and mind. It counts many victims in and outside of prisons. In the latter institutions Onany is practiced almost universally.

Cut off from the outside world, removed from home and friends, worrying and brooding over his (or her) troubles, the prisoner, upon entering a penal institution finds himself (or herself) in a most dejected frame of mind, utterly miserable and wretched. I have often heard a new prison-arrival exclaim, dejectedly, upon being advised by some fellow prisoners to take care of himself: "I don't care: I will not live out my term anyhow!" And yet their sentences were often real

---

* A. B.: *The reader will kindly permit me the freedom of coining this term—"Erotic Perversion"—to designate a practice, the specific scientific name of which is unknown to me. Writing as I do, in a prison cell without a single medical book of reference at my disposal, I am greatly handicapped in handling this subject.*

sinecures, as compared to my own,—a year or two, or three. I have found this state of the prisoner's mind a most potent factor in leading the unfortunate prisoner to Onanism. He begins this terrible practice even before his erotic desires are actually manifesting themselves— from sheer misery and dejection. But upon getting acquainted with the institution—his new home—its character and routine, and prob- ably receiving some employment, the new prisoner gradually gets over his dejection; his spirits rise, and he becomes animated with the hope of serving out his sentence and living down his shame. His returning spirits and good humor now prove a check on his self- abusing practices—until after the prisoner has become more or less assimilated with his new environments and got used to his daily rou- tine, when his, first psychological and then physiological, Erotic needs are aroused. A stranger among strangers, the only sympathetic link combining him with his fellow prisoners being their mutual trouble and suffering, the young prisoner comes to pity himself—and with pity and self-commiseration comes the craving for a sympathizer, the thirst for a kind word—a friendly hand to press, a loving heart to un- burden oneself to; in fine, the better nature of the prisoner is awak- ened, his inner self begins to assert itself, his purely psychical Erotic desires are aroused, the whole fabric of his psychic needs set into motion—he is thirsting for love—a mother's love, a friend's love, a woman's love—to love and be loved. But the inexorable prison "disci- pline" goes on; instead of the love, the friendship, and the kind word he craves for, the prisoner receives the stern command of the guard; he is commanded and insulted; his awakened manhood—aroused by his craving for love—rises up in arms against the offered indignities; the long suppressed bitterness of his heart may find vent in a rough answer to the received command; he is then promptly disciplined, punished, maltreated . . . The treatment he receives reacts upon his better instincts. Experience teaches him that he can expect neither

kindness nor sympathy from those in authority. As a result, he becomes sulky—and is again punished . . . He seeks consolation in his
powers of imagination; in the isolation of his cell he pictures to himself his home; the kind face of his mother arises before his mental eye;
he recalls to his mind the happy moments of his past—his mother,
his wife, his sweetheart haunt his dreams and reveries; he becomes
preabsorbed, is inattentive to his duties and is again punished . . . His
nature rebels, he thinks of things that "might have been," the saddest
note in the gamut of misery—of the happiness he had forfeited; his
imagination is untiringly at work . . . His psychic and physiological
Erotic desires now fully aroused, the prisoner falls back on his former Onanitic practices,—and another victim of prison discipline is
added.

But while his former self-abusing practices were rather mechanical and lasted only as long as the cause—dejection—that produced
them, the prisoner is now a victim of "mental" Onanism. This form
of Onanism, the subject's imagination at work of picturing the necessary surroundings of sexual cohabitation—is the most dangerous
one. If the victim does not possess the necessary strength of will—
and under the circumstances great will-power is required—his pernicious habit will grow on him with terrible rapidity; it will develop to
excess of all physiological needs; the nervous system of the victim will
soon be reduced to the permanent condition of unnatural tension,
his mind will become diseased to a degree that the mere sight of
a member of the opposite sex, or even a printed likeness of it—the
mere pictorial form—will unnerve and excite him and force him to
seek momentary relief from his unbearable sexual tension in Onanitic practices. The "mental" form of Onany here assumes a perfectly
mechanical character; it is no longer any physiological want that the
victim seeks to satisfy; he does so merely in obedience to a habit, already almost too strong and imperative to overcome.

The slave of Onany is doomed. The terrible drainage on the nervous system saps his vitality; he becomes fearfully emaciated, the tenor of his whole constitution is reduced to its minimum, the practice is speedily undermining his health and weakening his mental powers; his eyes take on a glassy expression, he is in a constant state of physical and mental lassitude, his memory grows weak, his nights are sleepless and his sleep restless and unrefreshing; terrible nightmares haunt his dreams and his already diseased mind begins to conceive queer ideas which assume the form of abnormal "physical" and mental idiosyncrasies often leading, if not checked, to imbecility, but more generally often developing into nervous disorders, culminating in insanity.

Primarily the queer ideas of the prisoner-Onanist manifest themselves occasionally only, at certain intervals, while he is apparently compos mentis the balance of the times. But his strange conduct, accompanied, as it usually is, with morosity, inattention to duty, and disregard of command procures for the prisoner punishment, ultimately resulting in solitary confinement. This last piece of discipline proves the most potent factor in intensifying the victim's Onanitic practices and landing him in the abyss of complete mental darkness. He is criminally left to take care of himself, though he is unable to do so. With his system in such a weakened state as described above, then microbes of disease find excellent ground to grow; when attacked, the patient, reduced by his Onanitic practices and insufficient nourishment to his physical minimum, lacks recuperative power, and the result is generally fatal.

Thus we see that prisons, by absolutely ignoring the physiological sexual needs of the prisoner, lead him to Onanism and Insanity. Statistics prove that the criminal classes supply the Insane Asylums with inmates, numerically exceeding those from any other class. It is to the solitary confinement feature of penal institutions, chiefly, that the greatest percentage of insanity among prisoners is due. Injurious as the practice of Onanism undoubtedly is, both to body and mind, *it cannot compare to the effects of solitary confinement* and deprivation of employment. My assertion is proved by the fact that Onanists not suffering solitary confinement rarely become insane. These, when released, find in natural sexual cohabitation their emancipation from Onany—either partial or complete. But Onanists—and fully 99 percent of [the] prison population are such—undergoing solitary confinement, without labor, will go insane in proportion to their ability to find means to employ their minds—thus illiterate prisoners, being unable to read or write and consequently having no employment *whatever,* constitute the greatest percentage of insane criminals.*

The above applies equally both to male and female prisoners. The latter have perhaps more to suffer from suppression of Erotic needs than the former. The Reformatories, where young girls are incarcerated, during the very age when their Erotic wants, of the psychical order especially, are the strongest, breed a morbid imagination, perverted desires, and an unnaturally strung nervous system and the specifically female hysteria, the results of which are most far-reaching and of injurious effects, fraught with prenatal influences on the coming generation. These Reformatories (so miscalled) are de facto schools of vice and immorality, only too often serving as stepping-stones to prostitution. The young female prisoner, suffering under the "reformatory" restrictions, actually looks to the day of her release as to her sexual salvation; she awaits anxiously her coming freedom and—she makes straightaway for the brothel. All this is too well known to the intelligent public to necessitate further dilation on

---

*A. B.: *The old Philadelphia system of solitary confinement provides work for the prisoner. But in the more modern prisons, fitted out with workshops, where the prisoners are congregated during the working hours, solitary confinement means total deprivation of employment.*

my part. The unfortunate girl hopes to find in the institution of prostitution—relatively remunerative and easily accessible as it is—speedy and certain Erotic satisfaction.—

B. Homosexuality

Extremes often meet.—The total suppression of natural Erotic wants—psychic and physiological—tends to produce the same effects on the human organism as over-indulgence in these functions does.

The Erotic gourmand soon tires of the "monotony" of the natural forms of sexual cohabitation; his sexual vitality being sapped and reduced to its minimum, he needs extra stimulus, which he seeks in nerve-rousing environments and new modes. Ultimately, having become sexually blasé, he completely loses the power to be charmed by the other sex; their society becomes a bore to him and even the very "ultima" ratio of Eros is powerless to drive away his sexual ennui.

But, though he is sexually dead to the opposite sex, his psychic Erotic needs are still strong within him, and he must find an object to place his affections upon—at this stage homosexual tendencies begin to manifest themselves; he enters the path leading to Pederasty.*

The identical result, though from very different causes, is produced by the other extreme—total sexual suppression and isolation. The results of the latter are by far more pernicious and immoral than those of sexual gourmandism; for, while the pederastic tendencies of the sexually blasé quite often remain as purely platonic in their nature as they were in the first stages of their development, pederasty in prisons, on the other hand, is always carnal.

This form of moral and Erotic degeneracy—Homosexuality in all its forms, from the "higher knowledge" of Parcival down to carnal

---

* A. B.: *Sexual overindulgence does not always lead to Homosexuality; also other causes cooperate with Erotic gourmandism in creating pederastic tendencies; this, however, can safely be left out of my essay, as it does not directly relate to the subject in hand.*

copulation of the same sexes—is by no means the exclusive product of our fin de siècle. It existed in old Biblical times and was then practiced far more extensively than nowadays, as witness Sodom and Gomorrah. The old Roman civilization also has the undisputed right to boast of these forms of civilized, human (specifically *male:* Pederasty) degeneracy. The historians and poets of those "classical" times unblushingly tell us of a very extensive practice, especially common with their "great" warriors, statesmen, and other public men, of having young pages, serving as "mistresses." The Mediaeval epochs also enjoy this unenviable distinction; Rome, especially, seems to have been the Eldorado of Pederasty; it is well known that the Vatican has been—up to the 18th Century—a very hotbed of unbounded license and perverted sexual practices of all kinds, among them Pederasty—counting among its "devotees" "holy" Popes, "pious" Cardinals, as well as other "Eminences," both of Church and State.

It would seem that inhabitants of warm climes are more susceptible to Homosexual influences than their Northern brothers. Be it as it may, Pederasty is undoubtedly practiced quite extensively in Southern countries, while it is almost unknown in certain cold climes.

It is not my intention to write at the present moment an historical essay on classical or contemporary Pederasty. My subject being "Homosexuality in Prison," I shall confine my remarks to that limit.

His Erotic needs absolutely ignored and suppressed, yet in no sense extinguished, the prisoner seeks some means to satisfy his cravings. He resorts to Onany. But this practice does not really satisfy his sexual wants; it does so for the moment only to reawaken his craving with redoubled force. I have pictured the morbid effects of total sexual seclusion on the mind of the prisoner; his morbid imagination constantly on fire, all his thoughts run in the direction of Eros, of woman; his heart is craving for something or somebody to love, but there's apparently nothing to fill out his psychic vacuum.

At this stage the influences of his environments begin to manifest their pernicious effects on the prisoner's mind. The prisoner—often quite unconsciously—enters the path, pointed out to him by his older fellow-sufferers. This attention is soon turned to the younger element of the prison population; among them he finds good-looking youths, whose appearance suggests to his diseased mind young members of the opposite sex. He mentally chooses one of these number and places his affections on him. At first the prisoner's Pederastic tendencies are comparatively pure; he imagines himself drawn to the particular youth, he conceives a liking for him and resolves to become his friend. If he is favored by his "choice," the two will generally form a true, strong friendship. The Pederast, still in the process of primary formation, will pay attentions to his young friend, shower gifts upon him and try to please him by anticipating all his wishes and satisfying the same to the extent of his ability. But the physiological Erotic desires are still suppressed and the work of the morbid imagination of the ongoing Pederast is advancing along the entered channels. The prisoner's primary, perhaps quite innocent, liking for the youth will become intensified with each day, and he will soon come to realize his semi-defined desires to have more of his "young friend's" company, to be in the latter's proximity, to feel the pressure of his hand; to embrace him, to touch his lips, in fine, gradually but certainly, he will pass through all stages characteristic of natural inter-sex (heterosexual) love, his pederastic propensities finally culminating in the desire for carnal, unnatural intercourse.

Homosexual cases have come under my observation where the Pederasts were apparently as much in love with their "young friends" as any man could possibly be with his lady-love: They manifested all the signs by which the lover is proverbially recognizable, inclusive of jealousy. The intensity of the Pederast's Erotic weakness for his particular "boy-love" often borders on self-sacrifice. I have known Pederasts so devoted to their "friends" as to actually deprive themselves of the necessities of life in order to please their young friends and make their prison life more comfortable. The Pederast will also often try to shield his "love" from punishment for a breach of prison discipline the latter may have committed, by claiming responsibility for the trouble and cheerfully taking the consequences.

The prison authorities are well aware of the immoral and bestial crimes of Homosexuality being committed inside the prison walls. They usually punish such offenders—when suspected or accused of having indulged in Pederastic practices—by dungeon and solitary confinement; but it is characteristic that prison-Pederasts are never brought to the bar and officially charged with their crimes; not even in cases where there is absolute proof of criminality, as, for instance, when the Pederasts are caught by the guards in the very act of homosexual copulation—and the reason for this shielding and protection of Pederasts on the part of prison authorities is obvious: the calling of public attention to such crimes being committed inside the prisons— prosecution and trial of a prison inmate on the charge of Homosexuality would necessarily prove a public sensation—would naturally tend to throw a very suspicious light—to put it mildly—on prison management, or rather on *prisons as a social institution.*

The prison authorities are powerless against this evil; the most they can do is discipline the offender, and possibly prevent further immorality of this sort on his part. But in place of every disciplined and isolated Pederast the penal institution breeds a dozen new ones, and the characteristic ingenuity of the criminal generally creates opportunities, in spite of all penal precaution and discipline—for the indulgence in his bestial desires. The congregating of prisoners for the several purposes of labor, learning, and religious services—a feature of all modern prisons—largely contributes to the dissemination of immoral ideas among prisoners, and the confinement of two or more inmates in the same cell tends to intensify Homosexual tendencies, as well as to encourage the confirmed Pederasts.

In Reformatories, both male and female, the practices of Homosexuality are even more common than in penitentiaries. There the inmates are accorded comparatively greater freedom of movement, mutual intercourse is consequently more facile and freely cultivated, with the same pernicious results as in penitentiaries. I have known many youthful prisoners, in this institution, who had previously been confined in various "Reformatories" of the States. They all assured me of the frightful extent to which Pederasty was practiced in those institutions. One young prisoner, who, having graduated from the Pennsylvania Reformatory, landed in the penitentiary after having committed some petty crime, relating to me his experiences while in the Reformatory, smilingly remarked (literally): "That's the place where I've lost my 'virginity.'"

The terrible revolting effects of criminal environments on the minds of the more innocent inmates are the worst feature of prisons; one that is in its essence and results a social crime. The youthful prisoner is generally completely ignorant of the existence of perverted sexual practices; and when, having more or less "acclimatized" under his new surroundings, he learns of the vice and immorality practiced in the institution, he never fails to evince his most unqualified, boundless abhorrence of and his unmitigated disgust at such practices. But as the years come and go, unseen influences are at work, undermining the young prisoner's moral stability. Three to four years of prison life generally suffice to completely transform the young innocent and create in him pederastic tendencies and fill him with those very desires, the mere mention of which had, a few years previously, disgusted and horrified him. The human mind is very susceptible to the influences of its environments and the youthful mind particularly so—the impressions made on the latter are generally permanent—the poison of vice and immorality having once penetrated the moral tissue, will speedily permeate the "soul's blood," diffusing its poisonous elements throughout the moral system, and will eventually carry intellectual degeneracy and moral death to the inmost chambers of the being. For such is human nature: We grow accustomed to the gruesome, the unnatural; Horrors grow to be familiar by their constant and commonplace character; familiarity no longer breeds contempt.

C. Erotic Perversion

Erotic Perversion is another form of immorality found in prisons. Prison life and environments produce Insanity, cause Onanism, and create immoral Erotic Tendencies, but Erotic perversion—i.e., that form of unnatural sexual proclivities which is not exclusively homosexual, usually being heterosexual with females—is not a product of prisons. The Erotic pervert, male or female, is rather the unfortunate victim of certain prenatal conditions stamping their effects on the offspring through the medium of the mother. Erotic perversion is probably also hereditary.

The Erotic pervert is to be pitied, rather than condemned; his (or her) sexual aberration is probably a physio-nervous anomaly rather than a moral disease.

As the various medical theories concerning this form of Erotic perversion do not directly relate to my subject, it will suffice to state here, without going into details, that cases of Erotic perverts of both sexes are frequent in prisons, and the exercise of their propensities— as far as male perverts are concerned—is by no means an impossibility in penal institutions.

Feb. 96

Prisons and Crime

Crime and Its Sources

CARL NOLD

S OCIETY MAKES NOT THE least effort to prevent crime, as it could and should by pursuing such methods which would tend to remove the conditions breeding criminals. It deals with criminals, not with crime. It concerns itself only with the classes or individuals already criminal—generally after the commitment of crime and occasionally while in the act of commitment—completely disregarding those standing on the precipice of criminality, ready to take their fatal leap.

Along the road of want and suffering and forbearance society's *les misérables*, those guilty without guilt are pushed forward by a strong and irresistible hand, forward and forward toward the yawning abyss, and there, pausing a moment on the brink, they behold the gaping chasm, illuminated by the sun of deceit, and through the eyes of misery and despair they perceive [a] fata morgana of lucrative ease, and while they are bending, half-frightened, over the dangerous brink, they are lifted up with irresistible force and pushed over the verge and sent flying down the steep incline, down and down, deeper and deeper into the yawning chasm, from which there is no returning. And all the while society is calmly looking on, never moving a single finger with a view of retarding the progress of the fallen, yet ever ready to stamp them with the label of criminality and to subject the bleeding and torn forms to the care of "Justice," to be punished for their fall.

And how does "Justice" take care of the criminal classes? How are the latter treated?

Concerning the criminal classes, the motto of Society has always been (and still is): "Get rid of them." And as the simplest way to get rid of them is to kill them, that was the method ordinarily pursued until a very recent period. In Great Britain, under Henry VIII, 236 different crimes were punished with death, and even so late as the close of the last century, 200 crimes were so punished. In the reign of Henry VIII, 200,000 persons were hanged in Great Britain. But we of the 19th century, have become too humane to carry on the process in that way. We banish men or imprison them to get rid of them.

Have the methods of the past or do the modern methods exterminate crime or even check its progress? By no means. If we would take the census of the criminal classes and those dependent upon the latter in the United States, we will find that 1 person in 70 belongs to the criminal class (in the broad sense of the term). And this criminal class has, on the whole, been increasing throughout Christendom. In Spain it has doubled in 13 years: in France it has increased several hundred percent within the last quarter century, and in the United States it has grown one-third faster, proportionately, than the population since the Civil War. The annals of criminality clearly demonstrate that our methods of treating crime are flat failures, and the effects of the treatment injurious to society, as a whole.

The fundamental principle of past and present methods is essentially wrong. The administration of Justice to criminals is immoral, brutal and brutalizing, and unjust, for by justice is meant the giving to every wrong deed its equivalent in penalty, a function which is but disguised revenge.

The deterrent power of fear is not the proper means of treating crime. It has been tried and it has failed. Men are not deterred from crime by fear. We have broken men on the wheel and buried them alive; we have hanged them; we have gathered the criminal classes all around the gallows to see the execution, and the victim has gone bravely to the scaffold and died game; he has become a hero in their eyes, and the men that have witnessed the execution have gone back to plunge deeper into crime than ever.

Capital punishment, which is advocated to deter men from crime, does not deter them. Severe penalty for crime does not prevent its increase.

The protection of society, sought directly by the (alleged) deterrent power of fear, is a brainless Utopia as to results. Methods of mere punishment cannot fail to be more injurious than beneficial. And aside from the questions as to society's right to punish and of the possibility that disorders heretofore classed as moral obliquities, vices, and simple depravity may prove to be diseases, society should deal with crime, not with criminals only. It is by learning the nature of crime and by ascertaining the divers causes leading men to crime that society might hope to eliminate this discordant factor of social progress.

If this compilation serves in any way to awaken the intelligent public to [a] realization of the injustice and costly and untenable impotence of existing methods of dealing with crime, if it excites sufficient interest to induce a further and fuller Study of this problem, then its object is accomplished and the author will consider his effort well repaid.[1]

"What's to be done?" the reader will probably ask at this juncture. If you expect me to dish up some cut-and-dried reforms, you might as well shut up the book and throw it aside, for I do not deal in universal panaceas.

The answer to the above question is simply this: adopt practical business methods, do as the doctor does, for instance: You have heard the complaint stated and you know that the social patient is seriously ill; now try to learn the nature of the trouble and the primary causes at the back of it; then the appropriate remedy will suggest itself.

What is, then, the nature of crime? Speaking from the standpoint of the existing state, all forms of crime could be broadly classified under three heads:

1. Injury to life and limb (including murder and assault).
2. Robbery (including all forms of theft, either by force or cunning).
3. Immorality (including, among other crimes, perjury).

To the first two classes belong all offenses against man, to the third those against morality—wrongs either perpetrated or contemplated (which is morally the same thing, seeing that a wrong is always first committed mentally even if the contemplated act of injustice had not found its expression in an actual deed).

These three classes of crime could further be generalized by bringing the crimes against morality under the head of those against man; it could be done, with justice and propriety, for what is morality but a conception of the world in accordance with which we regulate our conduct, in other words, morality is the principle of the relation of the individual to society—the accepted social etiquette—thus offenses against immorality are offenses against man; therefore crimes of all and every form could rightly be called—broadly speaking—Robberies, i.e.

1. Robbery of life or health
2. Robbery of property
3. Robbery of honor

Why are crimes committed? What leads men to kill, to rob, and to rape? What is the source of the most numerous class of crimes—of stealing?

Every effect has its cause; people do not, as a rule, steal for the principle of the thing; one does not risk his liberty—and occasionally his life—for this form of fun. What, then, causes men to steal?

It is the formidable eternal and universal battle for existence, the natural desire for self-preservation. Marching blindly along a false road to civilization, we have reached a state of affairs where one cannot live without robbing his neighbor, where one can neither climb up without pressing down others, nor fall without pulling down others with him into the abyss. Poverty and ignorance are sisters that always go together and where they reign, the battle for self-preservation goes on in the most dismal manner, for the inevitable circumstances under their reign demand it.

Ground down by poverty, often lacking the necessities of life, with no hopeful outlook for the future, miserable and despairing, the poor wretches have but one out of three choices: either to starve, or to become a burden to others, or [to] turn criminal. As there is still a spark of independence and manhood left in every individual no matter how wretched he may be, death by starvation is considered as a rule cowardice; to become a burden to others is against that spark of holy fire of independence still gleaming within the breast of the discarded, ergo, to become a criminal appears under the circumstances the most manly and courageous selection.

The hard battle for existence makes the ongoing criminal desperate. His own life is naturally of more worth to him than that of one that gives him cause to envy. Looking around he sees the costly mansions of the millionaires, the rich churches which do not want to be defiled by coming in contact with the poor, the fine carriages, filled warehouses, rich stores, luster and splendor everywhere, but the good things are not for him. And why not? Why only for a certain class of people? Why is his stomach empty as the pockets of his worn and torn garments; why is his home the underground sewer, the barn, the stable, while empty houses, hotels, churches etc. could give shelter to thousands; why must he pick his food from ash barrels in yards and streets, while corn and potatoes are so plentiful and cheap that farmers can afford to feed it to their hogs?

The moralist, the reformer, the preacher, the philanthropist, the capitalist, the statesman, and the man of science are always ready with an answer: "Work, work and economize; give up drinking and pleasure; the way to become wealthy is open to everyone."

Yes, indeed, the wretch behind prison bars had worked from his tenth year in order to help his parents feed his younger brothers and sisters; he had almost been brought up in the factory amid plenty of work, the rush of wheels, and noise of machinery. The 10-year-old child was so busy helping his parents earn a few cents that he had no time for regular school attendance, he had no time for pleasure, no time to play as other children did; he need not give up pleasure and drinking for he never enjoyed either the one or the other on account of his inability to earn enough.

Having been brought up in the factory, the young man at 20 is old in body and tired of working; besides he has to make room for new machinery which is a cheaper mode of production. He is therefore forced to join the great mass of the unemployed, he tramps the country and becomes in time a criminal.

His sister, having worked during five or seven years in a dusty cigar factory or cotton mill, contracts consumption; too sick to work, yet compelled to earn a living, she joins the ranks of prostitutes. And again, why should this young man do 60 hours' hard work for seven–eight dollars per week if he can make as much in one day in a comparatively easy way, and the girl, why should she not prefer the dive with no work to do, to a hard life on a small pittance?

But this is a life of crime and immorality! So it is, but the ruling question is not how to live virtuously but rather [how] to live well. The last question is superior to the first, because it is the natural impulse for self-preservation while the other is only the result of existing customs.

For this reason, people are virtuous and law abiding only when their interests demand it.

This is one source of crime.

Private property has created the conditions mentioned above as well as those which will be mentioned on the following pages. The institution of ownership can be considered as the primitive source of all evils, the spring of the majority of laws which are made according to the interests of private property for the protection of the few who possess and against the masses who possess not: the disinherited class.

Private ownership has created a class system, enormous wealth and horrible poverty; a state or government that protects the wealthy and oppresses the poor. It has created the present ferocious forms of the battle for existence and the antagonism between Capital and Labor.

Capital, in order to remain in possession, must rule, i.e. keep down Labor. Labor, tired of being ruled, aims at liberation or at least at equal rights; but where there are equal rights there can be neither master nor servant and as Capital does not want to give up mastership and Labor does no longer want to be the humble servant, it is most natural that crimes on both sides are the result, yet the difference is this: as Capital is the ruler, it considers itself infallible like the popes of Rome or William II of Germany, while the laboring classes suffer under the reign of these modern Caesars and fill as "criminals" the prisons. Such a class distinction has created one law for the poor and another for the rich.

This is the second source of crime. Another great source are the different laws made under the pretense of regulating society, restraining evil, protecting the good from the bad etc. etc. but in reality to hold the masses tight in hand, to hold back progress and to live against the supreme laws of nature, in order to serve like willing slaves to imaginary masters of this world and of another world, of which mankind knows nothing whatever save that it has its foundation in the mythology of nations long gone by.

The people have selected men as their representatives who are every year manufacturing new laws by the bushel in the name of the people; yet the very same people are constantly complaining of their liberty being more and more reduced; but law-making still goes on. The contradiction is amazing, and the courts are trying to do their best in mixing up disputed questions by rendering decision after decision. Why not participate in crime with others, then turn state evidence against the partners in crime and be rewarded for playing the role of traitor? Has not treachery become a virtue in our courts of "Justice"?![2]

In the name of Law and Order more crimes are committed than in the name of lawlessness. Law and order of today are more terrible inquisitors than those of the dark centuries. In the name of the law the child is taken from its mother, the father from his family, the mother from her infant, the lover out of the arms of his love, the son from his aged parents, the sick from the nurse, and so forth. Endless is the chain of crime, misery, poverty, starvation, cruelty, and barbarism caused in the name of Law and Order.

Every nation can boast of being guided by thousands of laws; still we are marching to a state of civilization which will turn in the end the whole world into a prison with a few infallible rulers in an air ship high up in the air, smiling and pointing down to us saying: "See our slaves; what great masters we are!"

There are so many laws that the best lawyer is unable to know them all; to the average citizen not nine-tenths of the existing laws are known. To expect that every citizen should know all the laws which he is supposed to obey would mean nothing less than to study law for about 10 to 15 years. The more laws the more lawbreaking—Is it a wonder, then, that crimes and criminals are constantly on the increase?

Today I am free to entertain a friend of mine with beverage stronger than water. If I do the same thing tomorrow I am a criminal fit for the prison, because overnight some body of "representatives of the people" has made a law to that effect. If I am unlucky enough to be out of work for a long time and consequently reduced in means and compelled by hunger to beg, the workhouse is open to me. Should I meet my sweetheart in the street and, animated by joy, kiss her, it is against the law; to step accidentally on the grass of a public park is against the law; to feed the sparrows is against the law; not to take off the hat in a courtroom is punishable; to sing in the street is punishable. Our wives are in danger of being arrested as prostitutes when out late in the evening; to look at a policeman from the side is sufficient to be arrested as a suspicious person; to refuse to work is conspiracy and to defend life against the bullets of Pinkertons is treason. Horses, cows, dogs, cats, birds etc. are protected by law, but that big animal "man" is shot down by official ruffians when he dares to protect himself.

And who are the men who are making such laws? Are they wise, old men, rich in experiences? Are they sociologists, philosophers, who have studied society and the wants and desires of its members? Are they profound thinkers who have sacrificed their whole life to the study of mankind and evolution? Not at all; they are men who have only one aim, i.e., to elevate themselves at the cost of others. They are politicians who serve themselves under the pretense of serving the people; they are men in nowise better and often worse than those

styled "criminals"; they are subjected to the same natural law ani-
mating the criminal and every other being in the pursuance of his
"business"—the law of self-preservation—yet, while the criminal is
simply trying to make a living by robbing and cheating individuals,
the politicians of State and Church are constantly robbing the nation
as a whole.

In the first article, reference has been made to the common characteristics of the Church and Prison; these two institutions do have
much in common.

The laws of the Church, derived from that obscene book called the
"Bible," have become to a great extent the laws of the state and must
be obeyed by all members of the state no matter whether they believe in the teachings of the Bible or not.[3] Thus we have laws which
would put the old Roman senators—when Rome was in the zenith of
its power—to shame. Laws which have been made 3,000 years ago are
still in force in the "enlightened" 19th century, laws which are directly
antagonistic to the laws of nature.

We condemn suicide and punish unsuccessful attempts at self-
destruction; we force husband and wife to live together when love has
turned into hatred; we teach the young man and the young girl that it
is a sin, a moral crime, to satisfy natural desires; to bear children without the knowledge of law or Church is called a shame and disgrace—
and suicide, criminal operations, infanticide, and other crimes are the
result of such false moral teachings and laws. Instead of explaining
the laws of nature concerning sexual matters to grown up boys and
girls, we try to keep them in absolute ignorance as to these questions,
and as a result of such ignorance, the missteps in this direction are
obvious. Instead of the great forgiving and excusing words of the
young Nazarene: "Go and sin no more," we hear the words of the
Judge: "Thirty days to the workhouse," and with true Christianity we
tramp the fallen down, deeper into the mud.

Obscene words and language we punish with fines and prison, yet the most obscene and foul passages of the Bible we call "inspired."

Indeed, Church and Prison have much in common. Both institutions are busy keeping their victims so deep in ignorance that the rays of the sun of truth should never penetrate their mind. The prize in the contest for darkness and ignorance justly belongs to the Catholic Church. The young prisoner knew it as he addressed his elder homosexual friend in the words: "Now is your chance; say what you want, for tomorrow I'll go to confession and be forgiven."

Other creeds need not rejoice, for their educational influence is not much better than that of the Catholic Church.

Not satisfied with the amount of criminality already created by poverty, ignorance, unjust and oppressive laws, social distinctions, party politics, Bible hypocrisy etc., our great leaders of every shade and color are at the present time busily engaged in creating still more criminals—or better—more sources of crime by concentrating the people into large cities: a greater Chicago, a greater New York, a greater Pittsburgh etc. are desired by these leaders in spite of the fact that the greater the city the greater is the poverty, the slums and crimes in her bosom, while on the other hand, even a blind man could perceive that in the smaller cities crimes are comparatively few. The slums and crimes of London, Paris, Vienna, Berlin, Chicago, Philadelphia are indeed frightful enough to discourage any attempts in trying to enlarge cities like Pittsburgh, for instance. Nevertheless, the great leaders and statesmen cannot see this, or if they do see it they find it more important to seek to gain their political points.

Laws compel men to break laws inasmuch as all laws are made for the sole purpose of upholding the present tangled-up social conditions, favorable to the few and injurious to the masses. Every new law creates new conditions in society which are a benefit to a small part of the people and a disadvantage to the majority; in other words, the more laws, the more crime. No man will willingly obey a law which is injurious to his interests; his first inclination is to evade the law. This is a natural inclination, not a criminal one, for to obey knowingly a law which is against my interests means nothing less than to give up my personal liberty and become a slave.

Prison, as a source of crime, has been sketched in the preceding articles. Another important source remains to be mentioned. It is intemperance, especially the excessive indulgence in alcoholic drinks.

Correctly speaking, there are no criminals. Man does what he is compelled to do; man is the product of circumstances; man is what his surroundings force him to be; therefore he is not entirely free, not to be held responsible for his actions. By nature all men are both good or bad, that is neither. It is the surroundings that make the man either good or bad, the influences of home-life, education, associates etc.

The Judge, who, in defiance of all man-made laws, shall sentence the young prisoner before the bar to a term at college instead of at the penitentiary, will make his name immortal.

As I have said before, I do not deal in cheap reforms like a Comstock or Pankhurst.[4]

Remove poverty and ignorance; remove class-distinctions and senseless laws as well as corrupt politicians; remove private property. Give the people economical independence and political freedom in the fullest sense of the word; throw the colleges open to all, poor and rich alike; away with religious training; away with the millions of the few and away with the rags of the many; reduce the population of the great cities, which is both a source of crime and a danger to health; hold on to the laws of nature and ensure every human being the satisfaction of his natural wants by instituting communism.

Take away all the conditions creating and fostering crime, and thus the evil will be abolished, for without the incentive, without the necessity of stealing, robbing etc., no sane man will turn criminal. In a society based upon the economical independence of every member, all problems of crime, criminals, and prisons will be solved by and through this very condition. Such a society will have no criminologists, nor the need of them either. There, crime will be a rare exception and not the rule, as it is today. Probable instances of crime will be regarded in the light of a disease and the subject entrusted to the care—not of a jailor—but of the physician.

Libertas: An Orthographical Study

ALEXANDER BERKMAN

L IBERTAS! LIBERTY! What a grand, majestic word! Nay, not a word, merely; more infinitely more! A large, inexhaustible gold-mine, as deep as the earth; an ocean of brilliant possibilities, the Niagara of joy! A word?! Nay, it is the Alpha and Omega of knowledge, the dictionary of wisdom, a very encyclopedia of happiness! "*Libertas!*" This word is *the* word; a whole word in itself, the Bible of Reason, the Messiah of Humanity, the only goddess worth adoring. Each individual letter of this Word—the essence of Life, the stone of the wise—treasures a thousand folios of unwritten wisdom under its unassuming garb, discernible only to the eyes of "the elected."

I will unravel for your special benefit a few of its Mysteries.

LIBERTAS

"L": This is a big L with a triple meaning; it stands for Life, Love, Liberty, the meaning of each different from those of the others, yet all three of parallel scope and absolutism, each reflecting and completing the other, bound by internal, inseparable ties, a veritable Holy Trinity, with the indisputable motto: "United we stand; divided we fall." Note the attitude of this L, the Leading Lady, the Prima Donna of the ensemble; her head is gracefully inclined toward the smaller "stars," and she is trying to encourage them with a kind smile, so that they do not lose their cue and follow in her tracks, while her beautiful feet are ready for the next step, forward.

"i": This is a small "i," a very small one indeed; it is a living "i" and it ought to be ashamed of its smallness, the more apparent and the greater because of its proximity to the big L. This "i" reads: I, you, he, she. What a small "i" it is, indeed, compared to the Lady at its side. Now please note the great diversity between these two "characters" (the L and i) apparent at the first glance. How plain and simple is L's outer garb and how unassuming her graceful, easy attitude. She is conscious of her infinite and absolute importance; even as the Leader (capital letter) of the Word; without her the balance would have neither meaning nor existence; she is aware of her superiority and priority and she is also fully confident of her ultimate triumph—yet, how modest she looks, how quietly she behaves!

You see no artificial adornments on her outer person, yet she shines and illuminates this whole word by that gold within her, which no Californian prospector thinks of seeking and which is, nevertheless, the only genuine article, the essence of all that for which this Lady stands. Now turn your eyes to the little fellow, hardly reaching to the beautiful Lady's hip; I mean the small "i," you know already that this "type" is a "he," the lord of creation, standing for the "whole of mankind," aye, for all creation and always speaking of himself and others as I, with due emphasis on the I, made necessary by his own smallness, with an I as big as he thinks himself. Reflecting on this gentleman's sorry personal appearance, you will at once perceive that he is placed in a rather uncomfortable position, highly poignant to his great sensibility on this point and to his vanity, which latter is second only to his infinite arrogance. Now, please don't interrupt, I tell you he is not the representative of John Bull, but he is, as before explained, the collective human gender, number and case, all in one. To improve upon his pygmy-like appearance—his bull-headedness does not improve it—and to add dignity to his person he has crowned himself with that crown, (the insignia of his divine right), you see on his head (the dot). It is replete with costly diamonds and gold, scintillating with a thousand rainbows and enfolding "Him" in brilliant clouds of light, which serve his purposes by blinding the other "characters" of the "cast" to the fact that the light is artificial and non-productive of warmth. Still, the brilliancy of the spectacle blinds them, and He, playing the hero, although in reality a "heavy villain," is fully conscious of his own importance, confident that he is being admired and wondered at. He rises in his own estimation with the homage he receives from others, his chest is swelling and he is trying to improve upon the work of Nature and correct its blunders by raising himself on his tip-toes. But in vain! Try as he may, he cannot efface the characteristics that Nature had ineffaceably stamped on his ego; in spite of all his "improvements" you will still perceive that He cannot disguise his real character by all his frippery: you see that his back is crooked, from a pernicious habit, no doubt, he dare not look up, while with his foot he is kicking those below him. He is a great man. He tries to look pleasant and happy, though he has, at times, the uncomfortable sensation of an empty head and overloaded stomach, places which He regards as the two central stations of civilization. Notice how his eyes fill with rage and hate as one of his admirers occasionally turns his head, as if in a dream, in the direction of the beautiful Lady. "He" angrily turns his back to her, trying—oh the poor, [con]ceited, vainglorious pygmy—to keep the big Leader from sight . . . But the great Lady only smiles, and there is a sad look on her beautiful face.

"b": This is a small "be," when standing by itself; it is of a double "character" (b, e) impossible without the "i" and undesirable without the "L." It reads: "to be" and its true mission is the same as that of the "L," whose vital principle it is. It is an universal factor; its essence is Life. It is the bottom and banks of the human river, while ("L")— Liberty, Love, Life are its life-giving waters; without these the river is but a dried-up, miasma-breeding swamp.

"r": This is an affirmation; it indicates that when you have the "be" and also the "L" then you really "are." As to what you are, it explains when taken in consecutive reading with the preceding neighbors: "L-i-b-e-r," you are "then" *Liber* (Latin: a free man).

Liber: When you have progressed thus far in the study of *the* word, the "liber" will suggest to you the advisability of keeping your head cool, so as not to get too much elated over your achievements. Acting on this well-meant suggestion, you will be able to discover the apparently superfluous letter "e" in the "Liber" and you will appreciate the great and important role this "character" plays in the "Liber" ensemble. Be careful not to displace this unassuming "type," watch him as you do the iris of your eye—"Liberty is bought at the price of constant watchfulness." It happened to our forefathers—long ago— to displace this "character" "e" in their attempts to spell the word "liber"; they spelled it "libri" instead of "liberi";* woe to them! Woe to us! They had thus driven the "liberi" to distraction—Liberty, the live Lady, was frightened and froze into a cold lifeless statue; education superseded natural intelligence, and Liberty changed into statutes. The "liberi" remained henceforward only on the "libri."

"t": This is a strong "character." Don't judge him from outward appearances; in his case they are deceptive; though he looks small, he is in reality a T-itan, with a big T. He stands at the side of "Liber" and calls "te," i.e. you (*te,* Latin, objective-case, you). He clearly says to

---

* *Latin:* Liberi, *free men;* Libri, *books.*

you: When you stand where I am, you will be "at Liber-te." This Titan is the gatekeeper of "Liber." His ample shoulders support the world; they are the pillars on which the Heaven of Life-Love rests. Now look at his extended arms; with the one hand he points at "Liber," his other he extends in the opposite direction. You surely notice that one of his arms is shorter than the other; namely the one pointing at "Liber"; you ask why he uses his *short* arm in this direction? Because with this one he leads those already on their way: he who has at all perceived the light, emanating from the "Capital" (L) will find the rest of the way by himself. But his long arm "T" extends in the other direction, endeavoring to reach out even further and further. He points to the "s" and utters a sad ah! (a) with a deep sigh; he is heartily sorry for the "s," for if you are as far removed from him as this "type" is, you are then an "s," indeed, an ass.

And this is the correct way of spelling "Libertas."

Its meaning: I have but partly, and that very feebly, explained to you, for it would take volumes to do justice to the deep wisdom of the word. It is a beautiful word, the essence, the very substance of wisdom. There is not a thing in the world worth knowing, that the careful study of "Libertas" will not reveal. Not a thing! But this is a skeptical world; I even see you smile over my assertion. You want proofs, you say? Good, you shall have them. Libertas is not of the fickle Fortuna-species of fairies. She never dodges those who seek her. Indeed, she is always at their command; like a loving woman she is ever ready to give herself for the asking. But she is more than a lover; she is your steady, faithful friend, truer than steel; sweetening your joys by her presence, lightening your burdens by her freeing love. And now to give you the proofs of the stability and justice of the claims of "Libertas" to universal wisdom. Look intently at the word—*Libertas*—and you will see in its mere orthography that happy solution of the whole question of woman's emancipation. You look surprised at the enor-

mity of my assertion, and well you may. The claim is enormous, indeed, but it is no pretense, merely; and how much more enormous
you will think "Libertas" when future study of the word will reveal to
you her right to far greater claims than the one I have just mentioned.
But I must not overtax your rather feeble brain, my friend, and therefore suffice for today to prove the above stated claim as to woman's
emancipation.

Now, look at the word again: *Libertas,* look with your mind and
eyes, and not with your prejudices, and you will perceive that it brings
you a message, written in that laconic language where certain figures
stand for whole ideas, yet saying none the less clearly: Li—berta—s! a
profound message; it reads:

"Li, li, berta, s"! which means "Li" (stands for Chinaman, that is,
man as the Barbarian of the opposite sex)—lies; Bertha—es (Latin:
thou art). It means then: Man is lying about the other sex; woman
(Bertha) thou art; in other words: Woman you are included in "Libertas," when taken as a whole, that is, in the whole Libertas, in the liberty of *all* is included the emancipation of the Berthas. Oh, the pro-
fundity and wisdom of this word, the word *Libertas!*

We have analyzed each "character" and the role it plays in this
grand "cast," one that could never be equaled by any other combination, on any other stage, in any other play. This—Libertas—is the
grandest play, the most beautiful spectacle humanity has ever seen. It
contains the wisdom of the collective Shakespearean productions; it
is the gamut of humanity, the Sun of Civilization. It will pay you to
acquaint yourself with Libertas.

Epilogue

We of the present epoch—spell "Libertas" in a different way, namely
Liberty. Our Anglo-Saxon forefathers had *invented* this way of spell-

ing it. It was then, and is now, merely an invention. It will be a new discovery, a great achievement, a regenerating rediscovery when we shall no more use this abridged thing (Liberty instead of Libert-as) but shall enjoy full, unqualified, untampered with, real Libertas.

West. Pent. of Pennsyl.
31 Dec. 95

The Vision in the Penitentiary Cell

CARL NOLD

TWO HOURS AFTER THE JUDGE had named my friend and
me "five-year state employees," I lay on my straw mattress in a
cell in the Western Pennsylvania Penitentiary. My glance fell through
the heavily barred windows and came to rest on the gray winter sky,
where clouds and bits of cloud were moving around. That was the
only view I had for the time being, so the slow, indolent clouds interested me quite a bit. They were evidently in the same state I was—
they weren't in a hurry, they had nothing to lose, their immediate future was taken care of, as was mine. Now they crowded together in a
thick tangle as if they had important things to say to each other. Suddenly they scattered apart like a group of Americans standing on a
corner scatters when a policeman wields his truncheon among them.
A truncheon, the modern symbol of order, wasn't visible here, but the
leaden canopy of the sky suddenly took on a white, then yellowing,
color, then the sky opened up and Helios in his resplendence smiled

down on the cold snow-covered earth. One of his rays penetrated my cell with such blinding light that I had to close my eyes for a minute. When I opened them again, the god of antiquity was no longer to be seen, but the cell walls and iron bars had also disappeared—I found myself inside a large, magnificent church of the kind I had seen in New York in which the renowned Four Hundred thank "their" God every week for not yet sending the Flood in the form of a popular uprising of the French kind of 1789. Every corner, every column, every door and window was abundantly adorned with flowers, wreaths, hothouse plants, and ribbons worked with gold and silver glitter. The gallery resembled a small forest and forest silence prevailed in the room, although all the soft padded chairs, covered in velvet and silk, were occupied by men and women who seemed to vie with each other in the cut of their clothing and the cost of their jewels.

At the place where one usually expects the main altar, there was a large stage, and on the lowered damask curtain were foot-high letters worked in gold, forming the words in English: "Praise them, praise them."

A bell signal sounded. The rosy light that had filled the room until now died away and a pleasant twilight took its place. Up went the stage curtain and in a sea of lights stood a silver altar of huge dimensions on which there stood three life-size wooden crosses. The Nazarene Jesus hung on the middle cross; on the cross to his right was nailed a figure that was not dissimilar to the American slave-worker. Over his head an inscription was emblazoned: "Homestead." At the upright of this cross, leaning against one of the heaviest steel armor plates under which a crushed man in worker's clothing lay struggling, stood a portly, finely attired, elderly man with a hammer in one hand, pointing to skillfully filled cast holes with the other, a smirk on his face. The "Rose of Virtue" in the buttonhole of his coat glittered.[1] On the cross to the left hung a figure that was suggestive of a foreign worker; over his head, the inscription "Coke Region." At the foot of this cross was a gilded coke oven with a fashionably dressed man in his prime sitting on it. On his vest pocket hung the ribbon of an unknown "Legion of Honor." His feet rested on a worker lying in a pool of blood and dressed in rags, like those one sees in the coke regions of Pennsylvania. His hand, frozen in place, still held the long, heavy, iron hook used to pull the burnt coke out of the oven.

When the curtain went up, those present threw themselves to their knees and now an old man with white hair stepped slowly, solemnly, up to the stairs of the altar, made a slight bow, and began: "Gods! Your servants have come to report. The rebellion has been put down; peace and security are in force again; the last troublemakers have been given into state custody for the next five years, by me, your obedient servant, oh ye Gods. Those who defiantly dared to conspire against your holy person are now paying for it. I was hopeful and fervently wished that those who are now sentenced would surrender bail and flee; we'd prefer the bail to them. But these criminals preferred to go to jail rather than let their bail fall into our hands and so it is to be feared that their punishment will bring about no reform. If you, oh Gods, deem it right, the next senate could enact emergency laws so that we would feel stronger."

The person on the plate of armor gestured toward his coat pocket with his right hand, where a large bank book was sticking out— the speaker put out his hand—the curtain fell. Rapturous music resounded and stormy applause mixed with loud cries: "Hallelujah, Hallelujah, Hosanna, Hosanna."

The noise died down; at a second bell signal the curtain rose again. The first speaker lay before the altar, his hands folded in a prayer of thanks. His head almost touched the floor. A young, beardless man now approached the steps, bowing deeply. His long hair fell into his eyes as he looked up to the gods and began: "Like the honorable speaker before me, who has served you faithfully, oh ye Gods, until his hair has turned white, I will pledge you my loyalty and be ready for any sign from you. My first trial I have passed, and though, sadly, in doing it, I posed the stupid question 'Do you believe in God,' oh ye Gods, do not be angry with me, for though we ourselves believe in nothing, yet the masses must be kept in their belief."

Casting a long, yearning look at the bank book that peeked out of the pocket of the one idol, the young man knelt down next to the old man. The gods sat immobile. With unsteady steps, like a drunk, a man with a flushed face now came in, two steps forward, one step back, up to the altar. He tripped over the two kneeling men, staggered up the steps, and began: "What purpose would judges and district attorneys have if it weren't for us detectives? We are the main g-g-g-guys. We have to swear false oaths and come up with witnesses and fabricate evidence where none exists; we have to make sure the innocent are found guilty." With that, and turning toward the idol with the "Rose of Virtue," he made the hand gesture for money. But the idol with the "Rose of Virtue" gestured toward his fellow idol with the "Legion of Honor" ribbon; the latter reached into his vest pocket and threw the speaker a quarter. The speaker, radiant with joy, bent over for it, lost his balance, and rolled down the steps next to the kneeling men.

The crowd shouted "Hosanna, Hosanna; Hallelujah, Hallelujah"; the music started up and the howls of joy were terrible.

Then the first of the kneeling figures, the old man, rose. Silence fell immediately. His arms raised up to heaven, his gaze focused on the carpenter's son, he called out, "It is finished." A smile passed over the features of the Crucified One; he opened his mouth and answered, "Finally the hour has come."

The gods and the worshippers looked at each other fixedly. The room darkened, lightning flashed through the air, distant thunder rolled, loud cries and gunshots sounded from outside, the three crosses on the altar started to sway. "The Deluge, the Deluge," several voices cried out. Wild pandemonium broke out around the church, the one idol fell behind the plate of armor, the other toppled into the coke oven.

The Sinking Ship: A Parable

ALEXANDER BERKMAN

O N THE OCEAN SHORE STOOD a tall tower in which two bachelors lived: Mr. Philosopher and Mr. Enthusiast. One day the two young men were sitting in their tower, each engrossed in deep study. Mr. Philosopher was comfortably settled down in a soft, broad armchair, a thick folio in one hand and a pencil in the other with which he made marks in his book from time to time. His high forehead, as wide as it was high, his facial features refined by scholarship, the cool and judicious expression of self-confidence and self-satisfaction on his face revealed to the observer the large brain that is tirelessly at work at the expense of the heart.

His companion, Mr. Enthusiast, was busily writing on a long roll of paper with fervent speed; he seemed riveted to his work and paid no attention to his companion. He was a tall, slim man, much younger than his companion. His soul flashed in his eyes; love-hate burned in them.

Considerable time passed while the two continued their own work. Then Mr. Enthusiast got up and stepped over to the telescope in the room. He positioned it and looked into the distance—at the ocean, then high up into the heavens. He stood like that at the telescope for several minutes, searching in the distance, and then, resuming his place again and turning to the Philosopher, said: "My friend, it seems that a storm is gathering. Big black clouds cover the sky; they have darkened the sun and the ocean is very turbulent today, swelling very high. The sight of the huge, black clouds—up above and down below—is really terrifying."

"It's very humid," answered the Philosopher, "and I see that it's getting dark."

"Yes, it is the dusk before dawn, as an Englishman would say. There will be a terrible thunderstorm, but—"

"No," the other interrupted, "I don't think we need fear such a big storm, just the usual, harmless thing, no danger to sailors."

"But you're mistaken; I've looked closely at the firmament. Danger, yes, I think great danger is at hand. The elements are angry; they have a force that no gods could master if it should come to that."

The Philosopher got up from his seat. "You are too enthusiastic, my young friend, as always," he said, then continued, "but let's take a look."

He stepped over to the telescope, turned it this way and that, and then, holding it in one direction for a while, he exclaimed: "There, a ship! That's surely our people's ship!"

"Our ship!? Really?" And the Enthusiast hurried over to the Philosopher. The latter made room for him.

His eyes fixed on the horizon, the Enthusiast continued: "Yes! That's it! Our ship! Right now it's in a dangerous spot; it looks like the roaring, rolling, wild ocean will have little trouble with that comparatively little thing."

"My friend," continued the Enthusiast after a short while, "the ship is in great danger; it's being hurled around this way and that between the thundering heavens and the glowering sea like a straw on the wings of the wind . . ."

"Over here, my friend, the ship is in peril of its life! Quick, we must rush to its rescue, otherwise it will soon go under."

The Enthusiast shouted these last words with a voice shaking with agitation. The Philosopher went to his companion and both fixed their gaze on the sea and the ship.

It was a terrible storm. However accustomed the two friends were to the water god's outbursts of rage—today it appeared to them that the sea was much more dangerous for seafaring than in an ordinary storm.

Considerable time passed. The storm gave no sign of weakening; on the contrary, it seemed to be working itself up into ever greater fury. The ship seemed to be tiring in its battle against Neptune's supernatural power; it was visibly spent, no longer aggressively fighting. It had all it could do to resist the onslaught of the churning, raging, torrential waves come alive.

The poor ship fought with a fierceness born of despair. It exerted its utmost power to force down the rising waters, but all in vain.

In vain! Angry Neptune grew more and more aggressive and hurled ever bigger and stronger masses of foam and water at the already sinking ship. Whole regiments of the water king's army seemed to fall upon the floating pygmy boat, coming aboard in compact form and driving it down to the depths with smashing force.

Now the poor ship seemed to be totally worn out in this unequal battle; it was still struggling, but without strength and without success; it seemed the ship's lifespan could be counted in minutes and then eternity . . .

And then the heavens opened and the sinister face of Janus, World-

Judge, appeared.[1] He cast a glance at the now almost exhausted ship, and a jeering, taunting, gloating laugh resounded thunderingly from on high ... and with his glowering face-of-the-past turned toward the ship, angry Janus nodded with his face-of-the-future to his fellow god Neptune.

And the poor ship fought on. Its main masts were already broken and the rudder was torn from its place and was being dragged into the sea—booty for those sure of victory.

Then a mighty crash—cunning Neptune had reached out one of his bony fingers and rammed it into the bottom of the ship. The ship shuddered all over like a criminal dying in the electric chair.[2] With wild, deafening howls, Neptune's bloodthirsty hordes began to rush into the opened breach, putting out the fire, and slowly pulling the ship into the depths.

Awakened by the deafening noise of the ship striking Neptune's finger, the passengers rushed to the deck, running this way and that, wild with fear and terror, confused by the unexpected and unimaginable calamity that had befallen them. Several began to lower the lifeboats. Terrible pandemonium ... savage howling, lamenting and wailing ... savage, hellish chaos ...

But soon several boats are safely lowered, and then an awful battle breaks out among the passengers over their personal safety; everyone wants to secure a life-saving place for himself. But there are few boats, far too few to hold even a tenth of the passengers. In droves, they jump into boats that are already overloaded, and those already "saved" start to push and throw themselves at each other ... Many fall overboard, but no one cares for them; instead, they thrust them deeper into the water and knock away the hands stretched out to those fortunate people in the boats.

"Quickly, friend," cried the Enthusiast in great agitation, "let us save the people! Hurry, come on, or they are goners."

"Save them?" answered the Philosopher somewhat sarcastically. "It's true, my studies have taught me how to battle these waves successfully and how to placate the gods. My knowledge could calm these people and save the ship, but this is not yet the right moment . . ."

The Enthusiast did not hear him; he ran out of the tower quickly and, hurrying along the ocean shore, he sounded the emergency signal, and the sailors who lived on the heights soon answered it. Then the Enthusiast threw himself into the water, a perfect swimmer, and headed out toward the ship to bring the foundering people the happy news of their coming rescue and to urge them to hold on to the masts until help should arrive.

Janus, now forbearing, clapped Neptune on the shoulder and said, "There's no hurry. Let's give these little human mites another test. Let them build a new and better ship that is more fitting for the spirit of the great Janus. Ignorant human creatures cannot escape the almighty will of the Past-and-Future-Seer. They could as well stop up the red-hot crater of Vesuvius with a little cotton! This is enough of a lesson for today."

Janus spoke and shook his friend Neptune's hand.

And Neptune raised his powerful arm and splashed the water, stirring up a mountain of phosphorescent bubbles near the sinking ship. The black clouds in the sky cleared away and a bright, shining sun strolled out into the world. Flooded by its brilliant rays, the mountain of bubbles seemed to the people on the sinking ship to be a green island full of the promise of life.

With a mighty thrust, Neptune pushed the ship up to the island and the passengers sang a heartfelt, fervent "Te Deum" in praise of the miraculous rescue as they fled safely onto the island.

"I was right," thought the Philosopher as he caught sight of the ocean oasis of bubbles. "It was just as I said; there was no danger of sinking. Meanwhile the ship is safe at harbor." And the wise Philosopher took up his thick book again and engrossed himself in it, paying no more attention to the ship and its passengers.

And when their initial fear was over and the storm had abated, and feeling themselves safe in the harbor, the passengers gained courage anew and thought and spoke like the Philosopher, and laughed over the imagined danger, which, as they said, had existed only in the minds of the fearful passengers who had needlessly lost their heads.

They quickly made repairs to the ship, but, unwilling to expose themselves to the terrible dangers of another journey at sea, the people anchored their ship at the green island—the water bubbles—and in their ignorance felt themselves safe again . . .

And the ship rocked back and forth on wily Neptune's back . . .

Winter Sun for My Prison Colleagues
M & G, 1 January 1896

CARL NOLD

Let Love Be Free

What you were and what you are—of what concern is that to me?
You love me deeply, you say, and so do I love you.
It is enough that we do not waste this hour
Nor worry about the past.
Give me the first kiss, roused by new love,
For what you were and are, I don't want to know.

Freedom

When I think back to the day when for the first time
We met, there in the assembly hall,
It's as if I had lost nothing
And had only gained much since that winter's night

When by the light of the fire in that familiar room
I pledged lasting friendship with you.

Since then many a storm has crossed our path,
And many an oak has fallen, that once defiant and bold
Raised its head into the ether's blue,
And many a good friend who once hailed you, a new dawn, freedom,
Now lies cold and dead,
His grave wrapped round with spiders' webs.

I think of many a brother, who so oft toasted you
With full glass, who loved, hoped,
But has long since forgotten us.
Many a dear young lady, too, once young and free,
Has since then sold herself but found no joy in doing so,
Since she was mistaken in love.

When I think back to that day, I feel your strength,
In my heart the passion of virtue arises ardently anew.
Only with you could I flourish.
You led me up to life's bright heights,
I saw your army of free men, saw the banner fly,
And saw the freedom of the future.

Murder!

Jeering, the moon throws ripples of light
Impudently in here,
Boldly, as if he wanted to ask:
Hey! Why aren't you falling asleep?

"Old friend, I have just
Slain a false idol

That dealt me many a blow
And on top of that, laughed at me.

"Whatever was won through his influence and companionship
Disappeared soon after.
Now I step forward as victor,
I've struck 'Humility' dead.

"I've already slain several
Who plagued me beyond bearing.
For the next who dare,
I'm keeping my sharpened sword ready."

Farewell

Leaves lie withered in the garden by now,
Summer's flowers have faded;
At the window a little bird sings to me
A soft, intimate song.

Ach! I feel, I understand
What he means by his song:
"To the South! To the South
I go. Good-bye, my friend.

"The whole summer long I've seen
You looking through the window
At the river, at valley and mountain,
At the forest and green meadows.

"Look, now the garden lies barren,
Autumn winds blow over it,
Farewell, my friend, I go
Away, to where warmer breezes blow."

Farewell, my little warbler,
You were a dear friend to me;
If you return with the spring,
You'll find me still here.

The Humble Church

She cleanses the infant of sin
Even before he fits into his shirt.
The dying man she ushers into heaven
By means of her Last Sacraments.
Whatever lies between these poles
In a man's short life—
That the preacher demands of every good Christian
Be given to *his* church.

Dance of the Guelphs

A ghostly scene grips me mightily,
It is the dance of the Guelphs at midnight:
A summer's eve—late—with earnest demeanor
I climbed up to the castle ruins
Where in dark and olden times, forgotten,
The Guelph dynasty once had their seat.
In the light of the moon stood the dark walls
That will no doubt last for centuries,
Overgrown by moss and tangles of ivy,
Inhabited by owls with their bickering and cawing.
On a pillar, fallen long ago,
I rested, tired, and thought of all
The knights, their squires and ladies,

Of their history and their name.
Now only the gray walls stand witness—
Oh! If only I could see them, watch them
At their feasts, their games and dances
In halls festooned with armor and wreaths;
The singers and bards with harp and rhyme,
The tankards and horns filled with wine,
The knights clad in iron and steel
And ladies arrayed in loose garments—
Lost in such thoughts, I stood on the old grounds
When from the valley the twelfth hour struck.
While the last peal still filled the air
And the moon hid behind clouds,
I heard a rattling like the clanking of swords,
Trampling and clamor and neighing of horses.
And lo and behold—as if from the edges of the clouds
On snorting steeds covered with foam,
An army of knights was coming to me through the air—
I opened my eyes wider and wider,
For in the saddle, leaning on his chest,
Each had a lady, laughing with zest.
In the castle courtyard they drew up their rows
And marched in, two by two,
Those knights clad in iron and steel,
The ladies arrayed in loose garments,
With wreaths adorning their curling hair,
Their eyes sparkling and so wonderful,
Those powerful women with noble features
Like Greeks atop the highest stair.—
In the middle of the hall, fire was made;
It bathed the armor in dazzling splendor
And bards struck up dances and sang
For the pairs swinging wildly around the fire.

The loose garments fluttered in dance,
Faces glowed—then sudden silence.
A singer stepped forward, his harp in his hand,
His song was tidings from a faraway land;
Of ancestors who fell there in battle,
Who once had built and decked out these halls,
Of the courage of knights, of wine and desire
And blissful death in one's lover's embrace.
Then the wild dance began anew.
Accompanied by harps and flutes and violins,
Amid loving and waving and joking and shoving
They leapt over the fire in pairs.
From mighty tankards and horns they drank,
Then, kissing, they sank into each other's arms—
Then suddenly I heard the command:
"Knights and ladies, one o'clock, call out your horse, call out your
    horse!"
The fire was extinguished, and the moon reappeared:
As they had come, so they did fade, that band of ghostly figures.
That was the dance of the Guelphs that one could watch
Between twelve and one in the Walpurgis Night.[1]

The Night of November 11
November 1895

The pavement resounds with heavy steps;[2]
You hear the muted sound of drums;
With steady tread there nears
A platoon of dead men, without end.
Herculean figures
Lead this terrible procession,

The torches in the lead
Are skeletons dipped in tar.

Following the drummers, who beat
Drum rolls, not on drums, but on skulls,
Comes a man in sandals flecked with blood
Who carries a flag of human skin
On which one can read
In the torchlight in the old script:
"We who follow this flag are
The slaves of Rome and Greece."

Following him in broad rows
Come the victims devoured
By the eternal city at whose feet
The whole world once lay.
With the slave in the bog, the rich man on top,
The soft earth gave way—
Both fell down, and in the struggle
The entire structure collapsed.

Gruff voices sound from afar,
And clearly comes the call: "Spears to the fore!"
Hanging on a rod you see
An old pair of shoes with thongs
It is the "Bundschuh" from German lands—[3]
The slaves of feudal masters are coming next;
And with them Konrad, Götz and Müntzer,[4]
The leaders of these peasant forces.

Swords, lances, sickles glint
In the moonlight of the November night.
The throng hurries past, followed by
A sea of flames whipped up by the wind.
As if hell had erupted,

As if the Last Judgment were already here,
So hot—it's the burning pyres,
The work of the Inquisition.

The victims that were burned to cinders
Because they opposed the Church's tricks,
Are bringing the burning pyres
As an indictment of every Christian.
There goes Savonarola, and there, Bruno,[5]
Laughing mightily over faith gone crazy;
Hus and Galileo[6] go
Undaunted on their way.

And onward push new waves of men,
Marat, Baboef, Danton[7] and
Flags whose inscription reads:
"Freedom! Equality! Brotherhood!"
Following the Sans Culottes[8] come the youths
Who fell in 1848.[9]
Here is Robert Blum,[10] surrounded by friends,
There, Füster[11] scoffing at exile.

After them, their measured steps blending well
With the sound of the "Marseillaise,"[12]
In shirts blackened by gunpowder smoke
The host of heroes from Père Lachaise[13] approaches.
Their General Dabrowski[14] leads
The ghostly army bravely still
And in the chorus there echoes loudly
The cry: "Long live the Commune!"[15]

Then, lit by no torch,
A crowd pushes forward,
In their midst a hanging gallows
With the motto: "Long live anarchy!"

Spies and Parsons[16] stride gravely ahead
Followed by fighters from every land
Whose graves are adorned every year
With greenery and laurel wreaths.

From Germany, France, and Italy
From Siberia's snow and ice
Even from the south, from beautiful Spain,
Heroes appear in droves
From every land and every region
And stand before Church, State, and Money Bag.
On the modern work-slaves' faces
One sees the banner of hunger flying.

Trooping along are women, daughters, children,
Loudly cursing the tyrants' might.
These are the victims that march
On the eleventh night of November;
These are the dead that every year
Remind us loudly of our duty.
And still they file past side by side,
No end of the procession yet in sight.

Winter Sun

Through the light fog, you could see clouds moving
For eight hours now, heavy
In the cold atmosphere
Quickly, as if fleeing from something.

There—in the ugly gray winter sky
A window opens suddenly
And the sun graciously, beautifully,
Charmingly smiles on the world's tumult.

Sparrows shake their feathers saucily
And, kissed by the warm rays
That no sparrow spurns,
They pipe in chorus the song of brotherhood.

In fellowship, a pair of tramps
Felt the delight of the sparrows;
Looking up to the golden sun,
They sang the song of vagabonds.

Last Days in the Penitentiary: Excerpts from the Diary of Alexander Berkman

April 1905:

Apr. 27. My neighbor Schwanson (4219) died in Hospital in sleeping jacket. Simple; sick but neglected; St. Vitus Dance, Dr. claimed fake. Had fit in 23Y (I in 22y) at 7 P.M. Apr. 25. I called Dr.'s attention but Dr. said "fake, put him in Jacket." Died in Jacket. Was in jacket and gagged (in cell) about 10 days before that, for moaning. A case of murder by neglect.

May:

Time passing at a lively gait. I could not tell off hand how many days I got—2 and a stump.[1] Other fellows count the days to the hour. . . . One of these days I'll surprise myself with "just 30 days."

June 4th Sunday eve.

—all is lovely. All is quiet on the Potomac.[2] It's "after lights," mine burns an extra hour. The sirens from the river reach my ear and the girls are giggling on the banks of the Ohio, but all is quiet here, and I am thinking of the terror looming in the distance. The Inspector will probably sit on my case this week—the result?? . . .

July 1, 1905 Sat. 3 P.M.

asked Deputy J. H. Corbett as to date of my discharge. Answer—19 July 1905. How happy it made me—the happiest day in 13 years. The anxiety is over. Who knows what Pennypacker might have done.[3] But now all is safe. Sent special message to chums to tell the good news. . . .

. . .

Saturday, July 15.

Inspector Diehl visited me; offered to go down to Workhouse to get me light work. Asked me to call on him upon release. . . .

Time is going. Only 2 more days after tonight. This is Sunday, July 16, '05, 9 P.M. Lights out, mine burning extra. Am wakeful. What new terrors has Workhouse in store for me? But I am not afraid—I feel strong in body and mind and above all, confident of final triumph. I go with a light heart. I ask no favors, no quarters. Freeman of Broom Shop volunteered to visit Workhouse in my behalf; so did Diehl. I did not ask the Dr.—as is customary—to eat in Hospital the last month or two. . . . Paid $2.00 for carriage to take me away. Hope we'll escape the reporters.

July 17.

. . . Solidarity of prisoners. My assistants and colored assistant on the range . . . give me nearly half of their milk to strengthen me for Workhouse. Chum sent fruit last night. Thoughtful as ever. Chum just sent note . . . also eye water[4] . . . but I don't need it . . . feel happy and strong in body and spirit.

July, 18, '05

Tuesday, 10 A.M.
Cell 22Y
South Block
Tomorrow this time I'll be on my way to Workhouse
Hurrah

July 18, 8:30 P.M.

Made rounds of South Block bidding all the boys goodbye. How sad it was to hear the dear fellows say—"3 years," "five years yet" etc., officers Jack Griffith, Hawkins etc. came around to bid goodbye. Feel happy, head shaved and ready to go.

Hurrah.

Alexander Berkman's Bibliography

"Les Miserable[s]" by Victor Hugo, 2 vol.
[Victor Hugo (1802–1885) published *Les Misérables* in 1862. Set in France at the time of the revolution in 1832, the novel tells the story of ex-prisoner Jean Valjean's search for redemption and is a plea for the humane treatment of the poor and for equality for all citizens.]

"The Man Who Laughs" by Victor Hugo
[Originally published in French in 1869 as *L'Homme qui rit,* this novel treats themes of childhood helplessness and poverty in the story of the doomed love between a boy and a blind girl he rescues from starvation.]

"The Rag Picker"
[This novel by American writer George Pickering Burnham (1814–
1902), published in 1855, is set in nineteenth-century antebellum Boston and describes parental tyranny and the moral abuses of slavery.]

"The Scarlet Letter" by Hawthorne
[The classic tale of Hester Prynne's punishment for adultery in
seventeenth-century Boston, by American writer Nathaniel Hawthorne (1804–1864), published in 1850, explores the nature of sin,
guilt, and redemption against the moral rigidity of a Puritan community.]

"Sunrise" by Wm. Black
[Subtitled *A Story of These Times,* by Scots writer William Black (1841–
1898) and published in America in 1881, this fiction is a drama of international political intrigue.]

"Oliver Twist" by Charles Dickens
[Published in 1838 by Dickens (1812–1870), the novel exposes the
baleful effects of industrialism in nineteenth-century England, told
through the life of an orphaned boy consigned to a workhouse and
forced into thievery.]

"Underground Russia" by Stepniak
[The author, Ukrainian-Russian revolutionary activist, lecturer, and
writer Sergius Michaelovitch Kravchinski (1851–1895), assassinated
the head of the Russian secret police, General N. V. Mezentsev, in St.

Petersburg in 1878. He lived thereafter in England, where he formed societies sympathetic to the radical underground revolutionary movements in Russia. *Underground Russia,* subtitled *Revolutionary Profiles and Sketches from Life,* published in London in 1882 and in New York in 1885, contains accounts of revolutionary activities and portraits of Russian revolutionaries, such as anarchist theorist Peter Kropotkin and activist Sophia Perovskaya, executed for the 1881 assassination of Czar Alexander II.]

"Under Sealed Orders" 2 vol. by ?
[Charles Grant Blairfindie Allen (1848–1899), a Canadian-born English socialist and evolutionist, published widely on many issues, including science, race, colonialism, and women's rights, and was also considered to have influenced the developing genre of detective fiction. *Under Sealed Orders,* a mystery-adventure story, was published in an American edition by the New Amsterdam Book Company in 1896.]

"Popes of Rome" by ?
[In all likelihood, Berkman read *The Popes of Rome: Their Church and State in the Sixteenth and Seventeenth Centuries* by German historian Leopold von Ranke (1795–1886), a multivolume work published in German between 1834 and 1836. Von Ranke, whose work is notable for initiating the study of history as a source-based practice, analyzed the political and social issues in the papacy, and coined the term "Counter-Reformation."]

"Cleopatra Queen of Egypt"; "Nero"; "Genghis Khan"; "Julius Caesar"
[These popular and highly readable biographies were among many written by Jacob Abbott (1803–1879), minister and educator, a prolific American writer of juvenile literature.]

"The Gracchi" by A. H. Beesly
[Subtitled *Marius and Sulla: Epochs of Ancient History,* by August Henry Beesly (1829–1909).]

"Lives of Ancient Philosophers" by Rev. J. Cormack
[Subtitled *Translated from the French of Fénelon* (i.e., Francois de Sallignac de la Mothe-Fénelon) *with Notes and a Life of the Author,* the American edition was published in 1842.]

"Lives of Mahomet and His Successors" 2 vol. by Washington Irving
[The American author, essayist, biographer, and historian Washington Irving (1783–1859) published his life of Muhammad in 1850, considered the first sympathetic biography of Muhammad to appear in America.]

"Väter und Söhne" von Iwan Turgenjew
[*Fathers and Sons* by Ivan Turgenev. The 1862 novel by Russian novelist Turgenev (1818–1883) reflects the growing generational divide between the political liberals of the 1830s and '40s and the nihilists, both seeking social change in Russia based on Western models.]

"Altväterliche Leute" von Nikolas Gogol[1]
["Old-Fashioned People" by Nikolai Gogol. This story by Russian author Gogol (1809–1852) was published in 1835 as the first tale in *Mirgorod*, a short-story collection in two volumes. It is an ambiguous portrayal of an apparently idyllic pastoral life with all its seductive appeal but all its vulnerability and limitations, too.]

"Russische Novellen" (von Nikolas Gogol)
[*Russian Novellas* (by Nikolai Gogol)]

"Onkel Tom's Hütte" von Mrs. H. B. Stowe
[*Uncle Tom's Cabin* by Mrs. H. B. Stowe. Published in 1850 by New England writer Harriet Beecher Stowe (1811–1896), this horrific account of slavery in America was internationally influential in promoting abolitionist sympathy.]

"Memoiren vom März 1848 bis Juli 1849" 2 Bände von A. Füster
[*Memoirs from March 1848 to July 1849* by Anton Füster. Anton Füster (1808–1881), priest and professor of theology and pedagogy in Vienna, member of the Imperial Assembly, participated in the 1848 revolution in Vienna and fled to England after its suppression. His memoir of the revolution was published in 1850 in Frankfurt am Main (Literarische Anstalt).]

"Die Regulatoren in Arkansas" von Friedrich Gerstäcker
[*The Regulators of Arkansas* by Friedrich Gerstäcker. The first novel of German novelist and travel writer Gerstäcker (1816–1872), published

in three volumes in 1845, described social conditions in Arkansas before the Civil War in an adventure featuring a vigilante group determined to end rampant horse rustling.]

"Ships That Pass in the Night" by Beatrice Harraden, George Munro's
Sons publ.
[This first novel by the British writer and suffragist Beatrice Harraden
(1864–1936), published in America in 1894, is a love story set in a tuberculosis sanatorium.]

*The New Normal Written Arithmetic Designed for Common and High
Schools etc.* by Edward Brooks A.M. Ph.D.
[The standard series of Brooks's school texts in mathematics was advertised in the *Pennsylvania School Journal,* published in Lancaster,
Pennsylvania, in 1888, as "adapted . . . to the needs of everyday business practice."]

"My Unkel [Uncle] Benjamin" by Claude Tillier. Transl. by B. Tucker
[This popular satirical and philosophical French novel, by Claude
Tillier (1801–1844), was published in 1842. The American edition was
translated by individualist anarchist Benjamin Tucker.]

"Prue and I" by ?
[This fictional biography was written by George William Curtis
(1824–1892) and shows a poor man's life to be infinitely richer in quality than the life of a millionaire.]

"Der Einzige und sein Eigenthum" Stirner

[Familiar in English as *The Ego and Its Own*, by Max Stirner. A more literal translation of the title would be "The Individual and His Property." Johann Kaspar Schmidt (1806–1856), better known as Max Stirner, was a German philosopher, one of the literary fathers of nihilism, existentialism, postmodernism, and anarchism, especially of individualist anarchism. This widely influential work, first published in 1844, is still in print today.]

Notes

1. Capital and the Battle on the Monongahela

Translated from the German by Bonnie Buettner. The first page of the text is missing; we adopted the descriptive title "Capital and the Battle on the Monongahela" based on the content of the article. The missing text may well have addressed the Great Railroad Strike to which Nold refers. Berkman indicates that Nold's first piece for their book was entitled "The Homestead Strike." In all likelihood this was the first chapter of *Prison Blossoms*. Alexander Berkman, *Prison Memoirs of an Anarchist* (New York: New York Review of Books, 1970), 285.

1. Founded in 1850, the Pinkerton company was an armed service of detectives, frequently employed as company spies by management to infiltrate labor unions and crush strikes. By 1892 they had been involved in some seventy labor disputes.

2. Marked by violent confrontations between workers and police, the Great Railroad Strike over reduced wages in the wake of the serious economic recession of 1873 began in West Virginia on July 14, 1877, and spread to Baltimore, Philadelphia, and across the Midwest to Chicago. Put down by local and state militias and finally by the intervention of federal

troops sent in by President Hayes, the strike ended forty-five days later. This uprising by railroad workers began a long period of labor unrest that culminated in the development of the labor union movement.

3. Recurrent public scandals over and investigations into what Nold calls the steel-plate swindle involved Bethlehem Iron and Carnegie Steel and focused on price-fixing and the low quality of the armor plate delivered to, among others, the U.S. military.

4. Hugh O'Donnell (b. ca. 1863 in Ireland) was chosen by the Homestead strikers as the leader of the Advisory Committee after the mill lockout at the end of June. Dates for Critchlow and Clifford are unknown.

5. Gallagher and Davidson (dates unknown), cooks in the mill kitchens, changed their stories several times, recanting testimony against Dempsey in July 1893 only to revert to their previous statements later. Robert J. Beatty (dates unknown) was one of the men who handled the food brought into the mill for the nonunion workers. Hugh F. Dempsey (dates unknown) had reached one of the highest offices (Master Workman) in the Knights of Labor, one of the most important national labor organizations in the United States in the nineteenth century. The Knights of Labor emphatically endorsed the efforts of the strikers, and perhaps because of his prominent position in that organization, Dempsey was accused of masterminding the alleged poisonings.

6. Several doctors testified that the same illness was raging outside the mill; it was suggested by some that it was caused by bad drinking water. Pinkerton agent J. H. Ford gave information against Beatty in December 1892; other Pinkerton detectives were involved in gathering "evidence" against them, and were charged by Gallagher and Davidson in their July 1893 recantations with having threatened and intimidated them into giving false evidence.

2. A Fateful Leaflet

Translated from the German, "Ein verhängnisvolles Flugblatt," by Bonnie Buettner.

1. Bauer calls Paul Eckert (dates unknown) "comrade," thus identifying him as a fellow anarchist. For Eckert's role in the convictions of Nold and Bauer, see Chapter 7, "Two Further Court Farces."

2. Formal organization among anarchists in the United States was often limited to local groups, collectives, or affinity groups, who might, as here,

band together for a particular reason. Nold's residence is referred to several times in the pages of *Prison Blossoms* as a meeting place for local anarchists, presumably the Allegheny Group I mentioned here.

3. The identities of Bauer's companions have never been clearly established. Rudolf Rocker names Bauer's companions as "Legleitener" and "Bower" in *Johann Most: Das Leben eines Rebellen* (Berlin: Der Syndikalist, 1924), 349. Max Metzkow (1854–1945), German-born socialist and anarchist living in Pittsburgh in the 1890s, may also have been involved in the dissemination of the leaflet. Candace Falk, ed., *Emma Goldman: A Documentary History of the American Years*, vol. 1: *Made for America, 1890–1901* (Berkeley: University of California Press, 2003), 543.

4. Bauer intended to include the text of the leaflet here in both German and in English, as is clear from a note in parentheses, but neither text is included in the archival material. We have supplied the English text from "A Fateful Leaflet," *Free Society*, April 17, 1898, signed H. Bauer, with the correction of one typo ("strutting" for "strotting"). Rocker, *Most*, 348–349, indicates that the German text was published in *Die Freiheit*, July 16, 1892, together with an article entitled "Wie man's macht" (How to Do It).

5. Jay Gould (1836–1892), American financier, speculator, and railroad developer, notorious for his ruthless and sometimes illegal business dealings.

6. The *Pittsburger Volksblatt* was the most widely circulated German newspaper in western Pennsylvania.

7. O'Donnell was chosen by the strikers as the leader of their Advisory Committee.

8. International Workers Association (IWA), a loose-knit federation of anarchist and socialist groups established in Pittsburgh in 1883, advocated revolutionary resistance to class rule, the establishment of an economy based on cooperation rather than profit, and equal rights regardless of sex or race. The IWA document produced at the Pittsburgh Congress in 1883, popularly called the "Pittsburgh Manifesto," was a landmark in American radical labor history; it appealed to both American and European social revolutionary traditions denouncing state, church, and education as repressive institutions serving a ruling elite and was translated into many languages and widely circulated.

9. The Turnvereins, or "Turners," were German-American social and athletic societies that served as athletic, political, and social centers for German communities in the United States.

10. The Amalgamated Association of Iron and Steel Workers was the industry's principal union at the time.

3. Autobiographical Sketches

Translated from the German, "Autobiographische Skizzen," by Bonnie Buettner.

1. Neither Johann Most (1846–1906) nor Louis Lingg (1864–1887) was hanged. Lingg was sentenced to death by hanging but killed himself in his cell the night before the execution. Most was not in Chicago at the time of the Haymarket bombing, nor was he indicted along with the other anarchists; at the time of the bombing, he was en route to Blackwell's Island prison to serve the first of three terms, having been indicted in New York for inflammatory rhetoric.

2. "Propaganda by deed," espoused by anarchist theorists in the late nineteenth century and largely abandoned by anarchists in America after World War I, was an act of revolutionary violence, such as the *attentat* or assassination or other act committed against authorities and institutions as a strategy to encourage more widespread resistance to oppressive social systems.

3. To protect his friends, Berkman presents his *attentat* as an act in which no one was involved but him. Others were, however, involved: Emma Goldman helped him raise money; Claus Timmermann (see note 4) helped prepare leaflets for distribution. Berkman's cousin Modest Aronstam (later Stein, 1871–1958), anarchist comrade and cohabiter with Emma Goldman, also knew about the plot, and after Berkman's arrest traveled to Pittsburgh to finish what Berkman had failed to do. He took alarm, however, and left the city when he learned that the police had been informed that another attempt on Frick's life would be made. Paul Avrich, *Anarchist Voices: An Oral History of Anarchism in America* (Oakland: AK Press, 2005), 55. Aronstam thought Roman Lewis (1865–1918), an anarchist from New York, might have been the police informant. Candace Falk, ed., *Emma Goldman: A Documentary History of the American Years,* vol. 1: *Made for America, 1890–1901* (Berkeley: University of California Press, 2003), 540.

4. Claus Timmermann (1866–1941), German-born anarchist, printer, first editor of *Der Anarchist.*

5. Maxim Berkman (dates unknown), Alexander Berkman's older brother, who sympathized with the populist revolutionaries, was (together

with their revolutionary activist uncle Maxim) an important influence on Berkman's early understanding. Paul Avrich, *Anarchist Portraits* (Princeton: Princeton University Press, 1990), 201.

6. Frank Mollock (dates unknown), Austrian-born anarchist, New Jersey comrade, sent money he owed Berkman by registered letter. See Chapter 4, "Jail Experiences."

7. With the "autonomous newspapers" Berkman refers to publications by anarchists who supported the Bohemian anarchist Josef Peukert (1855–1910) in his dispute with Johann Most. The disagreement, called the Brothers War, began in accusations made against Peukert, that he had acted as a police spy, but it may well have had at its core a rivalrous contention for leadership among anarchists in America, as well as different notions of anarchist collectivity. Bauer was a disciple of Most's and therefore suspicious of Berkman, who was sympathetic to Peukert and the Gruppe Autonomie (Autonomy Group). *Die Autonomie* (1886–1893) and *Der Anarchist* (1889–1895) were anarchist-communist newspapers with strong ties to the autonomists. *Die Autonomie,* published in London and edited by Joseph Peukert, advocated the anarchist communism of Peter Kropotkin, publishing some of his articles in German. Peukert joined *Der Anarchist* after he fled Europe; the paper later came out in support of Berkman's *attentat.*

8. That Berkman, even after three years, felt this insult very deeply is shown by his unusual use of two English words in Germanized form in the middle of his sentence: "Ich konnte nicht 'afforden' mit B. in Trouble zu gerathen." All three authors use some English words regularly (e.g., *strike, strikers, warden*) and incorporate some English phrases into their narrative when they want to emphasize the English. However, this Germanization of words is not only singular but also unnecessary, since Berkman elsewhere uses the correct German expressions.

4. Jail Experiences

Translated from the German, "Jail Erfahrungen," by Bonnie Buettner. An earlier title, "Acht (8) Wochen in der All. C. Jail" (Eight [8] Weeks in the Allegheny County Jail), was crossed out.

1. John McAleese (dates unknown), appointed inspector of the first police district in Pittsburgh in 1888 and warden of the Allegheny County Jail in 1891.

2. Roger O'Mara (dates unknown). Frank Mollock (dates unknown), Austrian-born anarchist. After leaving Worcester, Berkman, Emma Goldman, and Modest Aronstam stayed in Mollock's apartment in New York to prepare their agitation several days before the news of the battle with the Pinkertons fixed Berkman's resolve to assassinate Frick. Emma Goldman, *Living My Life,* vol. 1 (New York: Dover Publications, 1970), 86 and 99.

3. Hugh O'Donnell, leader of the Homestead strikers' Advisory Committee after the mill lockout at the end of June.

4. Berkman mistakenly wrote "September" instead of July.

5. Further Arrests

Translated from the German, "Weitere Verhaftungen," by Bonnie Buettner. Originally entitled "Die Verhaftungen von Nold und Bauer" (The Arrests of Nold and Bauer).

1. Nold is referring to their project to publish their writings as a book. The "fourth chapter" is clearly the section of Chapter 3, "Autobiographical Sketches," titled "3. In Allegheny, Pa."

2. Paul Eckert (dates unknown) lived on the first floor of the house, Nold on the second, and on the third was the printing press the Allegheny anarchists had installed. Henry Bauer identifies Eckert as a "comrade," i.e., fellow anarchist, in "A Fateful Leaflet" (Chapter 2).

3. John R. Murphy (1850–1917), chief of Allegheny police 1878–1881 and 1884–1891; after 1891, director of the Department of Public Safety. Called "Chief" even when he was no longer chief of police.

4. Frank Mollock, Austrian-born anarchist (dates unknown). Berkman, Emma Goldman, and Modest Aronstam stayed at Mollock's apartment in New York before Berkman traveled to Pittsburgh. This is one of the reasons the police suspected Mollock of involvement in the attack on Frick.

5. "Blessed are the poor in spirit, for theirs is the kingdom of heaven" (Matthew 5:3).

6. A defense committee raised funds for the legal defense of the three anarchists, like the defense committee organized on behalf of the Haymarket defendants in 1886. It continued its efforts on Berkman's behalf after Nold and Bauer were released, and after Berkman's release, on behalf of other anarchists charged with crimes.

7. Nold refers to Modest Aronstam (later Stein; 1871–1958), who set off for Pittsburgh to kill Frick after Berkman's *attentat* failed. Paul Avrich,

Anarchist Voices: An Oral History of Anarchism in America (Oakland: AK Press, 2005), 55.

6. An American Court Farce

Translated from the German, "Eine amerikanische Gerichts-Farce," by Bonnie Buettner. The two leading quotations were written in English and marked "For the English edition."

1. James Russell Lowell (1819–1891), American poet, educator, diplomat, and early abolitionist. The quotation is from the poem "The Present Crisis" (1844).

2. Berkman had expected that his comrades would make useful propaganda out of his deed, and was disappointed that they had not done so. See Chapter 8, "A Few Words as to My Deed."

3. John Brown (1800–1859), American abolitionist who tried to end slavery through armed slave revolt, most famously in the unsuccessful raid on the federal arsenal in Harpers Ferry, Virginia, in 1859.

4. Berkman means, of course, George III.

5. Clarence Burleigh (b. 1853), of the firm of Dakell, Scott and Gordon, became district attorney of Allegheny County in 1891.

6. Samuel A. McClung (1845–1915), a wealthy, conservative judge.

7. Philander Chase Knox (1853–1921), of Knox and Reed, legal advisers to Carnegie Steel.

8. John George Alexander Leishman (1857–1924), then vice president of Carnegie Steel, had been with Frick in his office at the time of the attack and had helped wrestle Berkman to the floor.

9. Because Berkman, acting as his own counsel, did not object to the multiplication of the charges against him, no future appeals on these grounds would be admissible. The two additional charges of entering the building with criminal intent (charges four and five) stemmed from the elevator operator's testimony that he had brought Berkman up to Frick's office floor three times.

10. Berkman refers to the five anarchists sentenced to death after the Haymarket riot: August Spies, Albert Parsons, Adolph Fischer, George Engel, and Louis Lingg.

11. It is not clear why Berkman is querying the text. Perhaps this was not what he had said. Perhaps he meant to draw attention to the fact that the

pronoun in the next sentence ("him") does not agree in number with its antecedent ("oppressors").

7. Two Further Court Farces

Translated from the German, "Zwei Weitere Gerichts-Farcen," by Bonnie Buettner.

1. Harry Goering (dates unknown).

2. Joseph Slagle (dates unknown). Paul Eckert (dates unknown) shared Nold's house in Allegheny and thus was as much Berkman's host as Nold. Bauer calls him a "comrade" in Chapter 2, "A Fateful Leaflet."

3. International Workers Association (IWA), a loose-knit federation of anarchist and socialist groups established in Pittsburgh in 1883, advocating revolutionary resistance to class rule, establishing an economy based on cooperation rather than profit, and demanding equal rights regardless of sex or race.

4. The identities of Bauer's companions have never been clearly established. See "A Fateful Leaflet."

5. Joseph Frick (d. 1891), anarchist and close collaborator with Johann Most.

6. Regarding Bauer's reference to "the fourth chapter," see Chapter 3, "Autobiographical Sketches," by Alexander Berkman.

7. In Chapter 5, "Further Arrests," Carl Nold gives an account of the conditions in the jail after their arrests.

8. Sylvester Critchlow, Jack Clifford, and Hugh O'Donnell were charged with murder for their leading roles in the Homestead strike and the repulsion of the Pinkerton agents. See Chapter 1, "Capital and the Battle on the Monongahela," by Carl Nold.

9. Hugh F. Dempsey and Robert J. Beatty were convicted, based on highly suspect testimony, of trying to poison nonunion workmen at Homestead in 1892. See "Capital and the Battle on the Monongahela."

10. *The Freedom* (1886–present), an anarchist-communist newspaper founded by Peter Kropotkin, among others, is the primary anarchist publication in English. *The Commonweal* (1885–1895) was a weekly journal that aimed at spreading socialism and advocated revolutionary socialism.

11. This note, in what appears to be Nold's hand, is in all likelihood addressed to Berkman, although the salutation is illegible. The signature initials at the end, K. G., most likely refer to the pseudonyms Nold (K., for

der Kleine) and Bauer (G., for *der Grosse*) assumed while collaborating with Berkman.

8. A Few Words as to My Deed

1. Berkman refers to events of the French Revolution and to the patriots of the American Revolution.

2. Czar Alexander II was assassinated in 1881 by members of the rural populist movement the People's Will *(Narodnaia Volia)*. An earlier incendiary proclamation issued in 1862 by "Young Russia" called for violence against the czar and revolution.

3. Anarchist Auguste Vaillant threw a bomb into the Chamber of Deputies in Paris in 1893.

4. Berkman is alluding here to *Faust,* act 1, scene 3, by Johann Wolfgang von Goethe. Faust struggles to translate John 1:1, "In the beginning was the Word," and rejects first "word" then "sense" or "thought" and finally "power" as that force that creates all and sets all in motion. He finally decides on "deed" as the actuating motive (as Berkman might express it). In Berkman's words (see Chapter 6, "An American Court Farce"), "The merit is determined by the actuating motive," and it is indeed Faust's socially useful actions on behalf of others that prove his merit and save him. The parallel to Berkman's view of his "deed" is unmistakable.

5. Berkman refers to the falling off of anarchist influence in the American radical labor movement from its high-water mark between the time of the promulgation of the Pittsburgh Manifesto, an 1883 proclamation for social revolution, and the agitation in Chicago for the eight-hour day, which culminated in the executions of prominent anarchists, convicted without evidence for deaths in the Haymarket riot of 1886. The executions, which took place without anarchist reprisals, seemed to signal the supremacy of the state, dispiriting anarchist activists.

6. Johann Most (1846–1906), German anarchist and prominent advocate of propaganda by deed.

7. Saverio Merlino (1856–1930), Italian lawyer and anarchist, addressed a mass meeting in New York on Berkman's behalf shortly after his attack on Frick and before his trial. The meeting was organized by Russian-Jewish anarchist Emma Goldman (1869–1940), already prominent in America as a spokesperson for anarchism.

8. By "individualist anarchists," Berkman refers to the American

anarchist movement, which often sanctioned private property and was wary of collectivist economies. Among these, the most prominent disavowal of Berkman's deed was the libertarian anarchist Benjamin Tucker's in the pages of his anarchist journal *Liberty,* on July 30, 1892.

9. Berkman refers to personal animus Most may have borne him or believed Berkman bore against Most because both men had been Emma Goldman's lovers. The earliest response Most made to Berkman's *attentat* appeared in *Freiheit* under the title "Fricktionen," in which Most assailed Frick and praised Berkman's courage. He published "Attentats-Reflexionen," his disavowal of Berkman's attack, in *Freiheit* on August 27, 1892.

10. August Reinsdorf (1849–1885), executed in Germany for attempting to assassinate the emperor, Kaiser Wilhelm I, in one of the first acts of political terror in Germany.

11. Berkman refers to terrorist attacks made in 1893 by three European anarchists: Auguste Vaillant; Emile Henry, who exploded a bomb in the Café Terminus, a restaurant with a reputation as a middle-class gathering place in the Gare Saint-Lazare in Paris, in reprisal for Vaillant's execution; and Paulino Pallás, a young Andalusian anarchist, who attempted the assassination of General Martínez Campos in Barcelona to revenge the garroting of four anarchists arrested in peasant and worker demonstrations for the eight-hour day.

12. Berkman refers to the anarchist group that derived its name from Austrian anarchist Josef Peukert's paper *Die Autonomie.* Although accusations of betrayal were made against Peukert for allegedly cooperating with police spies in Germany, at issue may have been differing notions of anarchist economy, different strategies for defeating capitalism, and rival attempts to dominate the anarchist movement in New York.

9. The Red Bugbear

1. August Spies (1855–1887), German-born anarchist, executed in Chicago for his participation in the Haymarket strike. John Peter Altgeld (1847–1902), governor of Illinois, pardoned the surviving Haymarket anarchists in 1893, calling the trial a miscarriage of justice.

2. "Some autonomistic matter" refers to the Gruppe Autonomie, named for the newspaper of anarchist Josef Peukert.

3. Local anarchist associations were often identified as "groups."

4. The English translation of Most's article was not included in this manuscript.

5. Robert Reitzel (1849–1898), German American anarchist, poet, and critic, had been a prominent defender of the Haymarket anarchists. His literary and radical weekly newspaper *Der arme Teufel* (The Poor Devil) was widely read in the German American community.

10. Tolstoi or Bakunin?

1. From "The Present Crisis" (1844), by American poet James Russell Lowell, calling on patriots to join the abolitionist movement against slavery.

2. Nold refers to the assassination in 1904 of the Russian czarist director of police, later minister of justice, Vyacheslav von Plehve (1846–1904), who was responsible for bloody reprisals against revolutionaries and terrorists. The date of this reference reminds us that while Nold, Bauer, and Berkman composed most of the *Prison Blossoms* during their shared years in the penitentiary, they continued writing chapters of their proposed book after Bauer and Nold's release.

3. Nold contrasts the violent revolutionary anarchism of Mikhail Bakunin (1814–1876) with the repudiation of violence of the great Russian writer and reformer Leo Tolstoy (1828–1910). Tolstoy did not call himself an anarchist because of anarchism's association with violence, but his rejection of both private property and laws of the state and his advocacy of a simpler life in harmony with nature were compatible with anarchist visions of a reformed society.

4. Von Plehve was assassinated by Yegor Sozonov, a member of the Socialist Revolutionary Combat Organization, which had attempted several prior assassinations of von Plehve.

5. Nold is excerpting a passage from an anonymously written article entitled "The Tsar," published in *Littell's Living Age* 242 (August 27, 1904): 519.

11. Our Prison Life

Translated from the German, "Unser Zuchthausleben: Zweite Hälfte (Feb. 1895–Mai 1897)," by Bonnie Buettner. Despite the title, the piece actually covers only the time up to December 1895. There is no continuation among the Berkman Papers in the archives at the International Institute for Social History to bring the account up to the release of Bauer and Nold in May 1897.

1. A note at the end of the piece clarifies "our" as Nold's and Bauer's prison terms.

2. Archival evidence suggests that "Schulz" is one John Schulz, a German immigrant, admitted to the Western Pennsylvania Penitentiary in 1894 on the charge of rioting, which was very often the indictment handed down for political agitation. "Friend H" is presumably the prisoner Berkman refers to as Horsethief, who carried messages between the three men. Bauer wrote "B" (probably to stand for "Bob," for Robert Richards, imprisoned in fact for stealing horses) every time this person is mentioned, but it was changed to "H" in Latin script (Berkman's editing?) throughout the manuscript. We have left the change as it stands.

3. Berkman was kept for more than a year in solitary. See Alexander Berkman, *Prison Memoirs of an Anarchist* (New York: New York Review of Books, 1970), 241. "Jim" is Jim McPane (dates unknown), deputy warden at the Western Pennsylvania Penitentiary. Berkman, *Memoirs,* 268.

4. J. Linn Milligan (dates unknown) was chaplain for thirty years at the Western Pennsylvania Penitentiary.

5. Benny Greaves was made deputy warden after McPane; Greaves released Berkman from solitary confinement and had him replace the coffee boy on the cell-block range. Berkman, *Memoirs,* 241.

6. The archival material does not contain the earlier writings mentioned here. Bauer used the abbreviations "Z Bl" and "P B," presumably for *Zuchthausblüthen* and *Prison Bird.* According to Carl Nold, *Zuchthausblüthen* was first "published" about March 1, 1893, and was kept up for two years (letter from Nold to Berkman, October 3, 1911, Alexander Berkman Papers, International Institute of Social History, Amsterdam). Their English having by then improved greatly, they gave it up and started *Prison Bird,* written in English. After a year, they decided to write the book Bauer discusses here, *Prison Blossoms,* and they no longer had time for *Prison Bird.* "Bird" is prison parlance for covert writing passed from prisoner to prisoner.

7. Probably a reference to the contributor referred to elsewhere as "'D' for *Dichter,*" "our poet laureate." Berkman, *Memoirs,* 183 and 283.

8. Emma Goldman identifies her as "Emma Lee," a freethinker ("Free lover") who had been imprisoned in the South on a trumped-up charge and was now committed to prison reform. Goldman, *Living My Life,* vol. 1 (New York: Dover Publications, 1970), 158–159 and 176.

9. The copied text contains many grammatical, syntactical, and spelling mistakes we did not try to reproduce in the translation. We did leave run-on sentences as they were, to give some idea of the illiteracy of at least one of their detractors—surely one of the reasons Bauer includes the text here.

10. For many anarchists, reliance on or use of any state agency or arm of the establishment was a repudiation of anarchistic principles.

11. Most likely *My Uncle Benjamin* by Claude Tillier, translated by Benjamin R. Tucker (Boston: Benjamin R. Tucker, 1890), a humorous genre satire first published in French as a serialized novel, starting in 1842, and very popular in Germany.

12. Penitentiary Administration and Treatment of Prisoners

Translated from the German, "Zuchthausverwaltung und Behandlung der Gefangenen," by Bonnie Buettner. The manuscript contains additional notations written in two different hands. The notes in the first hand—that of the author of the piece, Henry Bauer—are additions and corrections; these have been incorporated directly into the text. Those in the second hand, signed at the end "m"—i.e., Berkman—appear here as commentary in footnotes, except where he wrote whole sentences or paragraphs; those have been incorporated into the text and are identified with an endnote. Our own explanatory notes appear as endnotes.

1. George Kennan, *Siberia and the Exile System* (New York: Century, 1891).

2. New York's Elmira Reformatory opened in 1876 with Zebulon Reed Brockway (1827–1920) as its superintendent. The reformatory's rejection of punitive penology in favor of a rehabilitative focus earned it wide acclaim, but its very success led to overcrowding, excesses, and gross mismanagement. In 1893 Brockway was found guilty of "unlawful, unjust, cruel, brutal, inhuman, degrading excessive and unusual punishment of inmates, frequently causing permanent injuries and disfigurements." "New York State Correctional Officer Informational Page," www.geocities.com/motorcity/downs/3548/facility/elmira.html, accessed 2/24/09; not available online as of 11/29/10. A second investigation vacated the finding, and Brockway remained in charge at Elmira until he retired in 1900.

3. Recurrent public scandals and investigations into what Bauer calls the steel-plate swindle involved Bethlehem Iron and Carnegie Steel. See Chapter 1, "Capital and the Battle on the Monongahela."

4. Edward Smith Wright (1829–1916).

5. Benny Greaves (dates unknown).

6. Bauer is speaking here specifically of Warden Wright.

7. J. Linn Milligan (dates unknown).

8. Prison labor was a hot controversy at this time. Pennsylvania lawmakers and penal reformers had traditionally rejected it "on the grounds

that its principal motive was pecuniary in nature, and thereby, a corruption of the penitentiary's supreme, *moral* mission of spiritual reform." Rebecca McLennan, *The Crisis of Imprisonment: Protest, Politics, and the Making of the American Penal State, 1776–1941* (Cambridge: Cambridge University Press, 2008), 101. The prisoners were never paid, even though they were working for for-profit companies, but under the unpaid labor system both the state and the business owners made money—as did the wardens, though they were not entitled to any profit (ibid., 104).

   9. The Allegheny prison established common workshops instead of a system of work done in individual cells, "due to the small cells, which lacked adequate air and light, making solitary work impossible." Pennsylvania Correctional Industries, "A Historical Overview of Inmate Labor in Pennsylvania," www.pci.state.pa.us, accessed 10/15/09.

   10. Sometimes called the dungeon, a dark basement cell without bed or cot, where, according to the clarification Berkman added toward the end of this essay, prisoners were stripped to their underwear and held on a diet of two ounces of bread and two drinks of water per day.

   11. Founded in 1859, relocated outside Pittsburgh and renamed for Dorothea Dix in 1862, the Dixmont Insane Asylum was soon notorious for being severely overcrowded and underfunded, conditions that lasted into the early twentieth century. It was closed in 1984.

   12. Jim McPane (dates unknown), the deputy warden before Benny Greaves, was universally hated by the prisoners. See Chapter 11, "Our Prison Life."

   13. Paragraph added by Berkman.

   14. This paragraph and the next added by Berkman.

   15. Bauer's intention is clear; his sentence is not.

   16. Quoted in English in the German text.

   17. From here to the end of the paragraph the writing reflects Berkman's revision of Bauer's text.

   18. Quoted in English in the German text.

13. The Treatment of Prisoner A-444, in His Own Words

Translated from the German, "Die Behandlung des Gefangenen No. A-444—von ihm selbst geschrieben," by Bonnie Buettner. A note indicates that Carl Nold translated A-444's account into German (though the text is in Henry Bauer's hand), and we have translated it "back" into English for this volume.

1. A note at the end of the piece indicates that "the names of 8931 and 161 may not be made public."

2. The text uses the word "sodomy" throughout, but this was changed to "pederasty" in a note at the end.

17. A Morning Conversation between Dutch and Mike (Two Prisoners)

Translated from the German, "Ein Morgen-Gespräch zwischen Dutsch und Mike (zwei Gefangene)," by Bonnie Buettner. The piece records a conversation written down by Carl Nold.

18. Punishment: Its Nature and Effects

1. The Circassians, originally from the northwestern Caucasus, also known as the "Tscherkess," inherit a tradition of blood-revenge, to which Berkman makes reference.

2. The 1862 novel *Les Misérables* (or "The Miserable Ones," by Victor Hugo, 1802–1885), dwells on the nature of justice, morality, religion, and politics while telling the story of former prisoner Jean Valjean's search for redemption.

3. Berkman is citing the "The World's Need," by American poet Ella Wheeler Wilcox, 1850–1919.

4. "Poor Children of Westchester," *New York Times,* January 1, 1896, 9. The young boy, Henry Weeks, who had attempted to run away from cruel treatment, was found with chains around his feet.

5. In 1893 Zebulon Reed Brockway, superintendent of the reformatory in Elmira, New York, was found guilty of excessive and unusual punishments that often led to serious injury.

20. Crime and Its Sources

1. Two copies of the essay up to this point exist in the archive. One, in Alexander Berkman's hand and giving his name as author, concludes with this paragraph. A second copy, in Carl Nold's hand and giving his name as author, contains the rest of the essay. In his copy Nold omitted Berkman's final paragraph ("If this compilation . . ."), perhaps considering this as a conclusion no longer necessary since he was carrying the essay forward.

2. Carl Nold was sharing imprisonment with the Homestead strike union leaders, Knights of Labor master workman Hugh F. Dempsey and Robert Beatty, who were accused of poisoning strikebreakers by prosecution

witnesses who later retracted their testimony and claimed they had been intimidated by the state.

3. Nold mockingly implies that the Bible is in violation of federal censorship, since the enactment of the Comstock laws in 1873 made the dissemination of obscenity in publications through the U.S. mail illegal.

4. Anthony Comstock (1844–1915), moral reformer; Emmeline Pankhurst (1858–1928) and her daughter Christabel (1880–1958) were leading British suffragists and women's rights advocates.

22. The Vision in the Penitentiary Cell

Translated from the German, "Die Erscheinung in der Zuchthaus Zelle," by Bonnie Buettner.

1. With the "Rose of Virtue" Nold may be alluding to a gold presentation piece (not a lapel decoration as here) in the form of a rose, given by the Pope to an individual, church, or institution for services rendered to the Catholic Church.

23. The Sinking Ship

Translated from the German, "Das sinkende Schiff, Eine Parabel von M," by Bonnie Buettner ("M" in the title refers to Alexander Berkman). On the facing page in the manuscript is a note in a very faint hand: "Whoever is not able to write an article to M's [Berkman's] taste had best let M write the article. K. [Carl Nold]."

1. In Roman mythology, Janus (Ianus), with his two heads looking in opposite directions, is the god of gates, doorways, transitions, beginnings and endings, the past and the future.

2. Berkman attributes the finger thrust first to Janus, then to Neptune. As the more active god, Neptune is more likely to have acted here; the text has been changed accordingly. The electric chair, used only in the United States and the Philippines, was first used in New York in 1890 as a "more humane" method of execution, after a particularly horrifying hanging. The first execution by electrocution, however, took eight minutes in all.

24. Winter Sun for My Prison Colleagues M & G

Translated from the German, "Winter-Sonne für meine Zuchthaus Collegen M & G, 1. Janner 1896, von K," by Bonnie Buettner. Written by Carl Nold ("K") for his colleagues Alexander Berkman ("M") and Henry Bauer ("G").

1. The evening preceding the feast day of St. Walpurga (April 30 or May 1), when witches congregated and conducted pagan sacrifices in Germany's Harz Mountains, especially on the Brocken, the highest point in the mountains.

2. The eleventh of November refers primarily to the anniversary of the hanging of August Spies, Albert Parsons, Adolph Fischer, and George Engel, four of the eight anarchists taken to trial after the Haymarket riot (May 4, 1886). Secondarily, it also marks the beginning of the pre-Lenten carnival season (which begins at the eleventh minute of the eleventh hour of the eleventh day of the eleventh month, though most of the festivities are concentrated immediately before the start of Lent), a festival related to pagan rites to drive out evil spirits of winter and usher in life-renewing spring and summer. Among other things, it is characterized by masquerades and parades that symbolically subvert the rules and governance of normal life and turn the world upside down.

3. The *Bundschuh,* or peasant's shoe, became the symbol for a series of peasant uprisings in Germany against the nobility (1493–1517); the Bundschuh movement was a precursor to the Peasants' War (1524–1526).

4. Konrad, Götz, Müntzer: In 1514 German peasants in Württemberg rose up to protest, among other things, heavy taxation and feudal duties, calling their movement "Armer Konrad" (Poor Conrad). They were easily defeated, however, leaving the issues still festering and ushering in the greater uprising, a decade later, known as the Peasants' War. Götz von Berlichingen (ca. 1480–1562), a mercenary knight made famous by Goethe's play of the same name, led the peasants in Odenwald against the ecclesiastical princes of the Holy Roman Empire, though he was never actually a staunch believer in the peasants' cause. Thomas Müntzer (ca. 1488–1525), radical reformer and religious opponent of Luther, led a troop of some 8,000 peasants in the Battle of Frankenhausen; he was captured, tortured, and beheaded. One of his battle cries was "Omnia sunt communia" (All things are in common), a sentiment that appealed greatly to anarchists.

5. Savonarola, Bruno: Girolamo Savonarola (1452–1498) a Dominican priest, best known for his burning of books, preached vehemently against the excesses and moral corruption of many priests, and was excommunicated, tortured, and burned at the stake in Florence. Giordano Bruno (1548–1600) was an Italian philosopher who was a proponent of heliocentrism and was burned at the stake as a heretic by the Roman Inquisition.

6. Hus and Galileo: Jan Hus (ca. 1372–1415), Bohemian reformer, was

burned at the stake as a heretic; Galileo Galilei (1564–1642) was forced to recant his support of Copernican heliocentrism and spent the last years of his life under house arrest on orders of the Roman Inquisition.

7. Jean-Paul Marat (1743–1793), Georges Danton (1759–1794), and François-Noël (Gracchus) Baboef (1760–1797) were leaders in the French Revolution; the first was murdered in his bath, the latter two guillotined. Baboef is said to have been a forerunner of Lenin and Trotsky.

8. Originally a term of contempt referring to the poorer classes, *sans-culotte* ("without knee breeches") was adopted by the revolutionaries in the French Revolution as a popular name for themselves.

9. The year 1848 saw a series of political revolutions across Europe. Though most were quickly and often brutally quelled, there were long-term political effects in many of the countries.

10. Robert Blum (1807–1848), German politician and member of the German National Assembly of 1848; died by execution. He became a symbol for Germany's failed 1848 rebellion.

11. Anton Füster (1808–1881), professor of theology and pedagogy in Vienna, chaplain of the Academic Legion; as a member of the Reichsrat, he was involved politically in the German revolution in 1848, and he fled to England after its suppression.

12. Song, written in 1792 to protest the invasion of foreign armies, that became the rallying cry of the French Revolution and then, in 1795, the French national anthem. It has been one of the most popular revolutionary songs.

13. The largest cemetery in the city of Paris, named after Père François de la Chaise (1624–1709), confessor to Louis XIV; where the Paris Communards made their last stand and where their bodies were deposited. (See note 15 below.)

14. Jaroslaw Dabrowski (1836–1871), exiled Polish revolutionary, nationalist, and last commander-in-chief of the Paris Commune of 1871; buried in Père Lachaise.

15. The Commune of Paris (March 18 to May 28, 1871) marked the first advance of working-class power by anarchists and socialists. After government forces conquered the city, more than 80,000 Communards were killed or executed.

16. August Spies and Albert Parsons, two of the anarchists tried and hanged for murder after the Haymarket riot in Chicago. As they were taken to the gallows, they sang "La Marseillaise."

Appendix 1. Last Days in the Penitentiary

Berkman wrote these few notes in a diary he kept in the last weeks before his release from the Western Pennsylvania Penitentiary. From the prison he went to serve another year in the Allegheny County Workhouse near Pittsburgh.

1. Berkman means two months; "and a stump" is prison parlance for "and some additional time."

2. The familiar phrase "All is quiet along the Potomac" is taken from the Civil War poem by Ethel Lynn Beers, written in 1861.

3. Samuel W. Pennypacker was governor of Pennsylvania from 1903 to 1907.

4. Popular American slang for gin during the time Berkman was writing.

Appendix 2. Alexander Berkman's Bibliography

Berkman added this list of books as a bibliography to his essay "Punishment—Its Nature and Effects" (Chapter 18). We reproduce it here, as he wrote it in German and English, to suggest the wide range of his reading while he was in prison. Bibliographic information about these works, which are for the most part works of social criticism, is appended in brackets below each title.

1. Berkman gives Gogol's work a title not usually used except in the German translation by Julius Meissner, *Altväterliche Leute und andere Erzählungen* [Old-Fashioned People and Other Stories] (Stuttgart: Deutsche Hand- und Hausbibliothek, n.d.). The usual German translation is "Altväterliche Gutsbesitzer," or Old-Fashioned Landowners. Since Meissner also renders Gogol's given name as Nikolas rather than the usual Nikolai, it seems likely that Meissner's is the edition Berkman had.

Further Reading

Works by Alexander Berkman

Berkman, Alexander. *The Blast: Complete Collection of the Incendiary San Francisco Bi-Monthly Anarchist Newspaper.* Oakland: AK Press, 2005.

————. *The Bolshevik Myth.* London: Pluto Press, 1989.

————. "Hell on Earth . . . Alex. Berkman's First Speech after His Release From Jail," *KSL: Bulletin of the Kate Sharpley Library* 21 (February 2000), www.katesharpleylibrary.net/98sfwh (accessed December 2, 2009).

————. *Life of an Anarchist: The Alexander Berkman Reader,* ed. Gene Fellner. New York: Seven Stories Press, 2005.

————. *Prison Memoirs of an Anarchist.* New York: New York Review of Books, 1970.

————. *Registration, To the Youth of America, The Anarchist Movement Today,* in Anarchy Archives, an Online Research Center on the History and Theory of Anarchism. Dwardmac.pitzer.edu/Anarchist_Archives/very-selectbbiblio.html (accessed February 26, 2010). (This archive contains many unpublished letters and speeches by Berkman.)

————. *The Russian Tragedy.* Montreal: Black Rose Books, 1976.

———. *What Is Anarchism?* (originally *The ABC of Communist Anarchism*). Oakland: AK Press, 2003.

Glassgold, Peter, ed. *Anarchy: An Anthology of Emma Goldman's "Mother Earth."* Washington D.C.: Counterpoint, 2001. (Contains many contributions by Alexander Berkman written during his editorship of this leading anarchist journal, from 1906 to 1915.)

With Emma Goldman

Berkman, Alexander, and Emma Goldman. *Anarchism on Trial: Speeches of Alexander Berkman and Emma Goldman before the United States District Court, in the City of New York, July, 1917.* New York: Mother Earth Publishing Association, 1917.

———. "A Reflection on the Anniversary of the Deaths of Sacco and Vanzetti." See libcom.org/library/sacco and vanzetti-alexander-berkman-emma-goldman (accessed February 26, 2010).

Goldman, Emma, and Alexander Berkman. *A Fragment of the Prison Experiences of Emma Goldman and Alexander Berkman.* New York: Stella Comyn, 1919; www.archive.org/details/fragmentofprison00gold (accessed February 26, 2010).

———. *Nowhere at Home: Letters from Exile of Emma Goldman and Alexander Berkman,* ed. Richard Drinnon and Anna Maria Drinnon. New York: Schocken Books, 1975.

Archival Collections for Alexander Berkman

Alexander Berkman Papers. International Institute of Social History, Amsterdam. (Contains the most extensive collection of Berkman's letters and writings.)

Alexander Berkman Papers. The Tamiment Library and Robert F. Wagner Labor Archives. Alexander Berkman Papers TAM 067. New York.

Emma Goldman Papers: 1903–1940. Manuscript and Archive Division, Humanities and Social Science Library, New York Public Library, New York.

International Committee for Political Prisoners, Records 1918–1942. Manuscript and Archive Division, Humanities and Social Science Library, Box 25, New York Public Library, New York.

The Man Who Shot Frick (materials collected on the 100th anniversary tribute to Alexander Berkman's attempt to assassinate Henry Clay Frick). Labadie Collection, University of Michigan, Ann Arbor.

On Anarchism, Anarchists, and Labor History

Avrich, Paul. *Anarchist Portraits.* Princeton: Princeton University Press, 1988.

———. *Anarchist Voices: An Oral History of Anarchism in America.* Oakland: AK Press, 2005.

———. *The Haymarket Tragedy.* Princeton: Princeton University Press, 1984.

Brooks, Frank H., ed. *The Individualist Anarchists: An Anthology of "Liberty" (1881–1908).* New Brunswick, N.J.: Transaction Publishers, 1994.

Burwood, Linnea. "Alexander Berkman: Russian-American Anarchist." Ph.D. diss., Binghamton University, 2000.

DeLeon, David. *The American as Anarchist: Reflections on Indigenous Radicalism.* Baltimore: Johns Hopkins University Press, 1978.

Falk, Candace, ed., *Emma Goldman: A Documentary History of the American Years,* vol. 1: *Made for America, 1890–1901.* Berkeley: University of California Press, 2003.

Goldman, Emma. *Anarchism and Other Essays.* New York: Dover Publications, 1969.

———. *Living My Life,* two vols. New York: Dover Publications, 1970.

Kissack, Terence. *Free Comrades: Anarchism and Homosexuality in the United States, 1895–1917.* Oakland: AK Press, 2008.

Kropotkin, Peter. *In Russian and French Prisons.* New York: Schocken Books, 1971.

———. *Memoirs of a Revolutionist.* New York: Dover Publications, 1971.

Marshall, Peter. *Demanding the Impossible: A History of Anarchism.* London: HarperCollins, 1992.

Nasaw, David. *Andrew Carnegie.* New York: Penguin Press, 2006.

Rocker, Rudolf. *The London Years.* London: Robert Anscombe & Co. for the Rudolf Rocker Book Committee, 1956.

Stevenson, Billie Jeanne Hackley. "The Ideology of American Anarchism 1880–1910." Ph.D. diss., University of Iowa, 1972.

Wenzer, Kenneth C. *Anarchists Adrift: Emma Goldman and Alexander Berkman.* St. James, N.Y.: Brandywine Press, 1996.

———. "The Transmigration of Russian Anarcho-Communism." Ph.D. diss., Catholic University of America, 1992.

Woodcock, George. *Anarchism: A History of Libertarian Ideas and Movements.* Cleveland: Meridian Books, 1962.

Acknowledgments

We were fortunate to have the help and encouragement of librarians and staff at the International Institute of Social History in Amsterdam, particularly Eric de Ruijter and M. van der Pal, who transmitted copies of the manuscripts to us prior to our arrival in Amsterdam and made the originals available to us at the archive, even though they are in very fragile condition. In addition, we are grateful to Willis L. Shirk, Jr., and Jonathan R. Stayer at the Pennsylvania State Archive for their help in locating the prison records of the Western Pennsylvania Penitentiary for the time Berkman, Bauer, and Nold were there. For the identification of Robert Richards as Horsethief, we are grateful to researchers at the Emma Goldman Papers Project at the University of California, Berkeley. We relied as well on the help of librarians at the Tamiment Library and Robert F. Wagner Labor Archives at New York University and the Joseph A. Labadie Collection at the University of Michigan. And from its genesis to the completion of this volume we have had the invaluable support and encouragement of the excellent librarians and staff of Cornell University Library.

www.ingramcontent.com/pod-product-compliance
Lightning Source LLC
Chambersburg PA
CBHW051722260326
41914CB00031B/1691/J